Praise for Lawrence Brane Siddall's
Two Years in Poland and Other Stories

Lawrence Brane Siddall's memoir is the sort of book that, as Poles would say it, reads in "a single breath." In it, the 67-year-old grandfather takes his reader on a trip from today's Massachusetts to Poland, and then he travels back in time to his adventure of driving overland from Europe to India in the 1950's. Siddall's highly entertaining personal account is interwoven with his accounts of the rich history of the places he visits and his keen cultural observations.

In a letter of appreciation one of Siddall's Polish classes wrote: *You told us many exciting things and we know that they weren't only lessons of English, but also lessons about life.* Siddall's memoir gives its readers lessons about a life well led.

Marek Lesniewski-Laas
Honorary Consul of the Republic of Poland
Boston, Massachusetts

Lawrence Siddall is an excellent writer who has led an interesting life, even after retirement. While the primary focus of his memoir is the joys and challenges he faces as a Peace Corps volunteer teaching English in Poland in the late 1990s, Siddall also weaves in a fascinating tale of his travels across Europe and the Middle East on his way to India during the politically turbulent 1950s. This memoir will appeal to anyone who has an interest in life in the Peace Corps, post cold-war Eastern Europe, or the adventure of crossing the Middle East in a VW bug during the time Israel, Britain and France were drawn into conflict with Egypt over the Suez Canal in 1956.

Conny Jamison
San Diego, California

It has been a real reading pleasure to share the adventures of Lawrence Siddall. The sense of excitement with which he has viewed both opportunities and challenges that came his way has made for a lifetime of interesting and varied experiences. He brings to his writing not only his stories but also the optimism and pleasure in living that made them possible.

Betty Romer
Amherst, Massachusetts

Whether one is of Lawrence Siddall's generation now enjoying retirement or a younger person, this book will hold the reader in rapt attention. It is a story of his adventures that begins in Poland in 1997, and then looks back to the Middle East in 1956 when the world still held real adventures in abundance, a world without cell phones, internet communication, jet travel, and seamless ribbons of asphalt linking the far corners of the globe. Siddall's memoir is written in an engaging style and is full of thoughtfully-observed vignettes of faraway places that today are more important to us than ever before.

Walter Denny, Professor of Art History
University of Massachusetts at Amherst

This is a well-written and vividly-told story. Once started, it is impossible to put this book down. Lawrence Siddall has had an extraordinarily interesting life. He has an eye for character and a gift for bringing to life particular moments, which makes this memoir one of the best I have ever read! I am impressed that this work, rich in description, facts and atmosphere, is the author's first book.

Sylwia Mucha
Wrocław, Poland

At times both humorous and tender, Lawrence Siddall's contemplative memoir takes us on his journey to Poland as a Peace Corps volunteer at the age of 67. With a spirit of idealism and the energy of youth, he redefines traditional notions of aging and shows us that life in retirement can be fulfilling and meaningful. His stories are both inspirational and entertaining. I was entirely captivated by his honest voice and self-examination as he describes his many remarkable experiences. A must read.

Dorien Miller
Northampton, Massachusetts

I can highly recommend this memoir by Lawrence Siddall. It is well written and his stories will keep your attention from the first page to the last. You will get familiar with a variety of characters that include his students, colleagues, and friends, all of whom become very real. What I find most endearing is how this memoir describes our ordinary daily lives.

As an editor of a local newspaper, I am pleased and honored that, thanks to this book, my beautiful city will become more widely known. With its rich history, interesting architecture, and, of course, the Peace Church, listed as a UNESCO World Heritage site, it is a Polish city well worth visiting.

Anita Odachowska-Mazurek, Editor
Wiadomości Świdnickie
Świdnica, Poland

TWO YEARS IN
POLAND

and Other Stories

TWO YEARS IN
POLAND
and Other Stories

A Sixty-Seven-Year-Old Grandfather
Joins The Peace Corps
And Looks Back On His Life

A Memoir

By

Lawrence Brane Siddall

Pelham Springs Press

The author is grateful to the editor of the *Oberlin Alumni Magazine* for permission to include in this memoir a brief section from his article, "A Late-Life Adventure: My Two Years in the Peace Corps," Summer 2000.

ES, 13.
A
2008

Pelham Springs Press
129 Strong Street
Amherst, MA 01002

To contact the author, visit: www.lawrencesiddall.com

First Edition

ISBN-13: 978-0-9815297-0-7

Printed in the United States of America

Cover design: Pamela Glaven
Book design: Julie Murkette
Cover Photograph: M.H. Siddall
Maps: Serena Dameron

This memoir is dedicated to my children

Curtis, Mark and Jennifer

Author's Note

Photographs that accompany this memoir can be found at:

www.lawrencesiddall.com

Table of Contents

Acknowledgements

The writing of this memoir took over three years and would not have been possible without exceptional editorial assistance from Pat Schneider, Daphne Slocombe and Betsy Loughran. I worked with Pat for the first six months until her retirement, and then Daphne saw me through much of the remainder of this lengthy project. Betsy joined in toward the end. I am indebted to them all for their insight, patience, and mastery of the written word.

I am also grateful to the following for reading all or part of the manuscript: Betty Romer, Fred Wilson, Dorien Miller, Walter Denny, Conny Jamison, Sylwia Mucha, and Anita Odachowska-Mazurek. Their comments, corrections and suggestions made all the difference.

Polish Pronunciation Guide

sz: has an 'sh' sound, as in "should," Urszula, Tomasz.or Szopen

ś: also has an 'sh' sound, as in Świdnica

cz: has a 'ch' sound, as in "church," Częstochowa or Czajkowski

ch: has a guttural sound, like Bach in German and loch in Scottish

w: has a 'v' sound, as in "victory," Sylwia or Zawada

c: has a 'ts' sound, as in Świdnica (Shvidneetsa)

ł: sounds like a 'w', as in Wrocław (Vrotswav) or Michał (Meehow)

ck: sounds like 'itsk', as in Malicka (Malitska)

ę: has a nasal sound, as in Wałęsa, or proszę

ą: has a similar nasal sound, but more like "ouch"

ż: a 'z' with a dot is like a soft 'g', as in "garage" or Grażyna

ó: has an "oo" sound, as in "roof" or Kraków (Krakoof)

PART I

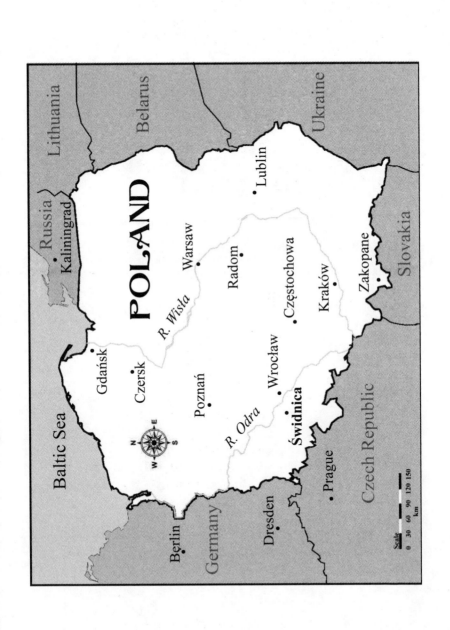

CHAPTER ONE

Świdnica, Poland: September and October 1997

It was past midnight and I couldn't sleep. A cold wind rapped at the leaky windows and what little heat there had been in my small fourth-floor apartment of the school had long since departed. The building was like a fortress, almost 100 years old, now empty and locked up for the night. In a few hours 650 adolescents would be roaring through the halls below. I was feeling restless and edgy. It had been my worst day. Going through my mind was what to do with the noisy and disruptive behavior in one of my classes. I was still having trouble keeping this class quiet during lessons, and my patience was weakening. I hadn't yet figured out what I was doing wrong. I was thinking of going to the director, but what would I tell him? After eight weeks I was having doubts about teaching for two years in this foreign land 3,000 miles from home. From under my covers I stared into the darkness and wondered what I had gotten myself into.

If any of my family or friends thought I was a bit reckless or naïve when I told them I was going to join the Peace Corps, they kept it to themselves. I'm sure they wondered why a sixty-seven-year-old grandfather would want to leave the comforts of home and live in some far corner of the world. But aside from what misgivings they may have had, and in spite of a few of my own, here I was teaching English in a high school in Poland. After eleven weeks of pre-service training during the summer, I had arrived in Świdnica (pronounced shvid-Neet-sa), a city of 65,000 in the southwest corner of the country near the Czech border. It was a late Friday afternoon in the last weekend of August, 1997. I would learn later that I was the only American and the only native speaker of English in the city. I was met at my school, where I would also live, by its director, Pan (Mr.) Henryk Zawada. He greeted me with a warm handshake and a small bouquet of flowers. "*Dzień dobry. Witamy w naszej szkole.*" (Hello. Welcome to our school.) As we walked up the wide staircase to my fourth-floor apartment, he explained that I would be meeting the next day with one of my colleagues for a brief orientation. He then gave me my keys; I would need all five of them. One for my apartment door, one for the lock on the iron gate down the hall, one for my classroom, and two for the main door downstairs. Since his English was hardly better than my limited Polish, our meeting was brief.

The next morning Pani (Mrs.) Grażyna Malicka (pronounced mah-Lit-ska), the head English teacher, arrived at my apartment. She spoke excellent English and I guessed that she was in her forties. She was good looking with prominent features, rather formal in manner, and casually but fashionably dressed. As a welcoming gift she brought some delicious Polish pastries. She was also the bearer of unsettling news. "You will be teaching four classes of third-year students, about 110 students. You will be their only teacher for grammar and conversation."

"Really? I thought just the Polish teachers taught grammar."

"Usually they do," she replied, "but the Peace Corps teacher before you requested permission to teach grammar and we are continuing that arrangement. Didn't they tell you in your training?"

"No, they didn't." I felt a jolt of anxiety in my stomach and tried not to shrink in my seat.

"You will need to buy the textbook series we use at the English bookstore in Wrocław. I have written down the name of the texts."

"I can't buy them here in Świdnica?"

"No," she said. "The bookstores here don't have them."

She explained that Wrocław (pronounced Vrots-waf) was a large city to the north, an hour by bus. I could buy the books the following weekend. "Until then," she said, "do anything you want with your students."

Alone in my spare two-room apartment I was left to contemplate my new situation. The thought of being the only teacher for 110 students was at that moment overwhelming. Until now I had the expectation, based on what we were told in our pre-service training, that the teaching load would be shared with a Polish counterpart, with most of the responsibility of teaching grammar in her lap. *And*, I asked myself, w*hy couldn't the school provide me the teaching* *tools I would need? Why should I have to spend most of a day looking for them, plus having to use my own money? Besides, what would I do on Monday in my classes?* With these thoughts in mind, I felt totally unprepared, not unlike the dreaded anxiety dream of not having studied for an exam. I needed something to distract me.

Putting aside further unpacking, I went for a walk to see what Świdnica had to offer. Directly across the street from the school was a park with beautiful old trees, and beyond the park, streets led into town, about a ten-minute walk. I passed old apartment buildings, some still showing a bit of grandeur from former times, while here and there were drab gray stucco buildings constructed during the communist era. By contrast, the façades of the town houses surrounding the central square, or *Rynek,* had been or were being renovated and colorfully repainted, some even with gold trim. Baroque architecture predominated, reflecting the tastes of the citizens who lived here when this part of Poland belonged to Germany until the end of World War II.

On the *Rynek* was the bank where I later opened an account, a variety of shops and small businesses, several restaurants, a large drug and cosmetic store, and an Internet café. A couple blocks away was Świdnica's Gothic cathedral with the second highest spire in Poland. I found a typical European market down another street. Under one roof was a collection of small stalls where shopkeepers sold vegetables, fruit, meat, poultry, fish, bread, and sundries such as stationery, batteries, and candy bars.

The streets were crowded with people rushing to finish shopping before 2:00 o'clock when most stores closed on Saturday afternoon. I couldn't help notice how many attractive, fashion-conscious women there were. The cosmetic industry was obviously doing well. Dying one's hair various shades of red was a popular fad. Young women liked to wear platform shoes and short, skimpy skirts. I located the post office and found other side streets with more shops. Though Poland was considered a poor country when compared to countries in Western Europe, there appeared to be no lack of merchandise. Traffic was heavy, too, zooming along at a clip faster than I considered prudent. Crossing the street could be dangerous.

On my way back to the school, I stopped to get groceries for the weekend that included a carton of milk, orange juice, a box of Kellogg's Cornflakes, a loaf of dark Polish bread, butter, a dozen eggs, and some rice and chicken to cook for supper. For three dollars I bought what turned out to be a thoroughly acceptable bottle of red wine from Bulgaria. Sales clerks all over Poland say "*Proszę*" when they are ready to wait on you. It literally means "I please," but takes the place of "Can I help you?"

After supper I did more unpacking and surveyed my new home. My apartment was down a long hall from my classroom. Along one side of the hall were dormitory rooms used for occasional guests of the school. Except for one other classroom, all the rest were on the floors below. Also on my floor, but on the opposite side of the building, lived the school custodian with his wife and four small children. He would be very helpful to me during my stay.

Immediately inside the apartment, in a kind of alcove, were the shower stall and sink to the left; to the right was a wooden cabinet for clothes. Beyond this alcove was the kitchen with an electric stove and cupboards with dishes. A small dining area was in the far end of the room, behind which was a window. On the counter was the telephone that was an extension of the school's number. Through a doorway to the right was my combination living and bedroom, with a couch/bed, a desk, a large bookcase with glass doors, an ironing board, and a television that received one channel. A casement window, like the one in the kitchen, looked out over gardens and rooftops of nearby homes. Neither window could be closed tight, a problem I hoped to solve before the cold weather set in. The walls were white, clearly recently painted. Down another hall in a different direction from my classroom was the toilet. Across from my apartment was a room under the eaves with a Russian-made washing machine and a small space to hang clothes to dry.

As I was getting ready for bed, I got to thinking about my children, two sons and a daughter, all now married and living in Massachusetts. I tried to imagine what they would say if they were there. *"Hey, Dad, are you really going to live in this tiny place for two years?" "I hope you can sleep on that couch. It doesn't look too comfy to me." "Sort of a long trek to the toilet, isn't it?" "This is pretty nice, Dad. You've got a shower with hot and cold running water. What more could you ask for?" "We miss you, Dad."* I missed them, too.

◆•❖•◆

On Monday I met Grażyna in the teachers' room, where she introduced me to a few of my future colleagues. Twenty-four teachers were on the staff, and except for the three other English teachers, none spoke much English. As one of the faculty, I had my own special place to sit at the long table that took up half of the room which was well lit by large windows on two sides. The other half was a kind of lounge with doors opening onto a small balcony where the cigarette smokers could take a break. It was evident that one didn't sit in someone else's seat. Soon we all left for an all-school assembly in the *aula*, or auditorium. This was the opening ceremony of the school year, with Mr. Zawada presiding. It was a lively affair with a variety of announcements interspersed with several student musical presentations that included a mixed vocal quartet and soprano solo with a piano accompaniment, both receiving loud cheers. I sat in the back with the other teachers. At one point Mr. Zawada read the names of the three new teachers. I stood up when I heard mine and the students all clapped. I took this as a good omen.

My classroom easily accommodated the twenty-seven to thirty students I had in each of my classes. Two aisles separated the six rows of desks. Large windows ran along one side of the room, letting in plenty of light. There were signs of neglect, however. Sections of the linoleum flooring were loose, pieces of drywall had come off the wall, and the room lacked the nice touch of having curtains like many other classrooms.

My students were a good looking group and typical of adolescents anywhere, being casually dressed in skirts and jeans, shirts and sweaters. Their class level corresponded to the American junior year in high school, though they were a year older since Polish schools begin and end a year later. Most would be nineteen upon graduation. One striking difference, at least compared to where I lived back home, was the total lack of ethnic diversity. Apparently Poland had not yet allowed much immigration. For reasons I never fully understood, one class had mostly boys and one was mostly girls; the other two appeared to be about evenly divided. The days I liked best were when classes were split up, usually twice a week, and the two halves scheduled at different hours. The atmosphere was more relaxed with no more than fifteen students in the room.

In that first week I improvised as best I could. I prepared a brief biographical piece which I dictated, while the students wrote it down in their copybooks. They learned that I was born in China where my father had been a medical missionary, grew up in a small town in Ohio, which I pointed out on the large map that hung on the wall in front of the classroom, and had three children and two grandchildren. One class asked, "Mr. Siddall, do you speak Chinese?" Another class wanted to know, "Have you been to Poland before? Do you speak Polish?"

I then asked, "Did you know that I live here in the school?"

"Yes, we know. The American teacher last year lived here. How do you like living here?"

"I like it fine," I said with as much enthusiasm as I could muster. Then I asked, "Would you like to stay overnight in the school?"

They laughed. "No! No!"

For the rest of the week I made up exercises and used lesson plans from my pre-service training. I was grateful when the week finally came to an end. I had survived.

I set aside Saturday to buy the textbooks I needed and made my first trip to Wrocław, an hour from Świdnica by bus. Fortunately the bus station was only a ten minute walk. With a population of over 700,000, Wrocław was the former German city of Breslau.[*]

---

[*] In 1163 the southwestern region of Poland, known as Silesia, was divided into Upper and Lower Silesia and ruled by princes of the Piast Dynasty. Wrocław and Świdnica were in Lower Silesia and for a time each city was capital of its own duchy. In 1335 the region became part of Bohemia (what is now mostly the Czech Republic), and then in 1526 came under the rule of the Austrian Hapsburgs. In 1742 Frederick the Great of Prussia, in a war with Austria, annexed Silesia, which eventually was incorporated into Germany under Bismarck in 1871. At the end of World War I Poland got back most of Upper Silesia, but lost it when Germany invaded Poland in 1939. In 1945, both Upper and Lower Silesia were returned to Poland.

In the center of its *Rynek* was the Gothic style Town Hall, now a museum, with a tavern that centuries ago was popular for selling the beer that was made in Świdnica at that time. Around the *Rynek* were colorfully restored former town houses similar to those in Świdnica, but on a much grander scale. The whole setting was impressive. With its restaurants, outdoor cafes, department stores and small businesses, it attracted locals and tourists alike. In time I would also get to know Wrocław well for its museums, symphony concerts, and massive train station.

At first I found my students more respectful than I had anticipated. For example, they always stood up when a teacher entered the classroom. With some notable exceptions, they were outgoing and friendly. However, it soon became evident that they liked to talk in class. I found this difficult to control, but they usually talked less the more they were engaged in their lessons. Other teachers said they had the same problem. I had to be strict, they told me. One day I asked a class why they liked to talk so much. "It's the Polish way," they replied.

Talking and other disruptions were most troubling with class IIIB (Third B). I felt most annoyed with three boys in particular. In my first encounter they were sitting together in the rear left corner of the classroom. After asking them to be quiet three times I walked down the aisle, and as I approached one of them looked up, leaned back in his chair and smiled. I took an instant dislike to him. The word slippery came to mind. In a flash my annoyance turned to anger. He said, "What's wrong? What did I do?"

"The three of you talking bothers everyone around you. You may have to sit up front by my desk if this continues."

"But I like to sit here with my friends. We'll be quiet."

I felt that I had little leverage, but I was more worried about losing my temper. I dreaded a confrontation, which I knew would be a bad idea. I wasn't about to lose control at this point. "I want to speak to you after class today." Looking at the other two I said, "I'll talk to you two tomorrow."

In elementary school my own report cards often had 'whispers too much' checked off. I can remember clearly one teacher we had who didn't say anything if we were talking, but instead went to the blackboard and wrote our names in the top right corner where they remained until some kind of punishment was meted out. Even two years later I sometimes felt a twinge of anxiety when a teacher went to the board even though it had nothing to do with anyone misbehaving. I didn't want to cause such a lasting effect, but my attempts at discipline, including making a mark by their names in the class grade book, didn't seem to make much difference. I was getting fed up.

Many of the students in IIIB were A students. Having studied English for several years, some were amazingly fluent and knew their grammar well. This was also the class that most of all missed the Peace Corps teacher who preceded me. When I first met the school director he gave me a letter from this young woman telling me, in addition to helpful information, how much she liked the students, and because she had enjoyed teaching there so much she extended her tour another year. My impression was that she already had experience teaching before she came to Poland. The clincher was that she wrote a letter to IIIB soon after I arrived, and the student to whom it had been addressed read it out loud. This led them to reminisce and tell me how she loved them and cried on the last day. She was a hard act to follow.

The morning after my restless night, eight weeks after I had arrived at the school, the students in IIIB could tell something was amiss by the look on my face. "I have something to tell you," I announced. I paused for moment. Silence filled every corner of the room. "I have decided to go to the director and tell him I don't want to teach this class any more. There is too much talking during lessons. You are too noisy. Some of you have been rude. I have reminded you enough." I stood there looking into their faces.

What is really going on here? I asked myself. Am I overreacting? Do these students deserve my harsh words? Am I punishing the whole class for my frustration dealing with the three most disruptive students? Am I being too rigid? Am I expecting too much of myself? Am I taking out on them my feelings of isolation in this foreign country?

Finally, Katarzyna stood up, her pretty face betraying an uncharacteristic look of dismay. Brushing back her long auburn hair and nervously clutching her desk, she said with as firm a voice as she could find, "Please, Mr. Siddall, don't go to the director. We'll try harder to be quiet. Please give us another chance." Again there was silence. Then Łukasz stood from his usual place at the back of the room. A tall, serious boy who looked older than his age, he said in his deep voice, "I think we can improve our behavior, but we want something different to do."

Then there followed pleas by Paweł, who had that week loaned me one of his favorite music cassettes, and Magda, one of the worst chattering offenders, but always cheerful. Others began to chime in, especially after I asked, "Are you bored?"

Before the session ended that morning the class made the decision, with my blessing, to spend one period a week in which they would take turns in pairs to make a presentation and lead a discussion on any topic they chose.

Later that day I decided to let Grażyna know what had happened. She was, after all, my counterpart to whom I should bring my concerns. I found her in her classroom, catching up on work at her desk. As she greeted me, I was reminded that she rarely smiled. I pulled up a chair and explained the morning events.

"I know that class well. They were my students for two years. I've had difficulty with the three boys you mentioned. I think everyone has."

She was not an expressive person, so it was difficult to know what she really thought. In our brief conversation her comments were noncommittal. If she felt critical of what I had done she didn't show it.

The next day IIIB told me that Grażyna came to their class and scolded them, quite loudly, they said, for making trouble for me. My initial reaction was to feel both annoyed and confused. I had assumed that my conversation with her had been between us, but she apparently had a different notion of what confidentiality meant. Thereafter I was careful about what I told her. Fortunately, IIIB didn't seem to be bothered much at all by her outburst, and a few even thought it was a bit humorous.

The following week, on the day when the class was divided in two, I asked Paweł and Tomek, "What are you presenting today for discussion?"

Tomek said, "It's about President John Kennedy. We found an article about him and his relationship with Marilyn Monroe."

"It's really interesting," Paweł added.

Though I had some doubts about the appropriateness of the article, which they had found in an obscure publication, it was obvious they were fascinated with Kennedy's personal life. More important, Paweł and Tomek did well in leading a lively discussion. With just fifteen students, almost everyone participated.

Overall my relationship with this class improved, though the irksome behavior of the three most troublesome boys persisted. If I had known the language better I might have had a meeting with each of them and their parents. At this point, however, I felt on shaky ground to try any sort of family intervention. Two weeks later I finally decided to send each of them to see the director. Over time their behavior mellowed, but for the rest of the year they remained a source of aggravation. I had a lot to learn about what it meant to be a teacher.

❖

In contrast to the interaction I had with students, my initial contacts with the teachers were much more limited. While most of the staff came to the teachers' room between classes, it wasn't until the mid-morning break that there was opportunity for much conversation. It would take weeks before I began to feel included. For one thing, I was still struggling to learn Polish. I learned later that a few of my colleagues, in addition to the three teachers of English, could in fact speak some English, certainly more than I could speak Polish. And I found it ironic that at the end of the school year I would learn that a young woman who taught Polish part-time knew English very well. Later, after we became better acquainted, she told me that what held her back was feeling shy and afraid to make mistakes in front of everyone. She guessed that applied to the others as well. Whatever the reason, I was the one who had to take the risk of making mistakes in Polish.

Even the other English teachers appeared to make little effort to include me in conversations. Besides Grażyna there were Krystyna, a long-time teacher at the school, and Ewa, a new member of the faculty. There wasn't the easy acceptance of someone new that I could imagine taking place in a high school back home. Grażyna sat two places to my left, and except for glancing up and saying hello in the morning, she rarely initiated a conversation. I considered the possibility that besides my limited Polish my age might be a factor in the overall equation. As far as I could tell I was the oldest person among them, and I had no idea what they were thinking. My colleagues were outgoing with each other, but it seemed obvious that if I were to become a part of this group it would be up to me, not them, to find a way in.

On a crisp October morning, as I was standing by one of the large windows in the teachers' room enjoying the autumn view, a woman whom I had not met came up to me and said, "Hello, my name is Urszula Tokarska. I teach English part-time. How do you like our school?"

I was momentarily speechless. I thought, *Not all that great.* But seeing her friendly smile I replied, "I like it pretty well, thank you. My name is Larry Siddall."

"Yes, I know."

"I'm delighted to meet you."

We chatted for a few minutes before the bell rang, and then she said, "I would like to invite you to my home sometime so we can get acquainted and you can meet my husband and two boys. They are both studying English."

"I would like that very much," I happily replied. This was my first invitation. Things were beginning to look up.

CHAPTER TWO

Radom, Poland: June to August 1997

I knew I wanted to do something out of the ordinary when I retired. I liked to travel and the thought of living abroad in a different culture was appealing. Over the years I often felt a kind of restlessness, a recurring urge to see what existed beyond my familiar world. Perhaps this stemmed in part from being born in China and growing up with stories of far-off places. No doubt it was intensified by my overland trip from Europe to India in 1956 when I was in my mid-twenties. There was little to hold me back. I was single and had the freedom to live where I wanted. I was in excellent health, I had no debt, my grown children were doing well, and my ex-wife was working.

The Peace Corps offered the allure of the unknown. It also had what I considered a good track record for its humanitarian projects. There was even the possibility that in some small way I might be a good-will ambassador on behalf of my home country. Two years in another country was also appealing because it would be totally unlike the conventional middle-class life I had lived in Amherst, Massachusetts, helping to raise three children, singing in my church choir, volunteering on church and town committees, protesting the Vietnam War, playing tennis, and running in 10K races. I was looking for a late-life adventure.

I applied to the Peace Corps in the spring of 1996 and retired that summer after thirty-four years working as a psychotherapist. I requested South America because I had never traveled there and I wanted to learn Spanish. My application to be an English teacher was accepted in August, but I wouldn't receive my official invitation for nine months in order to coincide with the next teaching year. To be free of all encumbrances, I decided to sell the house I had lived in for over thirty years. I held a massive yard sale, put the rest of my household goods in storage, and moved in with close friends who had a large house with a spare bedroom.

I was initially disappointed when I received my assignment to Poland the following April. All I knew about the country was the invasion in 1939 by Germany, the Warsaw Uprising in 1944, the resistance to the communist regime led by Lech Wałęsa and his Solidarity movement, and the fact that the Pope was Polish. Though there was a large Polish community in the town next to where I lived in Massachusetts, the only Pole I knew was my tailor. For some reason I was aware that learning the language would be difficult, certainly far more than Spanish. Then, as I got to thinking about living in Europe, fond memories of my two years in Munich in the 1950s came to mind. Poland was right next door. I would have the opportunity to look up old friends and travel in Central and Eastern Europe.

My first day in the Peace Corps was June 14, 1997, when I arrived in Washington, D.C. for a brief orientation. There were eighty in our group going to Poland, fifty to teach English and the others to serve as environmental consultants to non-governmental organizations. The next day we flew on three different flights to Warsaw.* High above the Atlantic Ocean I still felt the warmth of the farewell party given by friends the week before and the goodbye dinner I had with my children, Curt, Mark, and Jennifer, their spouses, and Jennifer's two small children, Parker and Caroline. Everyone's well-wishes stayed with me long after I arrived in my new home.

From Warsaw we went by bus to the city of Radom two hours south. There, for eleven weeks until the end of August, we would receive our "pre-service training," which included instruction in Polish, lectures on adjusting to the Polish culture, and for us teachers classes in teaching English. After we arrived in Radom, a drab, run-down-looking city of 250,000, we were met by our host families with whom we would stay for the summer. My "family" was Marek Duszynski, a factory worker in his late forties whose wife, I figured out in time, lived in a village thirty miles north where she taught school. They had two grown boys, one in the army and one in high school who lived with his mother. Since

---

* Since the name of Warsaw is so familiar, I use it instead of Warszawa, the Polish spelling. The names of all other cities I refer to are in Polish.

he didn't own a car, Marek had a friend drive us to his apartment fifteen minutes away. It was on the fifth floor of a large apartment building in a complex typical of many throughout the city. He spoke no English but was friendly and hospitable.

Most of the other host families lived in similar apartment complexes. All received a stipend from the Peace Corps to pay for food and minor expenses. Children or parents often gave up their rooms and slept on the living room couch to accommodate their American guests. I was fortunate to have more privacy than many of my Peace Corps friends and was spared being witness to family squabbles and pressure from "host moms" to eat more than some thought was humanly possible.

Marek's apartment was clean but small. We both observed the Polish custom of taking off our shoes inside the front door. My bedroom window, with its heavy red drapes and white lace curtains, faced east and looked out over a parking lot, then open fields, and beyond that the railroad tracks a mile away. The distant sound of frequent trains became familiar and even comforting at night. Since my room had no bed, I slept on a futon. The bathroom had plenty of hot water which came from one of three central heating plants in the city, but unfortunately it was turned off for ten days in the summer to service the pipes. The kitchen where we cooked on a gas stove and ate our meals was next to my room. Across the entryway were Marek's room and the living room with a balcony that looked out on the other apartment buildings, all connected by footpaths in the tall grass that was rarely mowed. I got a good daily workout walking up and down the five flights of stairs.

I was out of bed before 6:00 and left the apartment by 7:15 to catch the bus for a thirty-minute ride to the polytechnic school on the other side of the city where our classes were held. Its facilities were modest compared to what we have in the States, but adequate and provided ample space for classes and meetings.

At 8:00 we all met together for "check-in." In addition to staff announcements and other official business, it was a time for us to report on events of the previous day, which usually were about life with our host families. I got a laugh when I said I didn't know where Marek's wife was, and how, when I first plugged it in, the surge protector for my laptop computer blew up. We then went to our classes, which ended usually at 5:00. Many of our group then gathered at a beer garden near the school. Though I sometimes joined them, I usually preferred the quiet of Marek's apartment.

———————

Learning Polish turned out to be far more difficult than I imagined. I had studied German in college and learned to speak it fairly well when I lived in Munich for two years, but as challenging as I thought German was, I found Polish to be in a different league. Most of us struggled, though some of the younger volunteers caught on with less difficulty.

There were eight of us in each class. Several times in the summer we were assigned to a different group depending on how we were judged to be doing. We changed instructors several times as well. I did better than I expected in the first fifteen-minute oral evaluation and was put in a more advanced class. I was pleased at first, but then it became a strain to keep up.

We had several hours of instruction five days a week. Polish is a Slavic language and its grammar, spelling and pronunciation have little in common with English. Polish does have the advantage of being a phonetic language, so that once one learns the rules, pronunciation is always the same. However, it takes a good ear and some tongue twisting to get the sounds right. We started out with simple, everyday words: *tak* (yes), *nie* (no), *Dzień dobry* (Hello/Good day), *Do widzenia* (Goodbye), *dzisiaj* (today), *jutro* (tomorrow), *Dziekuję bardzo* (Thank you very much), *wszystkiego najlepszego* (best wishes), *Piwo* (beer), *Na zdrowie!* (To your health!).

Then we began to put together short sentences. *Mowię slabo po polsku.* (I speak a little Polish.) *Język Polski jest bardzo trudny.* (The Polish language is very difficult.) *Chciałbym kupic . . .* (I would like to buy . . .) *Jestem nauczycielem języka angielskiego.* (I am an English teacher.) And of course, *Jestem ochotnikem Amerikanskiego Korpusu Pokoju.* (I am an American Peace Corps volunteer.) The greeting, *Co słychac?* (How are you?) is not used nearly as much as in the

States when greeting someone because the inquiry is often taken literally. You are likely to hear how bad things have been lately.

In one of our other classes a staff member from the American Embassy gave a lecture on the economic situation in Poland, and said that in preparation for his assignment he was required to attend classes in Polish every day for a whole year before coming to Warsaw. He believed that only a few other languages, such as Chinese and Japanese, required this length of study prior to an assignment.

It was reassuring to learn that after we arrived at our teaching sites, the Peace Corps would reimburse us for the cost of a tutor. I planned to take advantage of this offer.

———◆◈◆———

Learning to teach English as a foreign language was not as difficult as learning Polish, but it required a lot of work. In addition to our classes, what I found most helpful were the three weeks of practice teaching, especially since I had never taught in a classroom before. Over 300 students from the community had signed up for the free classes, each to be taught by two volunteers. The students were evaluated and assigned according to their age and level of proficiency. Twelve eighteen- and nineteen-year-olds were in my class. The schedule was unrelenting. Each day we had to come up with a new lesson plan and get it approved by one of the instructors. I often stayed late in the resource room pouring over piles of old magazines and teaching aids, taking notes, then typing up a final draft in my room after supper. Sometimes I didn't get to bed until midnight.

One evening I was in the resource room and saw Aaron, a fellow volunteer, sitting in front of his laptop, staring out the window. I went over to say hello.

"How's it going, Ah-rone?" I asked, pronouncing his name like his students did.

He smiled, but he looked tired. "Oh, not too bad. I'm about ready to leave. I'm hungry. How about you?"

"I'm running out of ideas. I'd like something besides having the students buy train tickets, cook a meal, or learn about American holidays."

"I know what you mean. I overheard you talking about art the other day. Your students are older and more sophisticated than mine. Why don't you do something with that?"

I did in fact take Aaron's suggestion. Art history had been a life-long interest and I spent the next hour writing up a draft of a lesson plan entitled, "Viewing a Painting." The objective was to have the students gain an appreciation of a work of art by learning what to look for in a painting. It was fortunate that I brought with me an illustrated calendar of paintings by Johannes Vermeer from the popular exhibit I had seen in Washington, D.C. the winter before coming to Poland. I came up with several questions I would have the students consider. It turned out that I had enough material for two class sessions with lively discussion. Several students said they liked these lessons the best.

On the last day of the practice teaching, we had a party during which the students presented me with a book of beautiful photographs of the Tatry Mountains in southern Poland. Inside was inscribed, "Thank you for common time, hard work, and pleasant collaboration."

Lunch was in the school cafeteria. One day I was sitting across from Paula Miller, one of my new friends. In her thirties, she was attractive, good company, cheerful, and delightfully outspoken. She had just finished a masters program in higher education and was finally realizing a long-held dream of joining the Peace Corps.

"What did you think of Polish class this morning?" I asked.

"That stuff is really hard," she said. "Each day gets more and more frustrating. Trying to conjugate verbs is driving me nuts. How about you?"

"I agree. I'm not sure I'll ever be able to speak this language. It's a royal bitch if you ask me. By the way, are you going on the trip to Warsaw this weekend?"

"Yes, are you?"

"Definitely."

"Good. Why don't you come with Jenni and me? Shirley and Jon might come, too. Besides, we're all dying to get out of Radom. It's so gloomy."

This day trip was organized by the staff. In Warsaw we were first given a tour of the Peace Corps headquarters and then set free to see the sights on our own. Once called the "Paris of Central Europe," the destruction of Warsaw is one of the many tragic stories of World War II. The photographs and a film we saw at the Historical Museum in the restored Old Town (*Stare Miasto*) were shocking as they made vivid the heroic suffering endured by the citizens of Warsaw. In the first month of the war, over 40,000 inhabitants of Warsaw had already been killed and fifteen percent of the city severely damaged. Within a year the Nazis had created the Jewish Ghetto, which led to the futile rebellion in 1943 in which thousands of Jews were slaughtered. In retaliation of the failed Warsaw Uprising in 1944, Hitler ordered the systematic dynamiting of most of what was still standing of the city. By the time the war ground to an end a year later, more than 850,000 of Warsaw's inhabitants, two-thirds of the pre-war population, had perished.

After the war, as Warsaw began to rise from the rubble, the Old Town was slowly rebuilt using old architectural plans, pre-war photographs, and scenes of the city by eighteenth century artists. One was Bernardo Bellotto, an Italian who took the name Canaletto from his more famous uncle. With the aid of pollution, the buildings around the central square (*Rynek*), built in the architectural style of the seventeenth and eighteenth centuries, look truly authentic today. As we strolled along its cobblestone streets, I tried to imagine what it would have been like to wander through the desolate landscape that once stretched out for miles at war's end. Today the Old Town is one of Warsaw's most popular sites.

At one end of the central square stands the former seventeenth century Royal Castle *(Zamek Krolewski)*, now a museum. It lay in absolute ruins until the 1970s. In times past it had been the home of the royal family and seat of the Polish parliament, called the *Sejm*. It was here in 1573 that the *Sejm* passed a law that paved the way for Poland to become the most religiously tolerant country in Europe. In 1791 it established modern Europe's first constitution, having been directly influenced by the American Revolution. The Royal Castle, designed by Italian Renaissance architects, has been totally rebuilt, and it challenges one's imagination to consider how the art historians, restorers and craftspeople were able to bring such a beautiful structure back to life from utter destruction. The Canaletto Room is just one exquisite example, its white walls accentuated with decorative gold leaf moldings and wainscoting. The paintings on display include landscapes and views of the city by Bellotto. They survived the war because they were safely hidden away before the Nazis invaded. However, the Nazis did succeed in stealing thousands of works of art from museums and collections throughout Poland. Though many paintings and other objects were found safe in Germany after the war, untold numbers are still unaccounted for.

We headed for the central part of the city to have lunch. Away from the Old Town, Warsaw looked like an architectural wasteland. It was hard to shake my initial impression. A monstrous wedding-cake style skyscraper, a gift from Stalin in the 1950s called the Palace of Culture, dominated the downtown skyline. While a surge in foreign investment has financed many modern buildings since 1990, the older buildings constructed during the communist regime looked dull and unimaginative. But this was only my first visit. Later, when I returned to Warsaw on numerous occasions, I discovered many of its prize possessions, such as beautifully restored gardens and parks, the Philharmonic Hall, the Opera House, and Wilanów, the stunning seventeenth century palace on the city's outskirts.

———◆◈◆———

Since my arrival in Poland I had wondered how I would fit in with my younger colleagues. Though nine of us were over fifty, the average age was about thirty. (The husband in one of the few married couples was seventy-five.) I was impressed with these young people, some just out of college, for their courage to take on what would be for most a difficult job. I'm sure I couldn't have done it at their age. I wanted to get to know them and to see how they coped with the same problems I faced in adjusting to a different culture.

The lecture on safe sex jolted me into reality. It spared no details on the risks of sexually transmitted diseases and the importance of using a condom. In spite of the topic's seriousness, levity found its way in. The most hilarious part was getting someone to come forward to demonstrate how to put a condom on a plastic phallus on a table in front of the room. A voice from the rear said, "Hey, Ross, show us how it's done."

"Are you kidding?" Looking around he said, "Scott, you go up." Other voices chimed in. "Yeah, Scott, come on. Don't be bashful." So up to the table Scott came. He picked up the condom, deftly unwrapped it, and with great dexterity swiftly completed the delicate task. Smiling broadly, he was clearly enjoying the moment as he returned to his seat to cheers and clapping.

We were told that a certain percent of the group (I can't remember the exact statistic, but I was surprised how high it was) would have sex during their two-year tour. Glancing around at the women, I could see that I was probably too old to be in the running. Otherwise I found that my age wasn't an obstacle to getting to know my colleagues. Days passed when I didn't give it a thought.

One day at lunch, soon after our trip to Warsaw, I was sitting with Jon, a social worker from Seattle in his late twenties. Between bites of fish casserole he said, "I heard your announcement at check-in the other morning that you're starting a chorus."

"Right," I said. "I thought it would be a fun activity this summer for those of us who like to sing. Are you interested?"

"I think so."

I told Jon that the staff had plans for a concert at the end of the summer for the host families and our whole group. I thought the chorus might sing several pieces from an American songbook

I brought with me. In addition, the staff had lined up a variety of acts, including individual songs, recitations, and poetry readings.

"We especially need male voices. And no auditions, either," I added.

"I'll be there for sure," Jon said as he took a spoonful of watery custard dessert.

A couple weeks later Paula caught up with me after class. "If you're not busy this weekend, how about meeting in the city park for a beer. I need to get out of the house."

"That sounds great," I said. "Are you sure you can get away?"

"I'll find a way. No problem."

Paula chafed under the watchful eye of her overprotective host parents. She was expected to participate in all family activities, including frequent weekends to their summer home in the country, and it forced her to be creative in saying no in order to do things on her own. The household included a twenty-year-old son who had a steady job, and a mildly rebellious, sexually provocative teenage daughter. Paula told me once, her voice rising several pitches pretending to be shocked, "You would never believe what that girl wears when she goes out with her boyfriend!"

Radom was, as Paula said, a bit gloomy. It had a not-cared-for look like many Polish towns and cities. I sometimes chided myself for being affected by this aesthetic deficit, but on the way to the beer garden in the park, Paula and I agreed that a coat of paint would brighten things up.

The park turned out to be a popular gathering place for strolling among the shade trees and flowerbeds of impatiens, begonias, ageratum, and marigolds whose colors of red, blue, pink and yellow offset the drabness of the nearby buildings. Here and there sparrows hopped around in the grass. Sunday was a day to dress up and children were given special attention, particularly little girls who were displayed in their frilly dresses and white bonnets.

"Want another beer?" I asked.

"Sure, why not. You, too?"

"No, I think I'll just stick with this one. But how about splitting an order of kielbasa?" I suggested. "Just the aroma itself is worth the price. I think it comes with sauerkraut, dark bread and mustard."

"Okay. Sounds good."

After a rainy night the sky was cloudless and bright. We had decided to sit outside in the beer garden to feel the warmth of the sun filtering through the over-arching trees. We were among twenty or so other patrons that included a few families with children playing nearby. Several tables were as yet unoccupied, their shiny, dark green painted tops still holding pools of water from the previous night's storm. From inside the restaurant, its windows wide open, came the sounds of a boisterous party, with singing and accordion playing.

After the waitress had brought the beer and kielbasa, Paula said, "I overheard Brian and Jon teasing you about hanging out with host moms."

I laughed. "That's because Shirley told them that I visited her and her host family."

"When was that?"

"A couple weeks ago. I first met them at that outdoor museum on the edge of town, soon after we arrived here. Shirley was there with her host mom, Barbara. I was invited over for supper, and a week later Shirley and I cooked an American-style spaghetti dinner for Barbara and her daughter, Wioletta. It was a hit, but a bit awkward because of the language barrier. Barbara supplied the beer, and strawberries for dessert."

"What's Barbara like?"

I replied that she was a good-looking woman, probably in her late forties or early fifties. Shirley liked her a lot and was fitting into the family well from what she told me. She was not much older than Wioletta, who was about twenty. "Shirley's doing really well with her Polish," I added. "Mine's so limited."

"I've heard you in class. You're not so bad. Your pronunciation is better than most of us."

"Well, thanks. But even so I declined an invitation from Barbara to attend a gathering with her relatives next Sunday. For me, the strain of carrying on a halting conversation for a whole afternoon would spoil the fun. Really."

"Maybe she has designs on you," Paula said, grinning.

"Well, designs aren't going to go very far if you can't communicate."

"By the way," Paula said, "I hear Kathleen is now directing your chorus."

"Yes. She's doing a fine job."

I had enlisted Kathleen to be in charge of rehearsals because she was more musically trained than I. She and I had also become friendly because she lived just ten minutes from me and we often took the bus together. My stopping by her apartment led to getting to know her hosts, the Grzybowski family. In fact her host brother, Wojtek, was in my practice-teaching English class. He was a good student and talked incessantly about wanting to go to America. His older sister, Isabel, was quite fluent in English. She and her mother worked full-time, but unfortunately the father was ill and couldn't leave the house. He died the following year. They were a warm, close-knit family with whom I always felt welcome. During the summer I frequently shared a meal with them and Kathleen.

"Well," Paula said, "I'm coming by soon to hear what you guys sound like."

<hr>

Another staff-sponsored trip was to the city of Lublin, and, for those interested, a visit to the nearby concentration camp of Majdanek. By the sixteenth century Lublin had become a thriving cultural and commercial center. It was here in 1569 that the kings of Poland and Lithuania formally joined their countries to create the largest empire in Europe, stretching from the Baltic Sea in the north to the Black Sea in the south. The city also became one of Poland's most important Jewish communities. Its beginning dates back to the fourteenth century when King Kazimierz gave permission for Jews to settle. The Jewish cemetery is the oldest in Poland. In 1939, prior to World War II, there were over 100 synagogues; in 1945 there was one.

Lublin was a two-hour bus ride from Radom, and on the way I decided I wanted to see Majdanek (pronounced my-Don-eck), hoping in some way to understand better what took place in Poland under the Nazis. When I asked those around me on the bus, a few said they were considering going as well. Years before I had been to the concentration camp at Dachau, near Munich. Built in 1933, it was the first detention center under Hitler's regime. Majdanek was the first camp I would see on Polish soil.

Thinking about Dachau reminded me of my two-year stay in Munich in the 1950s. I became attached to the city and made good friends, but there was always the thought that I was living in the country whose Nazi government started the war that devastated Europe. Now here in Poland I would be confronted again with Germany's grim past.

After arriving in Lublin we had lunch and did a bit of sightseeing. Then a small group of us took a local bus for the short ride to Majdanek. The first thing I saw at the entrance was a gigantic sculpture commemorating the camp's victims. I couldn't tell if it was carved from stone or was poured concrete. It was a gray rectangle, rather ugly to my eye, about twenty feet long and several feet thick, supported by two short columns. It's called the *Monument to Struggle and Martyrdom* with the inscription, "Let our fate be a warning for you."

A long walkway led from the entrance into the camp. The inmates had called it the black path because it was paved with broken gravestones from Jewish cemeteries. Lush, green lawns gave the setting a tranquil atmosphere. It took me a few minutes to realize that little effort had been made to conceal the camp from the road.

Majdanek was built as a camp for Russian prisoners of war who had been captured during Germany's invasion of Russia early in the war. However, it soon became a major center for exterminating Jews and Polish political prisoners. It would also be a source for slave labor. Heinrich Himmler came to Lublin in 1941 to oversee the initial construction of what would be the easternmost concentration camp in Poland.

Twenty groups of barracks had been planned, but only six were built. Each contained twenty-four barracks, which were prefabricated horse barns. One of them could accommodate about 250 inmates, but eventually each housed 500 to 800. At any one time there were about 25,000 inmates at the camp. Each group was surrounded by barbed wire and electric fence. Eighteen watchtowers, many still standing, were placed around the camp. Only one group of barracks was preserved.

We first saw a film in the main visitor's center taken by Russian troops showing shocking images just after Majdanek was liberated. I was shaken by the sight of hollow-eyed women and men looking like walking cadavers, emaciated children, and charred remains of bodies. After the film I decided to see the rest of the camp on my own.

Nearby, former workshop buildings housed the exhibits. The one I saw first was of thousands of shoes that almost filled an entire room. It was reported that over 800,000 pairs had been collected. I could see some of them in detail, a scuffed work shoe, a man's brown dress shoe, a woman's finely made leather boot, a little girl's dark red shoe with a slender strap. Next door was a glass case full of human hair. Accumulated hair was sent to Germany to be used in making fabric. The uniform color of the hair on display was a result of the effects of the lethal chemical used in the gas chamber.

In another exhibit, besides the blue and gray striped garments the inmates wore, were personal items such as toothbrushes, combs, dolls, books, rosaries, crosses, homemade jewelry, drawings and poems. There were also photographs of camp life, some depicting guards and staff. The camp was run by SS officers, a number of whom were especially feared for their cruelty. Many of the guards were criminals brought in from Germany and described in the exhibit as "degenerate functionaries."

Among the most compelling photographs were pictures of camp survivors, with brief descriptions of what had happened to them. One was an image of a young woman taken in profile that showed off her 1940s hairstyle, her hair combed high on her forehead and long in back. Her name was Halina Birenbaum. In the brochure I bought, she described a moment after arriving at Majdanek, starved and exhausted after having ridden to Lublin in a filthy, stinking cattle car and transported to the camp in a truck. *We kept retreating, to postpone the moment of separation. Other families were doing the same. Sons, fathers, brothers and husbands, hastily said goodbye to their womenfolk. People embraced and kissed. The SS brutally pushed them, fired at those retreating, beating people blindly. We must have been harder than iron for our hearts did not break with the pain!*

Later a colleague told me that when she was looking at the exhibit of those photographs, a small group of visitors came in. An elderly woman said to her friends in German, pointing to the photograph of Halina Birenbaum, "That's me."

There was not much to see of the gas chamber but a concrete room with a door and an opening at the top where the Zyklon-B crystals were dropped in. It was simple in construction, but gruesome. It was mostly Jews who were gassed and sent to the ovens. Many inmates died of starvation or illness. Others were simply shot, hanged, clubbed, or drowned, often for a minor offence or at the whim of a guard. Those not cremated were buried in large pits dug in the ground. The worst massacre occurred on November 3, 4, and 5, 1943, in an operation called "Harvest Festival," when 43,000 people, mostly Jews from Lublin, were killed, abruptly ending 600 years of their cultural and religious history. In one day alone, beginning in the morning and lasting until nightfall, 18,000 people were machine gunned while music was played over loudspeakers to drown out the ghastly sounds. It became known as "Bloody Wednesday." Of the more than 300,000 people who came through Majdanek, representing over fifty nationalities, more than 250,000 perished. Incredibly, over 500 were able to escape.

In spite of all the cruelty, some inmates were allowed to receive packages from the Red Cross and other aid organizations. Goods were also smuggled in by resistance fighters. Local citizens tried to help as well. Inmates assigned work details outside the camp were among those most likely to survive. Survivors testified that a few of the guards treated inmates humanely. In the evening inmates could socialize and visit friends in other barracks. Religious gatherings were popular, as were group singing, informal concerts and plays.

The cries of crows overhead broke the stillness in the air as I walked to the crematorium. Five crematory ovens, each capable of accommodating two bodies at a time, stood in their original places. An eternal flame burned in one of them. When the ovens were in operation, ashes from the burned corpses were taken to the camp's compost pile, where they were mixed in with dirt and food scraps to be used on the camp's gardens. Nearby was another memorial; it looked like a large upside down bowl and contained the ashes of victims.

In the last year of the war, when the Nazis realized that Russian troops were approaching, they sent inmates to other camps. Some were transported by train; many of those who were made to walk died on the way. About 1,500 inmates were left in the barracks. The Nazi's final act was to round up the remaining political prisoners held in the Castle Prison in Lublin and bring them to the camp, where they were shot in front of the crematory ovens. Then they set fire to the wooden structure around the ovens. A scene from the film we saw in the visitors' center shows a group of women weeping over the remains. Liberation of Majdanek came on July 23, 1944. In America I celebrated my fourteenth birthday.

To this day I can recall the despair I felt walking alone down the black path on the way to meet my friends at the bus stop.

———◆•✕•◆———

A trip to Częstochowa introduced me to Polish Catholicism. Shirley, Kathleen and I were sitting in the Chapel of the Blessed Virgin in the Monastery of Jasna Gora, waiting for the next unveiling of Poland's famous icon, the Black Madonna. The pews were filling up fast. Excitement was definitely in the air here in this solemn, incense-filled holy place. We had five more minutes to wait. As Catholics, Shirley and Kathleen were fascinated by the occasion, though they told me later that they hadn't fully embraced what they had witnessed that day. I was finding our visit fascinating as well, but as a New England Congregationalist unaccustomed to revering icons, I was clearly in unfamiliar territory.

The Black Madonna, a centuries-old painting in the Byzantine style, portrays the Virgin Mary holding the Infant Jesus. It has darkened over the years from age and exposure to soot from votive candles. The painting is always shielded by a mechanized curtain that is raised only at specific times. This was the moment for which we were waiting.

In 1384 the painting was donated to the monastery two years after its founding. Many legends surround the painting's origin and the miracles associated with it. One legend says it was actually painted by St. Luke. Believers say that the power of the Black Madonna helped a small detachment of Polish soldiers repel a large Swedish army in 1655, saving the monastery from capture. Another legend says that when the painting was stolen in 1430, damage to the Virgin's face caused it to bleed. After its return it is said that the restorers made slash marks on the left cheek to maintain the legend. Because the painting has brought fame to Czestochowa, the city is one of the country's most sacred pilgrimage sites. In celebration of the Feast of Assumption on August 15, for instance, thousands of the Church's faithful walk for nine days from Warsaw to worship here.

In more recent times, Częstochowa became known as a center of the Church's opposition to the communist regime by encouraging pilgrimages as a way to show both patriotism and passive resistance. The fame of the monastery and the Black Madonna was further enhanced by a visit from Pope John Paul II, (whose name was Karol Wojtyła), the former bishop of Kraków. He came here in 1979 and worshipped in the same chapel where we were now sitting.

A recorded trumpet fanfare, sounding a bit tinny, broke the silence. Then the curtain began to slowly rise. Ohs and ahs were heard throughout the sanctuary. We had finally seen the Black Madonna.

------◆◆◆◆◆------

My stay with Marek worked out well. In spite of the gulf between us in language and culture, our daily lives meshed in a comfortable fashion, at least most of the time. He had a habit of talking in a loud voice, even when we were sitting at the kitchen table. When first addressing me he would begin by poking my arm and saying my name twice, which sounded like "Letty! Letty!" He spoke the language well and was always eager to help me with my Polish homework.

Marek was somewhat of a loner. Though he sometimes visited the couple who lived across the hall, rarely did he invite anyone to the apartment while I was there. I couldn't tell if he had any interests other than his job. I never fully understood just what kind of work he did; about all I could determine was it had something to do with working at a sewing machine in a factory.

Though I was soon preparing my own breakfast and doing some cooking, Marek usually had a light supper of soup, bread and cold cuts ready when I got home, for which I was most grateful. Traditionally Poles have their main meal, *obiad,* in the middle of the day, so I ate a good meal in the school cafeteria at noontime. I persisted in urging Marek to buy more fresh fruit and vegetables, especially since it was summer, with vendors filling the parking lot outside on Saturday mornings. He finally got the message after I came home one day with juicy tomatoes and fresh lettuce.

Marek liked his beer and always had several bottles in the refrigerator. I have a limited capacity for alcohol, so I never attempted to keep up with him. Once, when I came home late in the evening, he was sitting at the kitchen table, obviously drunk, his face flushed and his sad, watery eyes staring at the wall. "Letty! Letty!" he called out in a loud voice, but then began quietly muttering to himself. I sat with him for a while; it was an hour before I could get him to go to his room.

Only on two occasions did Marek and I go somewhere together. The first time was to a staff-sponsored Fourth of July event at the school for volunteers and their host families. This was an evening *ognisko,* a traditional Polish bonfire and picnic with plenty of beer and roasted kielbasa. Marek was quiet at first, but after a couple beers he loosened up and began socializing with other host families.

The other occasion was a Sunday visit in the country to see his wife, Wiesława. Accompanied by the couple across the hall, who had an automobile, we drove to the train station, then had a slow, forty-minute ride through the lush countryside under a warm sun. Finally, the train stopped in the middle of a woods, and from there we followed a well-worn path for a hundred yards that ended on an unpaved country lane, along which were several small dwellings. Wieslawa's home was what I would call a peasant's cottage that appeared to have very few amenities. It turned out that other friends and relatives, including Marek's two sons, were there as well. There were at least twelve altogether. By the time we arrived in late morning, preparations had begun for *obiad* that would take place around a large table under a tree in the yard. Cooking was underway in both the rustic kitchen and on a grill outside. Already beer and vodka were on the table, together with appetizers of cheeses, bread, and small slices of kielbasa and ham. Soon the women served the main meal of roasted chicken, boiled potatoes and vegetables. It was a happy scene, with much animated talking and laughter.

The only problem was I could hardly understand a word they said. All I could do was smile, say *dziękuję* (thank you) now and then, and eat. By the time we finished dessert, followed by more drinks, it was well into the afternoon and I thought Marek might give some indication when we would be leaving. While I waited for a sign, I wandered up and down the lane, strolled in the nearby woods, took more photographs of Marek's family and the guests, and became painfully bored. Then I noticed that more food and drinks were being brought out. My thought of leaving in the afternoon was a gross miscalculation. The sign from Marek to leave didn't come until 9:00 that evening.

<hr>

Our pre-service training ended with a swearing-in ceremony presided over by the American ambassador to Poland. First he gave a short speech in Polish and English, and then administered the oath of office, the same as our president says when inaugurated. I found the ceremony uplifting and felt truly proud to represent my country.

Volunteers, staff, teachers and host families packed the room. I was pleased that Marek and Wiesława were there. I took the occasion to give them a gift, a framed photograph of them together that I had taken during the picnic at her place.

A buffet supper followed. Afterward was a party at a nightclub, attended mostly by younger members of the host families in addition to staff, volunteers and some of the teachers. Paula decided not to go. I went and spent much of the evening with Shirley and her host mom, Barbara. We promised to keep in touch.

The next day we all departed for our sites scattered around Poland. A young teacher from my school and her uncle picked me up. I said goodbye to Marek and we set off for the six-hour ride to Świdnica, my new home for the next two years.

On the way I recalled Paula the evening before saying, "I know our assignments aren't very close, but I hope we can get together after we leave here and are settled."

"I hope so, too. In fact, I'm counting on it."

CHAPTER THREE

Świdnica, Poland: November 1997 to January 1998

It was a chilly but sunny Saturday in October. I was riding with
Urszula Tokarska and her family in their VW Golf, headed for a
day of hiking in the Karkonosze Mountains that separate Poland
and the Czech Republic, an hour south of Świdnica. We would be
joined by some of their friends. Alexander, Urszula's husband, was
driving. I was crammed into the back seat with their pre-teenaged
sons, Szymon and Marcin. This was my first outing with them and
it felt good to get out of town. The autumn foliage and the warm
browns and yellows of the farmland that stretched out before us
told of summer's end.

I felt at ease with Urszula and her family from the beginning.
They lived in a small fourth floor apartment in one of the newer
complexes next to open fields on the outskirts of Świdnica, feeling
like almost being in the country. The living room was furnished
with an overstuffed couch and two easy chairs upholstered in a large
floral pattern. Besides two floor lamps with ornate shades were
several large potted plants. A bookcase and the television occupied
the opposite wall from the couch. Heavy drapes surrounded a large
window that looked out over the courtyard below.

Urszula was of Russian descent and kept in touch with Russian
relatives. She had graduate degrees in Russian and English, and
spoke both fluently. Alexander, a friendly, thoughtful man, didn't
speak English, so Urszula translated our conversations. He was
an engineer and worked for the municipal water department.
Their two good-looking boys were equally personable, but shy
when mother called on them to speak English. Over time I was a
frequent visitor.

It was not long into our trip that I began to feel queasy because
Alexander, like other drivers, was going too fast. Unlike them,
however, he didn't pass around curves and in front of oncoming
cars. I began to wonder, *Will we all end up maimed and lying in*

a ditch? Will I have to be shipped back to the States with permanent injuries? At least we were wearing seatbelts.

To my relief we arrived without mishap. I was introduced to their friends, two couples with whom they often went hiking, and then we set out. We took a trail that led us up the mountain ridge. At first we trekked through thick stands of fir, beech and pine, but as we gained altitude we came to open spaces where we could look down on the serene valley below. The ascent was not steep, but for some in our group it became increasingly taxing. During one of our pauses Urszula said, "My friends commented how hiking up here doesn't seem to tire you out. They're impressed how fit you are."

"Well, at home I used to run almost every day. I'm still in good shape." In fact I had been a runner for almost twenty years. However, I felt self-conscious in Poland because I saw no other joggers, so I pretty much gave it up. I still got a good enough workout walking into town every day.

"We'll be stopping for lunch soon," she said. "We'll find a nice spot somewhere up ahead."

We could hear the waterfall before we saw it, a gentle sound at first, then more demanding, and suddenly it was upon us, crashing wildly over rocks and dead tree trunks, tossing up foam that glittered in the sunlight and spraying the ferns that clung to the banks of the stream.

"Let's have lunch here," we all agreed. In a nearby grassy area we spread out several blankets under the shade of a large fir. We were tired and relished the rest. While the men opened several bottles of beer and soft drinks for the boys, the women served lunch: fried chicken, egg salad, dark bread, pickles, olives, and tomatoes. Dessert was assorted fruit, cookies and sweets.

It was a relaxed time of eating and sharing stories of previous hikes. One of Urszula's friends said, "Maybe the next time we can take the gondola. It's a great view from the top."

As we came slowly down the mountain under a late-afternoon sun filtering through the treetops, a hawk high overhead kept us company. I felt content. It had been a perfect day.

My classes began every morning at 8:00. Given my preference for conservative dress, I wore a tie and sport jacket, or no jacket in the warmer weather. Our director, Mr. Zawada, always wore a suit, white shirt and tie, as did another older teacher. The younger male teachers wore open shirts and sweaters.

I tried to arrive early at my classroom each day and would be greeted by a clutch of students milling round and chatting in the hallway while waiting for me to unlock the door. Several would greet me before the door was opened. "Good morning, Mr. Siddall." "What are we doing today, Mr. Siddall?" "Are you still going to give us a test today?" By the time the bell rang, most of the students were seated. The occasional latecomer would arrive breathless at my desk to offer an excuse for being tardy.

The first order of business was taking attendance. I noted presence or absence in the class's *dziennik,* a large folio in which was recorded each student's attendance, grades and other important information for the entire year. The *dzienniks* were kept in the teachers' room where they were filed by class number and were picked up each hour before class by the teachers.

Depending on the schedule for the day, my classes ended between 1:00 and 2:30. Then I walked into town for the day's main meal, *obiad,* served in the basement dining room of a dormitory where commuting students stayed during the week. Those who ate there included a few students and teachers from my school, plus teachers from other schools and people from the community. The food was bland but the portions generous. A typical meal began with a large bowl of soup, then a steaming dish of veal cutlet, mashed potatoes with gravy, an over-cooked vegetable, and hearty bread. Dessert was often custard. Tea, coffee, or a weak fruit drink accompanied the meal. It was a real bonus that the school paid for my meals.

On my way to lunch I stopped at the post office to pick up my mail, so frequently I had correspondence to keep me company. Afterward I usually had grocery shopping and other errands to do, such as getting copies made for an exam. One of my favorite stops was a bakery where I could satisfy my craving for Polish pastries. I especially liked *pączki*, which are jelly-filled donuts.

Returning to my apartment, I spent what remained of the afternoon preparing for the next day, which if necessary continued after supper. Then, depending on what was left of my waning energy, I filled the rest of the evening studying Polish, writing letters, or making entries in my laptop diary. By 10:00 I was ready for bed and some light reading. My busy schedule helped to soften the loneliness I felt.

One night I had a dream in which I was sitting on the front porch steps of a house. I was a little boy. It was a warm day and I was waiting for someone. I wondered how long I would have to wait. No one was around. I didn't see or hear anyone. I woke up feeling anxious.

Later the image in the dream came back to me, and a memory that I connected with it. I was sitting on the steps of our house on Elm Street in the small college town of Oberlin in northern Ohio, not far from Cleveland. I was three years old. It was to this house where we moved in 1933 after leaving China following my mother's death. Until my father remarried a year later, my grandmother Siddall cared for my two older brothers and me, a responsibility she must have felt burdened by much of the time.

Once, after I had wandered off too far for the second time, my grandmother tied me to the front porch with a ten-foot piece of clothesline. I can dimly recall how helpless and frustrated I felt. While my grandmother was busy doing housekeeping or preparing meals, I often sat on the front steps waiting for my two older brothers and my father to come home.

Thinking back on this time, I have come to see that loneliness has always been a life companion, sometimes very much present as it was in those first months in Świdnica, other times a more shadowy presence like a distant fog.

——◆•◆✕◆•●——

I asked Grażyna, "When do I get paid?"

"The last Thursday of the month. The school secretary will give you your money."

A week later I was in the secretary's office. She kept all the teachers' salaries, in cash, in a cabinet behind her desk. It took her a few minutes to find my envelope. She then brought it to her desk where she slowly counted out the money. It looked and felt like a lot. To verify that I received it, she had me put my initials by my name on a list with everyone's name. If I had been so inclined, I could have easily seen what others were paid. *So much for privacy*, I thought. What I had in my hand was the equivalent of about $200, the salary of a beginning teacher. The Peace Corps supplemented this by $90 a month for travel to meetings and other expenses, which was automatically deposited into my bank account.

The Polish currency, the *Złoty*, at that time was worth about three to the dollar. Relative to the U.S., the cost of living was about a third less. Since I had no rent to pay and my mid-day meal was paid for, I lived comfortably on my school salary. The supplement from the Peace Corps I saved my first year. Though my living situation was modest, it was a long way from the primitive circumstances that many Peace Corps volunteers around the world endure.

<hr />

It was mid-morning on a cold, wet November day. The trees, now leafless and drenched from the rain, stood grimly watching over the end of autumn. I had finished taking attendance in IIIA, one of my better-behaved classes. The students were in a good mood, and so was I. Though I had initially felt overwhelmed by the thought of having primary responsibility for my students, I came to realize that this was a blessing in disguise. For one thing, I liked being independent and deciding for myself what to do in class. Also, in teaching grammar I had textbooks to provide structure, which meant that I didn't have to come up with a new lesson plan each day.

"This morning we begin Unit 7," I announced. "Please turn to page 48. The lesson today will introduce the present perfect and we will learn how it is different from the past simple."

I first called on Dorota, an excellent student whose plain features were framed by her closely cropped dark hair and complemented by a gold post in her left nostril. "Dorota, please read where it begins, *The present perfect is formed…*"

Even with a pronounced accent she read well. "*The present perfect is formed with the auxiliary verb has/have plus the past participle.*"

"Very good," I said. "Now we will read the examples of the difference between the present perfect and the past simple. They have to do with the short article we will be reading about a movie actress. Dorota, please pick someone to read the first example."

She surveyed the room. There were a few giggles and attempts to avoid her eyes. Reading out loud was not the class's favorite activity. She narrowed in on Andrzej. A shy, gangly boy, but a conscientious student, he read with some hesitation. I reminded myself that he and others needed more practice. *"She has made over twenty-five films. Charlie Chaplin made over fifty films."*

"Thank you, Andrzej. The first sentence he read is an example of the present perfect; the second is past simple. Now, Andrzej, pick someone to read the next example."

He found Darek, the closest boy to his desk. Darek raised his voice for emphasis, trying for a little attention. *"She has traveled to many parts of the world. She went to Argentina last year."* I thanked Darek on his reading and complimented him on knowing which example was the present perfect.

Ania, who sat near my desk, volunteered to read the last two examples, and then I asked her to tell the class again how the present perfect is formed. She checked her book. "It is formed with "has" or "have" plus the past participle."

"Excellent. Now look on the next page at the bottom. The rule tells us that the present perfect expresses an action that happened some time before now. The past simple expresses an action that happened at a definite time in the past."

I went to the board and wrote, *present perfect: indefinite time, past simple: definite time.* "After you write this in your copybooks we will then read about the Hollywood actress. Each of you will read one sentence. We'll begin in the back with you, Michał. Then we'll do some writing."

Learning verb forms in English required a lot of practice and review for my students. In their language they have basically three verb forms, past, present and future. They would encounter many more in English, such as the present simple continuous, the present simple passive, the past continuous, the past simple passive, and the past perfect. They also had to learn that English has no future tense; instead we use helping verbs such as will, going to, or the present continuous (I am seeing my doctor tomorrow). Even my best students often made the mistake of using the present perfect when they should use the past simple, for example saying "Last night I have watched television." Besides these verb forms were others such as conditionals (if I had a million dollars), the use of "might" and "should," the form of "used to," and others that contribute to making English a confusing language to learn.

Then there were nouns, adjectives and adverbs to master, getting word order correct, and trying to know which article to use, such as "a" or "the." This was another source of frustration because Polish doesn't have articles.

In the beginning I had much catching up to do when it came to being able to identify the various verb forms. Some of these terms I hadn't heard in fifty years, and I don't think I learned grammar in the same way in school. As the weeks and months passed, I came to realize more and more that English is a rich and expressive language.

The teaching texts the other three English teachers and I used were well written, with plenty of useful exercises and illustrated readings. We also used a workbook. Though I didn't give a grade for speaking, I always graded the students on writing exercises given as homework. Before handing back their papers, I called each student to my desk to explain my comments and answer questions. Some students may have found this intimidating at first, but I think they liked the few minutes of personal attention.

———◆◆✕◆◆———

My first experience with cheating was unsettling but not surprising. We were told in our pre-service training that students will cheat if given the chance, and that this phenomenon was endemic in Polish educational culture. I knew that saying anything to my students was most likely futile; nevertheless, as a warning I told each class at the beginning of the year that anyone I caught cheating on a test would receive a failing mark.

I soon learned that I couldn't monitor thirty students sitting close together. The first time I saw cheating came halfway into a grammar exam. I began to notice body movement, head turning, and eyes wandering. "Stop!" I said. "Put down your pencils. The test is over."

"Why? What's wrong? What did we do?"

"Too many of you are cheating. Turn in your papers. I'll give a different test another time."

There followed groans and denials, but they complied. I was surprised that even some of the better students tried to cheat, not for themselves so much as helping their friends.

When I brought up the issue with colleagues, they said they would definitely punish any student they found cheating. A few Polish friends said cheating was something of the past, while others said it definitely existed but was officially disapproved of.

I learned that cheating can be traced in part to Poland's tangled history, when the country was often under the domination of a foreign power. For many people, finding ways to thwart foreign control became a necessity of survival. After World War II, for instance, when Poland came under communist domination, getting jobs was not based on merit but on who you knew, so there was little motivation for hard work and honesty. Cheating in school was one way to beat the system.

I quickly learned to give an exam when a class was scheduled to be divided. With fifteen students I could seat them with a desk in between. Still, some occasionally tried to cheat. One time I had to fail four students in one class. It was an unhappy day, for them and for me. Fortunately, I didn't see students cheating that often. I think my vigilance paid off.

◆✦❉✦◆

It wasn't until Teachers' Day in mid-October that I first felt at ease with my colleagues. This occasion commemorated the founding of the National Education Committee on October 14, 1773. It meant a day off for the students. The teachers first met with the director for an hour in the auditorium, and then gathered in the teachers' room for socializing, eating, and drinking.

On the long table were a variety of cheeses, cold cuts, bread, fresh fruit, an assortment of pastries and crackers, fruit juice, vodka and beer. I was surprised to see alcohol served on school property. When I entered the room, Beata, who taught physical education, came over to me with a mildly flirtatious sparkle in her eyes, and taking my arm said, "Welcome! I give you drink. *Vodka, piwo* (beer)?"

"*Dziekuję. Chciałbym vodka i sok,*" I replied. (Thank you. I would like vodka and juice.)

Turning to her colleagues she said with a big smile, "Larry speaks Polish!"

After she poured my drink we held up our glasses for a toast. *"Na zdrowie!"* (To your health!)

And so began several hours of relaxed fun. Though I couldn't understand much of what others were saying, I was able to communicate with little bits of Polish and English. I was surprised when Marek, a young geography teacher with an open, boyish face, came over to me and said, "Hello. Glad you are here. Have something to eat." Though limited in his proficiency, he turned out to be one of the closet English speakers.

"Thank you. What do you recommend?" I asked, pleased with his interest.

"This cheese is Polish. Very good!"

I also found that my colleague, Krystyna, who taught English, became more animated. We sat next to each other every day, but I had often felt that our conversations were perfunctory and that she seemed reluctant to get too friendly. Today, however, she warmed up and we had a long talk about the group that she and her two adolescent children traveled with each summer. By bringing much of their own food, chartering a bus, and camping out when possible, they were able to travel inexpensively, even as far as to Greece and Spain. Though I could understand the savings in bringing food from home, it seemed a bit incongruous to imagine not enjoying a foreign country's local cuisine. (I would be reminded of this conversation months later when Paula recounted a trip to Paris with a colleague's family, taking with them their own food to save money. I thought, *Polish food in Paris?*) But it was clear that Krystyna saw these barebones group jaunts abroad as a way to provide opportunities for her two children that she, as a single mother, would not otherwise be able to provide on her own.

"By the way," she said with an impish smile, "you will have my son in one of your classes next year. You're lucky, though, my daughter is graduating this year."

With that we joined the others for another drink.

———◆◆※◆◆———

In November came a welcome break from school. For weeks I had been looking forward to the three days of Peace Corps meetings over Thanksgiving weekend in the historic town of Kazimierz Dolny, not far from Lublin. In observance of our American holiday we all enjoyed a traditional turkey dinner, cooked Polish style. It was a boost to my morale to see my friends again and hear their stories. I realized that, by comparison, I had a good teaching assignment.

The news from Paula, who I hadn't seen since we said goodbye in Radom at the end of August, was upbeat. "I love my kids, at least most of the time, and my counterpart has been great. I've even taken a couple trips with her and her husband. They're very friendly. Sometimes I wish they would leave me alone more, but it's not nearly as bad as it was with my host family in Radom."

I said, "Kathleen told me she wasn't very happy at her site. Problems with her director, I think. But Shirley likes her assignment. I visited her the weekend before Halloween. She's living with a family on a farm out in the boonies doing some kind of agricultural education for school children."

"Remember that couple in their fifties?" Paula responded. "I think he was a retired doctor. I heard they didn't last more than a few weeks after they arrived at their school. They seemed to do so well during our training."

"Counting the two who left last summer," I added, "I think we've lost five volunteers so far."

The dropout rate for our group was about average. (In Peace Corps parlance, to drop out is referred to as early termination, or ETing.) Worldwide, the number of volunteers who don't complete their two-year tour ranges from twenty-five to thirty percent. Our group would continue to lose someone every few months. We all heard stories of disagreeable directors, sassy students, unpleasant colleagues, illness, poor living situations, and for some of our women colleagues, being harassed on the street. Having one's apartment broken into was also an experience from which it was difficult to recover. Running afoul of Peace Corps regulations was another factor, like not getting permission to cross the border to another country. With Germany, the Czech Republic, and Slovakia not far away, making a visit on a weekend was a temptation some couldn't resist. This particular infraction by itself wouldn't lead to dismissal, but it could tip the balance if the volunteer had other difficulties with the administration.

"Well, it sounds like you're going to make it," I said.

"And you, too, right?"

"Right. I'm determined to hang in there until the very end. By the way, we've had so many meetings that you and I really haven't had time to get caught up. I want to hear more about your new life."

"I was thinking the same thing," Paula replied. "How about getting together for a weekend in Wrocław?"

"Good idea. We should do it before the holidays set in. Like early December."

"Okay by me. Since you go through there on your way home, you could find an inexpensive hotel and make reservations."

"Consider it done."

"Great! That'll be something to look forward to." Paula smiled and added, "Don't forget, two beds."

It turned out to be a fun, relaxed weekend. We even included a meal at the newly opened T.G.I. Friday's for a touch of the homeland. We thought it expensive by Poland standards and were surprised how busy it was. We played tourist and took in what sights were near the city center.

Lying in bed that first night I was feeling a bit keyed up. In the semi-darkness I could hear muffled sounds of the city. It had been an enjoyable day. I wanted to say something. "Paula?" No answer.

I looked over and could see that a narrow shaft of light from the window had fallen across her sleeping face.

———◆•▸◂•◆———

As fall faded into winter, Christmas vacation was in sight. With the accompanying cold weather, a haze settled over Świdnica from the burning of soft coal throughout the city, with the school's coal furnace contributing an abundant share of the pollution. We would have almost two weeks off over the holidays, and I was eager to leave town. On the last day classes ended at noon and the faculty gathered for a Christmas party.

This event was a fascinating mixture of celebration, religion, and levity, with a little vodka thrown in. The long table in the teacher's room was decked out in an array of food and drink, cheeses, bread, crackers, fruit, sliced meat, pastries, juice, vodka and beer, with holiday touches of red paper tablecloths and bright green paper napkins. What I found most unusual and a bit incongruous was the passing of the holy wafer, a combining of religion and education to which I was not accustomed. Adding to this Polish tradition was the presence of the Catholic priest who held a weekly class at the school. A young, affable man whom I had not previously met, he stayed for a couple hours and seemed to fit right in. To get things started, several boxes of wafers were opened and the white, thin squares were passed around. Each of us then greeted one another with W*ysołych Świąt* (Merry Christmas) and W*szystkiego dobrego w Nowym Roku* (Happy New Year), and exchanged a piece of wafer. This was followed by a kiss on the cheek, first one, then the other, then back to the other again. I limited my kissing to the women. In all it was a merry occasion. I stayed well into the late afternoon. Later I thought it curious that we didn't sing any carols.

The next day I was off to Italy and Germany, spending Christmas in Florence and New Year's Eve in Regensburg.

———◆•▸◂•◆———

Returning to classes was difficult. I dreaded the workload I would face. The end of the semester meant I had tests to give and grades to turn in. In addition to a grammar exam, I decided to give a writing exercise to be completed at home about how the students spent their holiday and celebrated Christmas. I told them, "I will be very interested in what you write. As a guest in your country, I want to know about the customs you observe."

Being a homogeneous and predominately Catholic society, Polish holiday customs are almost universal. Christmas Eve is the most important time, referred to as *Wigilia*, which means vigil. Many families wait until this time to decorate the Christmas tree. For their Christmas Eve dinner they prepare twelve dishes. Besides the traditional fish, usually carp, the dinner includes borscht with dumplings, sour cabbage, herring, boiled potatoes, egg and vegetable salad, and poppy-seed cake for dessert. No alcohol is served. It is also customary to set an extra place at the table for an unexpected guest. Dinner does not begin until the first star appears in the sky, and before sitting down the family shares the holy wafer and exchanges good wishes, along with kissing on the cheeks three times. Following the meal they open their presents and sing carols. Attending midnight mass completes the celebration.

After several long days and late nights I finally turned in my grades. School policy required that the end of semester grades be written out in the *dziennik*. For example, instead of a 4, the word *dobry* (good) was written, or *bardzo dobry* (very good) for a 5. This was time-consuming and required accuracy because erasures in the *dziennik* were not considered acceptable, though at times it couldn't be avoided.

The last day of the semester culminated in the *studniówka*, the Polish version of the senior prom. It was always held 100 days before the students had their final exams at the end of the year. It had started to snow in the afternoon, so I was grateful that one of my colleagues and her husband had offered to pick me up at 9:00 that evening. The students had festively decorated the large dance hall with bright colored streamers, and on the stage the band was already going full blast, playing music that was unfamiliar to me. Tables with bouquets of flowers were set up around the perimeter.

Students were already congregating on one side of the hall and the faculty had clustered on the other. At the far end the food was beautifully laid out. It looked as though there was enough to feed half the city. A number of parents were there to help serve the buffet-style supper.

Since students from the lower classes could attend only by invitation from a senior, few from my classes were there. I would have to wait a year to see them all dressed up in suits and long dresses. Still, I recognized many of the seniors and congratulated them on this spectacular occasion. Many of the teachers were present and elegantly dressed. I was delighted to find that several of the women were good dancers. Word got back to me later at school that some thought I was, too.

The occasion took me back to my younger years. I was instinctively drawn to dancing and can think of few physical activities more pleasurable than twirling around a dance floor with a woman in my arms. I can recall in my adolescence the exquisite feeling of holding a girl close as we moved together to the lush sounds of Glenn Miller's "Moonlight Serenade." My friends and I had taken up dancing in the eighth grade. We often gathered in each other's living rooms on Sunday afternoons, bringing a few of our own records of Big Band music that we bought at the local record store, where we would spend hours in the listening booths. As we got older we gave up Sunday afternoons for Saturday night school dances. We also held a few dances in our homes. At one of these parties was a girl with long red hair who I found attractive. It didn't bother me that she was taller than I, and was delighted when she came up to me with her dance card and said, with a sparkle in her eyes, "I want you to put your name here and here and here. You're one of my favorites to dance with."

By tradition this was an all night affair. I lasted until 3:00 in the morning. As I was leaving, a brief memory of my own prom in 1948 came to mind. Recalling the music my friends and I danced to, I couldn't help thinking, *Benny Goodman, Tommy Dorsey, Lionel Hampton, where are you?*

PART II

CHAPTER FOUR

Fort Knox and Munich: 1953 to 1956

The first time I lived abroad as an adult was courtesy of the United States Army. The morning of November 10, 1953 was mild and sunny when I reported to the induction center in Elyria, Ohio, nine miles from Oberlin where I lived. In those days there was little controversy over the draft. Like most young males, I saw military duty as an obligation to be fulfilled if called upon.

About forty of us were assembled, some looking hardly old enough to shave. I knew no one. The atmosphere was subdued. A local official said a word of welcome and congratulated us on serving our country. We first filled out forms, and then standing in our under shorts, we were given a brief physical exam. Soon we were on a bus headed for Fort Knox, near Louisville, Kentucky.

In looking back on my military experience fifty years later, I realize how easy it was compared to what it could have been like at a different time. By accident of birth I was too young for World War II in which my two older brothers served. Then the Korean War ended the summer before I was drafted. Basic training was rough at times, but the rest of my duty was spent in relative comfort. At twenty-three I was older than most of the other recruits, many of whom had never been away from home. Sometimes I overheard bits of their tearful calls home to mothers and girlfriends when I passed by the telephone booths in the PX, which made me wonder if they would survive the rigors and insults of basic training.

A no-nonsense but low-key sergeant, who had just returned from Korea, was in charge of our barracks. He yelled only when he was angry, which wasn't often. He had a room to himself at one end of our wooden barracks, while the rest of us co-existed in one large space with our bunks lined up in two rows. Even the showers and toilets were in one area without any dividers. Yet it was here I came to read or write letters after lights out.

First we were issued our military clothing at the supply depot. In lightning speed we were measured and handed fatigue shirts, pants, a jacket, two pairs of combat boots, two dress uniforms, a pair of dress shoes and an overcoat. I was amazed how well my boots fit. I never got a blister, even on long marches. We wore our fatigue pants tucked into our boots, called "blousing." Later we were given batteries of tests that lasted two days. The results would determine what path we would be assigned.

One of my new friends was Raymond, a twenty-year-old African American from Cleveland. We ran into each other one evening in the PX library. Slender and a little taller than I, he spoke in a deep, mellifluous voice. He had a knack for neatness that made him look well-dressed even in his fatigues. He was always reading and carried a paperback book with him in his jacket.

He asked, "What did you think of those tests they gave us the other day?"

"Not too bad, but exhausting," I replied. "Were you told anything?"

"Yeah. Told me I should apply to Officer Candidate School after basic."

"That's great! Are you going to?"

"I'm thinking about it." He grinned. "Then I can order you white boys around. Make your little white asses jump. You know what I'm saying?"

I laughed. "I do. I certainly do."

Lithe and quick, Raymond reminded me of one of my friends on the track team in high school. Growing up in Oberlin, Ohio, I had gone to school with African Americans since first grade.

I said, "Our drill sergeant was pretty rough on us today."

"Sounds mean," Raymond replied, "but I don't think he really is. I tried to talk to him yesterday during a break. Sort of brushed me off. I was a bit surprised seeing as how we're brothers."

The drill sergeant could make laggards feel like scum. Yet when we were finally in condition, I could tell from his bellowing voice that he was pleased as our company marched smartly in step for two miles at a clip. The singsong of the cadence he set rang in my ears as I fell exhausted into bed at night. "Left right, left right, your left, your left, sound off one, two, three, four . . . three-four!"

A couple weeks later Raymond and I were in the mess hall standing in line with our trays and silverware. Serving the food behind the counter stood three cooks in their culinary outfits. I had become acquainted with one of them during the two times that I had KP duty peeling potatoes in a smelly corner of the kitchen. He had a large grease stain on the front of his white apron, and I also noticed band-aids on two of his fingers, one still seeping blood. His moustache had flakes of flour on one side.

"How are things, general?" he asked.

"Fine," I replied.

"I'm looking forward to having you back again next week."

I laughed. "Maybe I'll go AWOL to get out of it."

As we moved down the line Raymond nudged my arm. In a hushed voice he said, "This army food is getting to me, man." Grimacing, he pointed to what looked like ground hamburger in gravy on toast. "Look at that stuff. They call that food?"

I said, "Do you know what it's called?"

"No, what?"

"SOS. Stands for shit on a shingle. My brother told me that's what they called it in the navy during the war."

"Well, I'm not eating it. No way. My mama would drop over dead if she saw that."

We both decided to pass it up.

One rainy night our sergeant lost his temper at several recruits for messing up their end of the barracks. "Get your jackets on men, because we're going outside for a little exercise."

"But it's raining."

"All the better. Now hustle."

Raymond came over to where I stood at a window watching the small group of waterlogged soldiers march in a circle in the drenching rain. His comment was, "That's crazy shit, man, crazy."

Next to me bunked a redheaded, eighteen-year-old from a small town near Detroit who had never been more than a hundred miles from home, let alone traveled to any other state. He had a peculiar last name, so we called him Michigan. I wondered at first whether he would complete his training, but after a shaky start he proved to be one of the best soldiers in our platoon. Coming into our barracks late one afternoon after rifle practice I took one look at him and said, "My God, Michigan, what happened to you?" Others gathered round, wincing.

Sheepishly he said he didn't hold his rifle right. I knew what he meant. The instructor told us to put our cheek against our right thumb while holding our rifle. This was to absorb the weapon's kick. Michigan obviously hadn't listened. The result for all to see was a mammoth swollen upper lip. Raymond came over to take a look. Shaking his head slowly he said, "I don't believe what I'm seeing. Man, you are one ugly mother."

The next morning was a chilly twenty-eight degrees, now early December. We were lined up in the company area for reporting in. As squad leader I had to make sure no one was missing, fatigue jackets were buttoned, caps were on straight, and no one had toothpaste on his face. Michigan was in my squad. He looked tired and pale. With his fat lip staring me in the face, I smiled and said quietly, "You're going to make a good soldier. You're one tough bird." He blinked his eyes as if to say thanks.

Then the platoon commander, a young lieutenant, probably an ROTC graduate about my age, called out, "'Ten-hut!'"

In turn, along with the other three squad leaders, I saluted and said in a loud voice, "All present and accounted for, sir!"

Michigan could hardly speak or eat for two days.

I had my own misfortune while we were on a three-day bivouac. We had been on a night maneuver and I was given charge of one of the portable radios. This meant that though I still had to carry my rifle, I didn't have to use it and it would be clean and ready for inspection before bedtime. With warmer weather coming after weeks of sub-freezing temperature, the ground had thawed. The company area was now a muddy mess. While we were marching back from our night excursion, I slipped on a buried rock and fell headlong into the cold morass, throwing my rifle-carrying arm forward and burying my M1. I was up until 1:00 A.M in my pup tent cleaning the mud from every tiny crevice.

I hated bayonet practice the most. We were supposed to scream some inane epithet as we lunged toward a straw dummy, trying to plunge the bayonet up to its hilt, twisting it and then pulling it out. I couldn't imagine doing this to a real person, as our instructor tried to convince us was a real possibility. Other exercises were more benign, even humorous at times, like when we had a lecture outdoors and someone fell asleep. The instructor would quietly tell everyone to stay seated, and then he yelled, "Ten-hut!" Of course, the lowly recruit stood up like a shot, to great laughter. Then the instructor took a hand grenade from his pocket, pulled the pin, and gave it to the embarrassed recruit to hold. He didn't dare fall asleep again, though we all knew the grenade wasn't armed.

One evening our sergeant told me, "Siddall, you're off duty tomorrow. I put your name in for Soldier of the Day, so report to Headquarters at 08:00."

"So what's this about?"

"Just do as you're told. And don't forget to wear your dress uniform."

The next day a general's aide drove me around Fort Knox in a jeep. We stopped at various departments where someone explained what they did. I actually found it fascinating to learn how a large base operated. The day ended with an informal chat and photo op with the base commander, General Beischline. He commented on my being older than most of the recruits. In the photograph of us together, my thinning hair is already evident.

<hr />

After two months of military basics, I was assigned to eight weeks of clerk typist school, also at Fort Knox. Here I learned the intricacies of how to prepare military correspondence. I was then sent to stenography school at Fort Benjamin Harrison in Indianapolis for five months, where we had classes in typing, shorthand, and English. Most of us were draftees with college degrees, but adding a bit of color to our group was a sprinkling of regular army soldiers. I particularly remember two young paratroopers from the 82nd Airborne Division, Fort Bragg, North Carolina, who were always smartly dressed in tailored uniforms and boots so shiny you could almost see your reflection. They didn't have college degrees, but in typing and shorthand achieved as well if not better than many of us reluctant warriors.

Though I had learned to type in high school, had typed many college term papers, and had the benefit of clerk typist school, I was still having difficulty with both speed and accuracy. The teacher put up a chart in the front of the classroom that listed each of our names once we could type an exercise at thirty-five words a minute with three or less errors. It was several weeks before I finally got my name on the list, but by then I could type sixty words a minute.

I didn't like shorthand. Learning to write the script required unending practice, and because of my poor handwriting, it was hard to read what I had written after taking a dictation. We were under constant pressure to be accurate while maintaining speed. Fortunately, our teacher, a middle-aged civilian woman, had great patience and a sense of humor.

English classes were more fun. We did a lot of writing and I still have stories I wrote then. Our instructor insisted on expanding our vocabulary by introducing a new word each day. "All right class. Today is review. Who can use vicarious in a sentence?"

No one raised his hand. The teacher surveyed the room. His eyes finally landed on the private next to me. By the look on his face, I could tell he was in trouble. He whispered, "What does it mean?" The only thing I could think of at the moment was "second hand." Then came his response. "I went out and bought a vicarious car." Muffled chuckles ran through the class.

Armed with typing and shorthand skills we were given an MOS (Military Occupational Specialty) that guaranteed an assignment to an army division headquarters or some special branch. We were anticipating that we would be sent to Korea, where most of the previous classes had gone. Then we got the news that we were going to Germany.

On August 13, 1954, nine months after my induction, I left Indianapolis with orders to report a week later to Camp Kilmer, New Jersey. In the meantime I could visit my family in Ohio for a few days. Once I had arrived at Kilmer, I had little to do before we shipped out. I went into New York City twice to see a Broadway show and eat some decent food. I also had the foresight to pack a few civilian clothes in my duffle bag.

Our troop ship finally got underway on August 31. After a crowded but uneventful five-day crossing, we arrived in Bremerhaven, Germany. By September 7, I was in Stuttgart at the Headquarters of the 66th Counter Intelligence Corps Group. Within two days I was sent to its unit in Munich.

I liked my new life. The military atmosphere was relaxed and, except for those of us in the administrative offices, everyone wore civilian clothes during the day. Our offices and sleeping quarters were housed in the same *kaserne*. It was a permanent structure built before the war, and compared to my previous life in wooden barracks, it was almost luxurious, with central heating and only two or three of us to a room. Many of the regular army personnel were married and lived off base with their families.

My job in the unit's personnel office required paper shuffling and a lot of typing. I was busy from 8:00 until 5:00. Several civilian women stenographers were employed in other administrative offices, so I didn't have to use my shorthand. One of my tasks was to prepare a monthly report accounting for the money given to the field agents that was used to pay informants. This report had to be in six copies with no erasures. Fortunately, speed was not required. I also had to make monthly reports accounting for money the agents spent from their civilian clothing allowance. Years later two of my friends were still wearing sport coats they had tailor made.

Not long after I arrived in Munich I found a tutor to help me improve what elementary German I had learned in college. Rudi was a medical student at the university and spoke excellent English. We would become good friends. I found it amusing when he spoke the American slang he had picked up while working at one of the military hospitals. Unruly reddish hair and wire-framed glasses gave him a scholarly appearance. He lived at home with his parents in their modest apartment. For my Thursday evening lessons I paid him with two cartons of cigarettes that cost me very little in the PX. He made a good profit selling them to family members and friends.

Several weeks after we met, Rudi said, "I've invited some of my friends over on Saturday night. I would like you to come, too. I know someone you might like to meet."

"That sounds great. Who do you have in mind?"

"You'll see. Come around eight."

I was the last to arrive. Rudi first introduced me to his freckle-faced girlfriend, Rosie, a quiet, pleasant girl. Then I met his childhood friend, Siegfried, a student in economics at the university. Tall and blond with a friendly, though slightly pompous manner, he preferred his nickname, Sigi. Across the room were two other guests pouring themselves a glass of beer. Rudi took me over to meet them. Frances was a war widow who, I learned later, was Sigi's thirty-five-year-old lover. She spoke English and introduced me to her good friend, Ursula. In her late twenties, Ursula had dark brown hair and wore a gray sweater with matching skirt, a red belt, and silver earrings. A touch of lipstick accentuated her smile. I thought she was very attractive.

It was a delightful evening. Rudi had the radio tuned to a station with American music, which he liked. The dining room table was laid with several cheeses, a variety of cold meats, bread, pickles, mustard, and beer. "We also have fresh *Apfel Kuchen* that Rosie made this morning," he announced.

Later, Rudi took me aside. "So what do you think? Do you like Ursula?"

"I think she's very nice. But she doesn't speak any English."

"That means you'll have to work harder on your German. Your pronunciation is good already."

I knew enough German to let Ursula know I would like to see her again, but not enough to make arrangements. So we enlisted Frances's help. "Why don't you two meet at my apartment next weekend?" she suggested. "Ursula said it was fine with her. I'll prepare some supper. Then you two can go out somewhere."

I was thrilled. By the time final arrangements were made, the party was breaking up. Ursula came with me to the door. She

smiled and said in German, "Good night. Until next weekend." I
knew it would be difficult waiting a whole week.

The days passed more quickly that I expected. Soon after I
arrived at Frances's apartment, she and Ursula served the meal
while I poured the wine I brought. Ursula worked in a bank, as
did Frances, and independently they had joined many others from
northern Germany who came to Munich after the war. The city
offered opportunity for work and the countryside offered beauty
and recreation. For our date afterward, Ursula and I went to a café
nearby where we had coffee and ice cream. It was an enjoyable
time.

It was difficult at first getting acquainted because of my limited
German. At times Ursula got a bit exasperated, but usually she was
patient and good humored. Once she laughed and said, "Sometimes
I have to speak to you like a child." As my fluency slowly improved,
however, our time together became more relaxed. Since she didn't
have a telephone, we had to plan ahead for a weekend when we
were both free.

Even with our limited incomes we could afford to attend
concerts, which we both enjoyed. Good seats for Munich's
symphony orchestra cost no more than eight *Deutschmarks*, about
two dollars. Once early on in our concert-going, I picked up our
tickets at the box office. "See these tickets?" I said, holding them
up.

"Yes, what about them?"

"I actually ordered them on the telephone, in German."

"See? I told you that you were improving." Taking my arm as
we went to find our seats she said, "You must feel very proud." She
was right. I had made it over what had felt like a huge hurdle.

There were also plenty of inexpensive restaurants. I had
developed a taste for *Bratwurst* and beer, which I liked best with
cold potato salad. But usually I preferred something like *Kalbfleisch*
(veal) or *Schnitzel* (a small cut of meat, usually pork, dipped in egg
and breadcrumbs and fried), along with a Bavarian specialty called
Kartoffelknödel, which is mashed potatoes cooked in a ball that
ends up like a dumpling. Though a bit sticky, or glochy as I would
say, it was delicious.

Once while I was observing her eating she asked, "What are you looking at?"

"You hold your fork and knife differently than we do at home."

"How do you mean?"

I explained that in the European style she held the knife in her right hand and ate with the fork upside down in her left hand.

"You don't do this in America?"

"No. But I like the idea." I demonstrated my new skill.

"See? Now no one will know you are a foreigner."

On a glorious late fall Sunday I rang Ursula's doorbell. She lived in one room that she rented from an elderly woman with whom she shared the bath and kitchen. Among her furniture were a single bed, a bureau with a mirror, an easy chair, and two small tables, each with a lamp. As in all old apartments, there was no built-in closet, so she hung her clothes in a large wooden wardrobe, or *Schrank*. A window looked out on the street two floors below.

I announced, "I have a surprise. Put on your coat and come downstairs."

Her face lit up as it did when she was excited. "What on earth do you have to show me?"

Getting her coat she followed me down to the street. "An auto! Is it really yours?"

"Yes indeed."

"I'm so impressed!"

Though Ursula was probably being diplomatic, she was clearly pleased. I had recently bought a 1950 German Ford *Taunus* from a departing soldier for $200. It looked a lot like a downsized 1938 American Ford. It had a dumpy look with numerous dents and a faded pea-green paint job. However, it got twenty-five miles to the gallon, and with gasoline at fifteen cents a gallon at the motor pool pump, I had inexpensive, and according to its previous owner, reliable transportation.

"Can we go for a ride?"

"Certainly."

Off we drove into the countryside. We headed south from Munich and stopped an hour later in the picturesque town of Mittenwald, with the snow-capped Alps in the background. It was one of the many charming Bavarian villages where houses and public buildings were painted with colorful murals. After strolling and window-shopping, we found a restaurant where the waitresses were dressed in traditional Bavarian peasant attire. Knowing how much I liked the hot, spiced wine called *Glüwein,* Ursula said, "This will be my treat. In honor of this special day. Now there are three of us. You and I and the little *Taunus."*

Our relationship developed easily enough. Neither of us was demanding of the other's time. Since we couldn't talk on the telephone, there was no communication between visits, which was frustrating. Ursula volunteered little about growing up, but mentioned several times that as a girl she liked sports. As an adult she stayed physically fit by going to a health club twice a week. Though she rarely referred to her father and older brother who were killed in the war, she did talk about her mother. Other than her friendship with Frances, with whom we often spent time, I heard little about other acquaintances or her social life, which seemed limited. We talked mostly about ordinary events in our lives, books we were reading, and films we had seen. There was no discussion about the future of our relationship, and though I felt genuine affection, I never considered marriage. We lived with the unspoken expectation that we would be together until I left Munich. As the weeks went by, I stayed later and later in the evening.

Compared to the drabness of how most Germans dressed at that time, Ursula liked color and could do a lot with what few clothes she could afford. I remember a red and blue wool jacket, with touches of white, which she wore on chilly fall days when we went walking in the *Englischer Garten* or when we drove to the foothills of the Alps in the winter. She liked to wear nail polish, and the only thing she ever asked me to buy for her at the PX was Revlon "Love that Red."

The worst moment between Ursula and me came after about six months. We were in her room on a Saturday afternoon. She had made tea and small, open-faced cheese sandwiches. We had plans that evening to see a Charlie Chaplin film that had come to the art movie house near the university.

"I have something to tell you," she said.

"What's that?"

"I missed my last period. I might be pregnant."

"But I don't think that's possible. I've always been so careful."

"Well, maybe something happened."

I felt a strong pang of anxiety well up. Before I knew what I was saying, I blurted out, "Have you been seeing anyone else?"

"What in heaven's name do you mean?"

"I don't know. Maybe you have another friend." Tears came to her eyes. I regretted immediately what I had said. "I'm sorry, I shouldn't have said that." I went over to comfort her, but she turned away.

"You don't trust me," she murmured.

We sat for a while in awkward silence. I felt awful. I had never been in this situation before and didn't know what do. It was true that I knew little of her life outside of our relationship. Still, why would the thought of her seeing someone else pop into my mind so easily, and why did I verbalize it? I was puzzled, confused, and feeling wretched.

I took her hand and told her again I was sorry. (Literally translated, the German expression for "I'm sorry" means, appropriately enough, "It does me pain.") She gently squeezed my hand and said, "Eat something, Larry. I'll be all right in a minute. Then we can talk." Finally, wiping her tears and turning toward me she said, "I'd like some tea."

I had to wait a week before Ursula found out she wasn't pregnant after all, much to our relief. In time this painful experience faded into the background, but it stayed with me a long time and led me to do some serious soul-searching about what vulnerable spot in my psyche caused me to react the way I did.

———◆⋆⋈⋆◆———

As with all major cities in Germany during World War II, Munich suffered terribly from Allied bombing. Now, ten years later, with the rubble cleared away, uninterrupted re-building had brought the city back to life with construction cranes crowding the landscape. However, there were still many empty tracts of land and several large government buildings stood in ruins. Munich's landmark, the *Frauenkirche* (The Church of Our Lady) with its twin onion-shaped domes had been restored, as well as the *Glockenspiel* on the façade of the *Rathaus*, where mechanical figures performed several times a day. The famous *Hofbräuhaus* survived the war and continued to be a popular restaurant for locals and tourists alike. The *Englischer Garten*, one of the largest city parks in Europe, dated to the late 1700s and was a true beauty spot. Unlike other parks such as at Versailles that had formal plantings, there were forested glens, broad lawns, ponds and streams. Its beer garden was always crowded on a warm, sunny day.

While I felt at ease with my small group of German friends, I was less comfortable around other Germans, who, though honest and hard working, often appeared stiff and humorless. There was a dull, oppressive atmosphere that I didn't really notice until I visited nearby countries. My first trip to Holland was like a breath of fresh air. Going to Italy was almost like being on another planet. Nevertheless, I became very fond of Munich and for years afterward referred to it as my second home.

<hr>

My American friends and I were having a drink in a small restaurant called *Meine Schwester und Ich* (My Sister and I), one of our favorite evening gathering places for a beer or glass of wine. It was located in *Schwabing*, known as the artsy section of Munich, not far from the university, though this was not a student hangout. With its dimly lit interior, blue and white tablecloths, and German pop music playing quietly in the background, it had a cozy atmosphere that is best described by the word *gemütlich*. I was sitting with Tom Bradley, Lee Striker and John Westergaard. It was late February, 1955, six months since I had arrived in Munich. I was a draftee with a two-year commitment. My colleagues were in for three years, having volunteered so they could be guaranteed special training for the Counter Intelligence Corps and attendance at the army language school in Monterey, California. My friends spent their days wearing civilian clothes while doing their clandestine work. We all had top-secret clearances, but I knew little of what they did other than investigating the backgrounds of Germans applying for visas to the U.S.

John had recently arrived from the States. He was telling us how much he liked Munich, and was glad to learn that local Germans were hired to do our KP and guard duty. He was disappointed, though, that he wouldn't have much chance to use the Polish he learned in language school. Soon, however, he was getting up every morning at 5:00 to teach himself German.

Tom said, "Too bad you missed the *Oktoberfest* this year, John. That's when you get another picture of what the Germans are like. It's a wild scene. The amount of beer and *Knockwurst* they put away is staggering."

Our conversation turned to taking leave time and where to go. Tom and I had recently driven in his German *Opel* to Zurich, Switzerland for a long weekend. He and I had arrived at the same time the previous fall, were roommates and had become good friends. Tall, slender and handsome, he could easily pass for Gregory Peck's younger brother.

Lee was asking when he and I were going to take a trip in my "fancy new car." So far the *Taunus* had performed well. It wasn't until I sold it to Lee the following year that its weaknesses surfaced, causing it to break down when he was in Italy. His colorful story, of how he had to abandon the car and later talked a friend in Munich into driving to Italy and towing the failed *Taunus* back over the Alps, is still alive in our collective memories.

That evening I told my friends that I had decided to stay another year in Munich and study art history at the university. Though I had taken an introductory course in college, it was visiting the museums in Munich and other European cities that inspired a fascination with the visual beauty of art that would continue throughout my life.

"C'mon, Siddall, don't you miss the good old US of A?"

"Not really. I like it here."

Lee said, "You've talked about it a few times. I didn't think you were really serious."

"Well, I am."

John smiled. "I don't blame you for wanting to stay. I hear that you have a nice girlfriend."

I realized then that with my two groups of friends I led a kind of double life. Rarely did they cross. My German friends knew little of my military life and never saw me in uniform. Of my American friends, it turned out that only Tom and Lee met Ursula, once briefly after a concert.

By the time my separation date came several months later on November 9, 1955, my passport had been issued through the American Consulate and my application to the university had been accepted. I had sold my *Taunus* to Lee because I couldn't afford the high insurance rates for a civilian. I found a room to rent for twenty dollars a month on *Josephs Platz*, not far from the university. With four *Deutschmarks* to the dollar I could live comfortably, as long as I was frugal, on the $125 a month I would receive from the GI Bill. Ursula was pleased that I was staying, but without my car our activities would be restricted. It was a long ride on the *Strassenbahn* to get to her place on the other side of the city.

And so began my year as an American student abroad. I was twenty-five. I bought a French beret, an English duffle coat, and rode a used German bicycle. I also grew a beard, which was not common then. I thought it gave me a Hemingway-like look. My small rented room was in an apartment that belonged to a friend of Rudi's. I had the use of the kitchen and prepared breakfast everyday. Usually I ate lunch in the university *Mensa*, or cafeteria, where I could be adequately fed for less than a dollar. Suppers were either at home or in an inexpensive restaurant. The apartment building had no central heating, but a tiny coal stove in my room took the chill off in the winter. The water heater for the tub in the bathroom required several coins, plus there was no shower, so I frequented the neighborhood public bath, where I could take what felt like a luxurious shower for only twenty-five cents. There were about ten stalls, and I remember the attendant would walk up and down knocking on each door when the time was up. There was also a sauna and a swimming pool where I occasionally treated myself.

The university was officially called *Ludwig-Maximilians-Universität Münchens*. Though my German had greatly improved, it took several months before I could fully understand the lectures. Fortunately, tests weren't required, since in the European system one usually doesn't begin to take the comprehensive examinations until the second or third year. My courses included Greek sculpture, fourteenth century Italian art, the art of Michelangelo, and architecture of the Middle East. A whole new world was opening up.

By January of 1956 I was well settled into my expatriate student life. Early one evening the doorbell rang. It was Lee at the door. This was his first visit.

"Will you join me in a cup of tea?" I asked.

"Sure. But first show me around."

There wasn't much to show. I had the smallest of the apartment's three bedrooms, which hardly had enough space for a single bed and a bureau. "As you can see, there's not much to the kitchen and bathroom either, but they're adequate."

"You seem fairly comfortable here," Lee said.

"Well, it's not bad for twenty dollars a month."

"I came by to ask if you would like to go to Salzburg later this month?"

"What's the occasion?"

"It's Mozart's birthday. On the 27th."

Lee and I shared an interest both in classical music and art history, his college major. He eventually earned his doctorate and became a university professor. Though serious, with intense dark eyes, he had a good sense of humor. We took several trips together in the *Taunus* that included Amsterdam and Paris.

"I remember now. It's his 200th anniversary."

"Right. There'll be a weeklong celebration, but we could go for just a couple days. What do you think? Interested?"

"Definitely."

It had been a cold winter with frequent snowfalls. It was a two-hour drive to Salzburg, and after finding a small hotel, we bought tickets to a chamber orchestra concert that evening. The next day there would be concerts in several churches, and in the evening an orchestra performance conducted by a young Herbert von Karajan, later of the Berlin Philharmonic.

After the concert that first evening, Lee and I stopped at a restaurant for a light supper. It was after 11:30 by the time we left and it had begun to snow. As we approached a church, spotlights lit up the bell tower.

"Look!" I said, pointing to the tower. "Something's about to happen."

"Let's stop and see."

We waited. The church loomed high above us, like a dark gray apparition in the cold night. Then suddenly on the stroke of midnight, amid the swirling snow, an unseen brass choir in the tower began to play, ushering in Mozart's birthday.

———◆•✕•◆———

Not long after my trip with Lee to Salzburg, John and I were having a beer at *Meine Schwester und Ich*. I was taken aback and laughed out loud when he said, "Would you be interested in driving to India next fall?"

"Now, just what do you mean, drive to India?"

"I mean just that. We'd go in my new Volkswagen. We'd have to do some research into how the roads are."

"Whatever gave you this idea anyway?" I asked skeptically. "I'm up for about anything, but this sounds pretty wild."

"Well, I got to thinking about what I would do after my tour ends in August. I'm interested in international trade and business. Here I am in Europe. Why not see what other countries are doing? I'm in no hurry to go home. Obviously you haven't been either."

"You're right, but this calls for some thought." I was definitely intrigued, but I had no idea how one got to India overland.

John said, "I've been looking at maps that show some roads. The cities in the Middle East have to be connected somehow."

"It would be quite an adventure, wouldn't it?"

"It sure would. Think about it. We ought to make a decision within the next couple months. Your second semester ends next summer doesn't it?"

"Yes, in July."

"Were you thinking of staying in Munich for another year?"

"No, I think it's about time to go home and get a job."

"Well then. Let's talk some more next week."

John's interests were along the lines of business and foreign trade; mine were in history and art. I was intrigued with the thought of exploring the world of Greece, Rome and the Middle East. I was also captivated by the ancient exploits of Alexander the Great.

By late spring we had both done enough reading and talking to people to be convinced the trip was possible. John knew two German businessmen who had recently returned from southern Turkey. They invited us to see photographs and hear about their trip. They also proudly displayed several beautiful carpets they had bought. They traveled by car and found that driving was not difficult.

Another source of information came to our attention by chance. One day I saw a man parking a Volkswagen with Baghdad license plates on a street several blocks from where I lived. I introduced myself and he turned out to be a German physician home on leave. I explained our plan and asked how the driving was.

"It's not that difficult," he said, speaking English, "but there is no direct route from Beirut to Baghdad. You will have to go into Jordan and get on the paved road that follows an old pipeline. Of course, you will encounter many unpaved stretches between here and there. And you should have a good automobile."

"We'll have a Volkswagen like yours, only newer."

"Well, you're all set. Good luck. *Gute Reise.*"

This fifteen minutes conversation convinced me that if we could get to Baghdad, why not the rest of the way to India?

———◆•◆◆•◆———

It was now March 1956. I decided to go to Italy for six weeks during the two-month university semester break.

"I wish you weren't going to be gone so long," Ursula said the night before I left. "Will you write?"

"Of course. I'll send you a hundred postcards."

On the thirteenth of March I took the train over the Alps to Trento, and from there began hitchhiking. I was headed for Sicily where spring and warm weather had already arrived. I stopped in Verona and then went down the coast via Genoa and Pisa. After a short stop in Naples, I took an overnight boat to Palermo.

The Sicilians and their way of life were clearly different from the rest of Italy. They seemed more temperamental, but no less hospitable. In Palermo I wandered the narrow back streets and was especially drawn to the congested outdoor markets. I can still hear the seafood vendor who was calling out his wares, a platter of squid. Many years later, in a photography exhibit, I included the photograph I took of him, mouth wide open.

Further around the coast in Agrigento, I visited a well-preserved Greek Doric temple dating from the fifth century B.C.E. Another of my favorite photographs was taken here. A gnarled olive tree is in the foreground, and from there a path winds its way up a hill to the temple, amazingly well preserved for its age. (Years later I saw the exact same view in an exhibit at the Museum of Modern Art in New York City.) I spent several days on the east coast of Sicily, first visiting Syracuse with its Greek and Roman amphitheaters. Further on was picturesque Catania, nestled between Mount Etna, still an active volcano that rises up 10,000 feet, and the blue Mediterranean. Everywhere wildflowers were in bloom. The views were spectacular.

My five days in Rome and two weeks in Florence were delightful, but I often felt lonely. This was the first time I had traveled for so long a time by myself. In those days these two glorious cities were less crowded with tourists, less noisy from motor scooters, and less polluted. I couldn't believe they could be home to so many art treasures. In my postcard to Ursula from Rome, I wished she could have been with me to see the Coliseum in the moonlight. In another postcard I told her I was still able to live within my budget of a few dollars a day by hitchhiking and staying in youth hostels. The one in Florence was a lovely converted villa. I lived mostly on bread, cheese and fresh fruit, with frequent dining in inexpensive restaurants. I also found cheap meals at university student dining halls, similar to the one in Munich.

Compared to the Germans, I found the Italians more outgoing and friendly. They were also far more fashion conscious. Even in small towns women dressed up when going to market. And in Rome and Florence the university women students wore dresses and high heels.

On my way to Venice, I stopped in Ravenna on the Adriatic coast to see the famous mosaics in the Church of San Vitale, which date from the sixth century. At that time Ravenna was the administrative capital of Byzantine Italy,* a province in the eastern Roman Empire whose seat of power was in Constantinople (formerly Byzantium), having been moved from Rome and renamed by Emperor Constantine in 330 C.E.

The mosaics I came to see at San Vitale were in the sanctuary apse, the semicircular space at the far end of the church. The church is an eight-sided structure with a beautiful central dome supported by large inner piers, around which runs an ambulatory with second-story windowed galleries. Passing under the dome high above, I entered the sanctuary and then into the adjoining light-filled apse. There on the north wall to the left I saw Emperor Justinian standing with church officials and soldiers, while his wife, Empress Theodora, was standing with her attendants on the opposite wall. Both Justinian and Theodora wear jeweled crowns and purple cloaks, with her crown enhanced by long strands of glistening pearls. Rich colors of white, green, orange, beige, and turquoise are seen in the robes worn by those in the royal court and in the decorative designs surrounding the two scenes. These mosaics are also remarkable for their state of preservation. Years later they would be restored to their original brilliance, and when I stopped there again on a trip to Italy forty-one years later

---

* Byzantine is the term used by scholars to refer to the art and culture of the eastern Roman Empire from the fifth to the fifteenth century.

in 1997, during Christmas break while teaching in Poland, I was overwhelmed by the dazzling color and exquisite detail. Indeed, these mosaics are among the most beautiful works of Byzantine art I have seen anywhere.

◆◆❈◆◆

Back in Munich, the second semester was passing quickly. My fluency in German had improved and I felt that I blended in with the campus scene. One of my new friends was Marianne von Lieres, a German student whom John, Lee, and I met through Tom. She and Tom had been a couple until he broke his leg while they were skiing in Austria the previous winter and had to be sent home early for treatment. Tall and good looking, she was studying German literature and spoke excellent English, having spent a year living with an aunt in Washington, D.C. She had heard John and me talking about going to India, and one afternoon in late spring when she and I were having coffee in the university cafeteria, she asked, "Would you and John consider taking me with you as far as Istanbul?"

It took me a moment to let the question sink in. *She was certainly pleasant company, friendly and outgoing. She had a delightful sense of humor. But how would the three of us get along?*

"Sounds like a nice idea," I said. "Let me talk to John."

Several days later John and I agreed that, since neither of us was romantically involved with Marianne, having her along would be fine. Later in the week the three of us met. "We would be delighted," we told her.

With classes over in late July, I set off in early August hitchhiking to London to get my visas. John was now a civilian and had gone north to Oslo, Norway to visit relatives and begin buying equipment for our trip. I would meet John in Oslo, where our trip would officially begin. Hitchhiking was easier than in Italy because I had made a sign that read "American Student." It cut my waiting time in half.

◆◆❈◆◆

Even before I left the States I was a veteran hitchhiker. In those days, hitchhiking was a safe and inexpensive way to travel for a young person. My most memorable trip was in the summer of 1950, after my sophomore year at college. I had taken a week off from working for a local contractor building houses to visit two college friends, one on Long Island and the other in Connecticut. To get back to Ohio I picked up Route 20 in Massachusetts and headed west. The Massachusetts Turnpike and the New York Thruway had not yet been built.

It was late Friday afternoon by the time I had reached Pittsfield near the New York border. A light rain had begun to fall. Fortunately, it wasn't long before a middle-aged man in a new-looking Chevy stopped and I got in. Almost immediately I could smell alcohol and was relieved when soon he asked, "Can you drive?"

"Sure."

"Good. I'll pull over so you can take the wheel."

After a few miles he asked, "Where are you headed?"

"Toward Cleveland, in Ohio."

"Fine. Drive on," he said as he took a bottle from under the seat.

My companion for the next fourteen hours was a Mr. Chenevert. Where he lived and what he did for a living, if anything, I had no idea. All I knew was that he liked his whiskey and looked like he hadn't shaved for several days. As I drove across the border into New York State, he took another swig from his bottle and moved over toward me, his fetid breath almost curling my eyebrows. Putting his arm around my shoulder he said, "It's you and me together, right?"

"Right," I replied, as I wondered if we were even going to make it as far as Albany. He then leaned back against the door and dozed off. Soon the clouds began to clear and the sinking sun set the sky ablaze. He was sound asleep when I stopped hours later at a truck stop near Skaneateles for a snack and a brief nap. When I started the engine Mr. C. woke up, and seeing a soldier hitchhiking, he said, "Pick that young feller up. We'll take him home."

"How do you know where he lives?"

"Doesn't matter," said Mr. C.

It turned out that the soldier lived about an hour further west, somewhere near Canandaigua. He was most grateful to be delivered to his doorstep in the middle of the night.

Underway again, Mr. C took another drink, climbed into the back seat and fell dead asleep. Over the next few hours I drove in solitude except for occasional burps and gurgles emanating from behind me.

Dawn came as we passed through Erie, Pennsylvania. By 7:00 we were coming into Cleveland. I was tired and a bit foggy, but still alert. Mr. C was now awake but clearly drunk. He slowly climbed back to the front seat. I was in a dilemma. With another hour to go I didn't know what to do. I could leave him with his car in a parking lot somewhere, but I was afraid he would drive away and cause an accident. When I told him that I would have to get out soon he said, "This isn't my car, ya know."

"What do you mean? Whose is it?"

"I dunno. Name's here somewheres." He then opened the glove compartment and took out a paycheck. Showing it to me he says, "This guy, I guess."

"Really? How come you have his car, anyway?"

"I stole it. I mean I borrowed it, yesterday, before I picked you up."

"For God's sake! You mean I've been driving a stolen car from Massachusetts?"

"Yep."

Though I knew that we had committed an illegal act, what I didn't know until later was that it was a federal offence to transport stolen goods across state lines. What to do? By this time we had driven through Cleveland. I could still leave Mr. C. somewhere with the car. But I finally decided to call the state police. A few miles from Oberlin, where I lived, I stopped at a roadhouse and told Mr. C that I was calling my home. A state policeman from the Lorain barracks showed up in about twenty minutes. He took Mr. C. with him and I followed in the stolen car. My interrogation was friendly, lasting about thirty minutes. I was told afterward that Mr. C didn't contradict my version of the events. Apparently he was a drifter and had no criminal intent to implicate me. I was then driven home in the state police car, arriving in time to tell my story at lunch, much to the astonishment and amusement of my parents.

I thought the matter was closed. But the next morning a reporter from a newspaper called and asked if she could interview me. Reluctantly I said yes. The guys I worked with either saw the article in the paper or heard it on the radio, so the first thing I heard when I showed up was, "Hey, Siddall! This man gives you a ride all the way from Massachusetts and you turn him in? That's pretty ungrateful, if you ask me." And so the razzing began and continued on and off all day. After a couple days it stopped and things got back to normal. But not quite. Two weeks later, my boss came over to where I was nailing two-by-four studding and said, "Siddall, the FBI is here to see you."

Mr. FBI was standing in someone's future living room. He looked like the typical gumshoe in his dark suit, white shirt and tie. He said he wanted to confirm some information in his file before he closed out my case. We chatted for ten minutes, then shook hands and said goodbye. He waved as he climbed into his nondescript government car. I returned to my hammer, ten-penny nails, and the rolling of eyes and muted snickering.

———◆◆◆◆◆———

It took me three days and over 600 miles to reach London, where I arrived at 1:00 in the morning. I had picked up a ride with a truck driver in Dover, and now I was walking along Belgrave Road near the Thames River. Halfway up the block I came upon a soldier standing in a lighted doorway. He was not much taller than I and had a long mustache that curled at the ends. I stopped for a moment and he said, "Good evening. You're out late tonight."

"Good evening. I've just arrived in London. I'm looking for a hotel."

"There aren't any around here. Where are you from, Canada?"

"No, the United States."

"In that beard you don't look like an American to me."

"Well, I am, and a tired one, too."

"I'm on duty here tonight. Why don't you come in for a cup of tea? This is the guardhouse for the Royal Army Medical College. We're not far from the Tate Gallery."

I gladly accepted his invitation. My first cup of tea on English soil couldn't have been more welcome. We chatted a while and then he said, "Look, mate, you could sleep in my bed for a few hours. But I'd have to roust you out at 6:00. What do you say?"

"Really?"

"Why not. It's empty."

I was grateful for the offer, and as with the cup of tea, my first hours of sleep were most welcome. To my surprise another cup of tea and a cookie were waiting for me when he got me up at 6:00. As I was ready to leave the sergeant said, "Here's some change for the bus. You can get it at the next corner. Number 7. It'll take you to Victoria Station. You'll find hotels around there."

"Thank you. You've been most hospitable."

"Not at all, old chap. Drop by again sometime."

My three weeks in London went quickly. I spent many hours going from embassy to embassy to get the visas I needed. In between I wandered through London's museums, did some sightseeing, and took in plays at night if I had enough money. From London I headed back over the English Channel and hitchhiked on to Amsterdam, Hamburg, Copenhagen, Stockholm and finally Oslo.

John had been there for two weeks and had some work done on his light blue Volkswagen Beetle that included having a mechanic alter the backrests of the front seats so they could lie flat, allowing us to sleep in the car when needed. He also had a metal sign made and attached to the rear that read "Oslo to Calcutta." We bought other equipment such as a Coleman stove, a few pots and pans, sleeping bags, and a water bag for the desert. This was a heavy canvas bag to hang over the front bumper that let water slowly seep through, the evaporation helping to cool the water. We would see them on vehicles all through the Middle East.

During my week in Oslo I met several of John's relatives, including his mother who had come over from Long Island.

Both of his parents were born in Norway. Before his death two years before, John's father headed an import business in New York City and was a director of the Norwegian-American Shipping Company. John was interested in the pulp paper industry abroad and had made up a list of firms he hoped to visit during our trip. We left Oslo on September 24. Our plan was to spend a brief time in Munich before continuing our big adventure the beginning of October.

In the afternoon of my last day in Munich, Ursula and I took a walk in the *Englischer Garten*. We always enjoyed the serenity of this splendid park, with its broad lawns, meandering streams, and patches of shady woods. On that autumn day, with the leaves beginning to turn, it was a pleasant haven where we could reminisce and begin to say goodbye.

As twilight came, we found a quiet restaurant near the park's entrance. We were tired and ready for supper. The dining room was dimly lighted, providing a cozy atmosphere for our last meal together. We sipped wine while waiting for our food.

"It's hard to believe I'll be leaving tomorrow," I said wistfully.

"Maybe we'll see each other again one day," Ursula replied with a faint smile. "One never knows." Pausing a moment, she said, "I have something for you to take on your trip." She handed me a small box. Inside, between two layers of cotton, was a silver medallion attached to a key ring. I recognized the imprinted image.

"Isn't this St. Christopher?"

"Yes," she said. "He's the patron saint of travelers. He will help keep you safe."

"It's beautiful. It will be my lucky charm." I turned the medallion over several times, admiring the artistic design. "Thank you. I'll treasure this."

I wondered if I would ever see Ursula again. I also wondered about her friend, Frances, and my tutor, Rudi. It turned out that when I returned to Munich twenty years later in 1976, I did see Ursula and Frances, but not Rudi. The story was that he had become a successful physician, but had an unhappy marriage, became an alcoholic and committed suicide.

Frances still lived in the same apartment and worked at the same bank. However, her circumstances had improved dramatically. She told me she could hardly believe how much more she was earning. By this time the German economy was going full blast and everyone's standard of living had vastly improved. People were better dressed, they looked happier, and the city had become a lively business and cultural center.

In the intervening years, Ursula and I had both married. Unhappily, her husband died suddenly several months before my visit. When they married he was a widower with two small children whom she helped raise. With her still grieving, it was a sad reunion. My later visits to Munich in 1982 and 1988 found her doing well. She was living in a comfortable condominium in a suburb of Munich and seemed content with her life. She still had the postcards I sent from Italy.

The Author's Overland Trip Begins in Oslo, September 1956

auto

CHAPTER FIVE

Munich to Istanbul: October 1956

The morning of October 3, 1956 began cloudy and cool. With our packing finally done, Marianne, John and I climbed into the blue Beetle and set out for Salzburg, Austria, two hours to the east. As we waved our final goodbye to Munich, I looked back and could see the twin onion-shaped towers of the *Frauenkirche* silhouetted against the gray skyline. Marianne insisted on being the first to sit in the back seat, wedged in against her suitcase and two boxes of food and cooking gear. The rest of the luggage, sleeping bags, extra shoes, and miscellaneous items were crammed into the compartment under the front hood. Books, maps, sweaters, jackets, and cameras were stored in the well behind the rear seat. Later, John and I would take our turns sitting in back while spelling each other with the driving. When my turn came after lunch, I soon dozed off to the distinctive purr of the Volkswagen's air-cooled rear engine, a sound that would become as familiar as my breathing.

From Salzburg we crossed Austria and by mid afternoon were in Graz. Traveling south through hilly, wooded terrain we crossed the border into Yugoslavia. By early evening we were in Zagreb, where we found a small hotel just off the main street. The middle-aged woman in charge knew a little English, and after taking our passports and showing us to our plain but clean rooms, she said in a hushed voice, as though not wanting to be overheard, "Life is difficult for many of us here. I hope you will find the beds comfortable. We see few foreigners." With a slight smile she added, "I've never met an American before."

Marianne's room had a bedside table with a lamp, while the light in John's and my room was only a bare bulb hanging by a frayed cord from the ceiling. Pointing to it John said, "I guess there's no reading in bed tonight."

We then went in search of a restaurant. What we noticed most about Zagreb was that there were not many people on the streets and very little automobile traffic. The atmosphere seemed even more subdued because of the sparse displays in store windows and drab-looking buildings, some still showing signs of war damage.

Our objective for the next day was to get to Belgrade, with a side trip on the way for John to visit a paper mill. Once off the main highway we occasionally passed farmers working in the fields and saw almost no automobiles. Few people took much notice as we went through small villages. It was not until we stopped in Prijedor, where the paper factory was, did a few adults and a gaggle of children gather around the car after we got out. Two smiling boys, one with half of his shirttail hanging out from under his worn sweater, were especially curious about us and wanted to try out the bit of English they knew. "Hello." "What is your name?"

We had parked in front of a café, one of the few in town. John would meet Marianne and me at the café later. He had dressed that morning in his suit, white shirt and tie. Smiling and looking confident he said, "Wish me luck. This is my first foreign business meeting. I'll see you in a couple hours."

Marianne and I found a table in the café and ordered coffee and sweet rolls. The place had no frills, but its atmosphere was inviting enough, with red and white-checkered tablecloths and the aroma of freshly baked bread. The other patrons gave us curious glances as we sat down. Staring into her cup, Marianne seemed quieter than usual, even a little melancholy. She said, "There are so many people here with blank faces. Much the way it was in Zagreb yesterday. Only the children look at all happy."

"We're in a different world here, aren't we?" I said, adding that there was certainly a huge difference economically between this communist country and Germany. Yet I sensed there was more on her mind. I asked, "Does being here remind you of the war?"

She was silent for a moment. "Yes. Especially when we had to leave our home in Golkowitz in what is now Poland. I was fourteen then. It was a difficult time for everyone. It took our family almost two weeks to reach Munich, walking most of the way. I saw many sad faces. Just like here." She paused and then said, "Sometimes it's hard to think about." It wasn't until many years later that she would tell me the whole story.

When John returned he was clearly pleased with his tour of the paper factory. "I don't think I would want to work there," he said. "The equipment appeared primitive and the workers, many of them anyway, looked pretty glum."

Marianne said, "We were saying while you were gone that life seems grim here."

"I agree," John replied. "Yet the people I met were friendly and certainly pleased to have a visitor, especially from the U.S."

To return to the main highway we had to negotiate more back roads. After about forty minutes the road abruptly came to a halt by a small river. To get across we would have to drive the car onto a rickety ferry that was fixed to a cable stretched across the river. With the boatman using the rudder, the current would take us to the other side. The other passengers were two farmers and a cow. Off to the side were two soldiers, obviously security personnel, watching what was going on. As John drove the VW onto the ferry, I took out my camera and snapped a couple of shots. Only then did one of the soldiers come over and by his hand gestures indicated that taking pictures was not permitted. And he wanted the film. I was about to protest, but immediately decided against it. As I was thinking over what to do, I realized I was at the end of a roll, and since I could rewind the film by hand, I thought I had a solution to the problem. I began rewinding and then stopped just as I felt the tension release. I opened the camera and was relieved to see some of the film showing. In front of the soldier I pulled three inches of the leader from the cassette and cut it off with the scissors on my pocketknife. With a friendly smile I presented the piece of film to the soldier, who readily took it and walked back to his comrade, obviously satisfied. The ferry then shoved off and soon we were on our way to Belgrade with the forbidden film safely in my pocket.

Over the next two days we frequently saw soldiers, a reminder of the Soviet-style government in Yugoslavia under its president, Marshal Tito. His given name was Josip Broz, but he took the name Tito as a code name after he joined the Communist Party at a time when it was illegal. Later, in 1937, he was appointed general secretary of the party. He was long remembered for his courage in leading the resistance against the Nazis in World War II, and for breaking with Stalin in 1948 over lack of economic aid and political differences. His split from Russia eventually led to Yugoslavia receiving aid from the West beginning in the 1950s. Tito's relationship with Russia was more cordial after Khrushchev came to power following Stalin's death in 1953, but cooled as a result of Russia's brutal repression of the Hungarian Revolution in 1956. (This tragic event was about to occur a few hundred miles to the north of us that October.)

Enjoying the view from the front seat Marianne said, "The countryside is certainly beautiful here. But the most beautiful part of Yugoslavia I've been told is along the Adriatic coast. It's too bad we don't have time to see it and visit Trieste."

From the back seat John said, "We'll go there on our next trip."

Yugoslavia as a country did not exist until after the end of World War I in 1918. Prior to that time much of the region had been part of the Austro-Hungarian Empire, which was dissolved following the war. This whole Balkan region had always been one of the most ethnically diverse in all Europe, a mixture of East and West, of Christian and Muslim. (The eastern segment had been a part of the Ottoman Empire until into the 1800s.). Yugoslavia was always a potential political powder keg, but under Tito's tight rule ethnic conflict was kept under control.

In a letter home I wrote: *The communist government has a definite effect upon the people, and one has the impression that everyone is so listless and the atmosphere austere. Even in the cities there is little activity on the streets, for there are few automobiles or even bicycles. The change from the relatively prosperous countries in Western Europe left quite an impression on me . . . The apathy of the farm people was so apparent that it was pitiful. When we were driving off the main highway, it was almost like being at the far end of the world. Our car was probably the only one to pass through some of the villages during a whole day, yet the people along the road in the horse-drawn carts often ignored us, even when we waved to them. Some of this outward indifference usually dissipated itself, though, when we stopped in small towns, for immediately a few people would gather around the car and show great interest in the fact that we were from Germany and America.*

During our brief visit to Yugoslavia, we were not as aware of its different ethnic states as we are today following the political explosions of the 1990s, which involved NATO intervention and led several states to gain their independence. We first entered the country by way of Slovenia and from there into Croatia, with Zagreb as its capital. Our side trip to Prijedor had taken us into a small section of Bosnia-Hercegovina, whose most famous city is Sarajevo. It was there in June of 1914 that the heir to the Austro-Hungarian throne, Archduke Franz Ferdinand, was assassinated by a young Bosnian who was a member of a Serbian terrorist group. This set off a chain of events that led to the outbreak of World War I.

We spent our second night in Belgrade, capital of both the country and the state of Serbia. Here there was more activity on the streets, and at a restaurant near our hotel we met a man at the table next to ours who was eager to talk. His English was quite good. We invited him to join us for coffee after dinner. He shook hands firmly and said, "It is my pleasure to meet the three of you. Welcome to my city."

Under his worn brown suit coat our guest wore a freshly ironed white shirt that contrasted with his ruddy complexion and two-day old beard. His uncut graying hair spilled over his ears and coat collar. He was a retired schoolteacher and lived on a small pension with his wife, who was away for a week visiting her sister. Our conversation eventually shifted to daily life. "Most people have a job of some kind," he said, "but few have extra money to spend, except officials in the Communist Party. What really makes our lives different from yours is we have less freedom. We have to be careful what we say." With a slightly mocking smile he leaned closer and lowered his voice. "You never know who is listening."

Our new acquaintance was fascinated by our trip. Turning to Marianne he said, "Women here don't travel much on their own. Even in the restaurant you see mostly men. You're fortunate." As we departed he smiled warmly and said, "I wish you all a happy journey."

From Belgrade the highway south was unpaved, giving us a dusty and bumpy ride on our way toward Pristina in Kosovo and then

Skopje, where we stopped for the night. It was there that we found we had picked up a nail in one of our tires. Amazingly, it turned out to be the only puncture we had during the whole trip. We easily found a garage where the tire could be repaired. John and I decided to sleep in the car that night to test out how comfortable it would be. (He had the backs of the front seats modified in Oslo.) We found a room in a rustic inn for Marianne and then had supper in the inn's small restaurant. Though crowded, noisy and smoky, the atmosphere was friendly. The hospitable innkeeper had his chef prepare a delicious chicken and rice dish, a favorite among locals he told us. To our delight three men began singing folk songs. One played what looked like a balalaika, a three-stringed instrument with a triangular shaped body. Two lively songs included rhythmic clapping that brought enthusiastic shouts from many of the other diners.

In the morning John and I agreed that sleeping in the car was actually quite comfortable. We then went in to meet Marianne for breakfast. Coming down the stairs, she was unsmiling with shadows under her eyes. "How did you sleep?"

"Terrible!" she exclaimed. "There were bedbugs! I had to sit in a chair half the night." However, after she had some breakfast and a nap in the back seat, by midmorning she was again her usual cheerful self. Fortunately, that was the only sleeping disaster we encountered.

The next day, October 7, the highway followed the Vardar River as it passed through a low mountain range and finally took us across the border into Greece. We were now in the province of Macedonia and soon arrived in Thessaloniki, the capital, situated on a bay in the upper reaches of the Aegean Sea.

———◆♦✕◆———

What a change from Yugoslavia to Greece. We woke up to a cloudless sky, bright sunshine, and garrulous, friendly people. Much of Thessaloniki is built on a hillside, so from our tiny hotel we had a marvelous view of the bay's blue water sparkling in the warm sun. We spent two days here enjoying the balmy weather and getting cleaned up after our dusty ride. Anticipating more dusty roads in the weeks to come, I decided to shave off my beard.

The first morning John wanted to do some reading about Greece's economy, so Marianne and I went to admire the mosaics in two Byzantine churches, dating from the fifth and eighth centuries. They had been spared from a disastrous fire in 1917 that leveled much of the city. We returned to the hotel for lunch with John and afterwards we all walked down to the harbor. On the way we passed through a noisy, bustling market place where a vendor called out his wares of copper pots and pans in a strange-sounding, high-pitched voice. We found a harbor-side café where we had tea and *baklava* while we watched fishing boats come in with their catch of the day. As we lounged under the sun's warmth, a treat for three travelers from often-cloudy northern Europe, the afternoon light gradually faded and finally ended in a magnificent sunset.

<hr />

Here in Thessaloniki we were not far from ancient Pella, the birthplace of Alexander the Great, one of the greatest military strategists in all history. He had captured my imagination when I began reading about him in Munich and served as a kind of guide during the trip.

Alexander was just twenty when he became commander of the fearsome Macedonian army upon the death of his father, Philip II, in 336 B.C.E. He was relentlessly driven to fulfill his father's ambition to conquer the Persians, who had invaded Greece a century before.

In 334 Alexander crossed the Hellespont (Dardanelles straits) into present-day Turkey with more than 30,000 Macedonian and Greek soldiers and 7,000 cavalry. By 326 he had gained control of the entire Persian Empire as far east as what is today Iran, Afghanistan, Pakistan, and western portions of India. During his campaigns he founded more that thirty cities, the most famous being Alexandria in Egypt. His most far-flung city was in Afghanistan, called "Alexandria the Farthest." He also introduced Hellenistic culture and the Greek language throughout much of the empire. He would have gone further into India, but his otherwise loyal troops threatened mutiny, so he turned back. On his return in 323, he fell ill in Babylon after a bout of excessive drinking and possibly having contracted malaria. He died ten days later. He was thirty-three years old. Upon his death, his general Ptolemy accompanied his body, carried in a gold coffin, to Alexandria.

Alexander's empire could not survive without his leadership and eventually, after decades of infighting between his generals, it was divided up among them. Ptolemy took control of Egypt where he established the Ptolemaic Dynasty that endured for 300 hundred years. The last sovereign of this Macedonian line was the notorious Cleopatra.

———◆◆×◆◆———

After watching the sunset we were hungry and found a nearby restaurant. We ordered beer and then scanned the menu. We agreed that seafood would be our choice for the evening. Our young waiter told us in excellent English, "Yes, the fish of the day is fresh as of this afternoon. I highly recommend it."

While we waited for our dinners, John said, looking around, "This is a great place. And I really like the Greek beer, though it's not quite up to what you get in Germany. What do you think, Marianne?"

"It tastes pretty good," she said. "But I agree. It's hard to beat what we have in Munich."

I said, "Since we have to come back through Thessaloniki after seeing Athens, we could come here again."

"That's a great idea," Marianne said. Then she added, "Here's something interesting I learned today. Thessaloniki was named after Alexander's half-sister, Thessalonika. She was married to the Macedonian general Kassander, who founded the city. The name means 'Victory in Thessaly.'"

From this point on we would be traveling over many of the same routes that Alexander took, beginning here in Greece and, with the gods on our side, ending in India.

———◆◆×◆◆———

From Thessaloniki we headed south toward Athens. We took two days in order to pay a visit to Delphi, home of the famous Delphic oracle. The ruins, which are nestled against the side of Mt. Parnassus some 2,000 feet above the valley, were not discovered until the early 1800s, having been buried under a small town. In ancient times common folk and mighty rulers alike consulted the oracle, as did Alexander, who was told that he was invincible. The oracle was a priestess, called the Pythia, and before making her prophesies she spent time in a chamber beneath the Temple of Apollo. While in a trance, she often prophesied in riddles that were difficult to understand. It was long believed that intoxicating fumes emanating from under the chamber had a significant influence. In fact modern geological research has identified one of these vapors as ethylene, which if inhaled can produce a trance-like, intoxicating state. The last recorded oracle occurred in the fourth century C.E., during which time Christianity became the official religion throughout the Roman Empire under Emperor Constantine. He himself had a vision in 312 C.E. that lead to his conversion. Finding no one who might have the qualities of an oracle to give us either advice or a blessing, we decided to leave and look for a place to stay the night.

We found Athens to be a bustling and noisy place. I was surprised to see that many of the taxis were shiny new American cars, and it seemed that on practically every corner there were five or six shoeshine men. With plenty of sidewalk cafés, we had our share of the coffee and sweet cakes that the Greeks relish. The streets I found most interesting were those with sidewalk vendors that sold everything from rugs and copper ware to hairpins and religious icons. I was especially drawn to these decorative paintings on wood, not so much for their religious significance, but for the deep colors and haunting faces as seen in the images of church saints or the Madonna with the infant Jesus. I was tempted to buy one and was told it was over 100 years old, but even at only twenty dollars it was more than I could afford, so I passed it up.

Throughout our trip, we had to forego seeing many important places in order to keep within our travel plan. We experienced this first in Greece, particularly in Athens, since we would be there just two days. There we limited our sightseeing to the Acropolis, two major museums, and a few other sites around the city.

It took the Greeks decades to rebuild the Acropolis after the Persians destroyed it in 480 B.C.E. The Parthenon, with its magnificent statue of Athena, was completed in 438 B.C.E. Centuries later it became a Christian church, and then a mosque under the Ottoman Turks. The Parthenon still commands its place as one of the most beautiful and perfectly designed structures in the world. This "gleaming marble ruin" is truly a wonder for its balance and harmony that has been rarely matched anywhere. At the time you could wander around freely. I was interested to learn that it has no straight lines, which I verified by sighting down the length of the steps and seeing the slight curve. A bit of architectural trivia I picked up was that, because the columns lean a bit inward, their axes would intersect a mile above if extended. I saw this beautiful structure for the first time early in the day. As I stood among its magnificent columns, the Parthenon almost glowed in the golden morning light.

In 1675 Sir George Wheler published the first account of a visit to Athens by a European. At that time it was an unassuming town of 10,000 inhabitants, having "disappeared from history" by the third century C.E. By the 1600s the city was part of the Ottoman Empire, and though under a Muslim government, the population was predominately Christian with over one hundred churches. Wheler described the Parthenon as having a minaret inside and its roof intact. He also observed that gunpowder was being stored within the temple. This would be the cause of a disastrous explosion and fire in 1687 when the Venetians shelled Athens and hit the Parthenon, blowing off its roof and destroying several columns and many of its sculptures.

The English poet Lord Byron, who visited Athens in 1809, is reported to have been horrified to see agents of his countryman, Lord Elgin, dismantling sculptures from the Parthenon. The Earl of Elgin was Thomas Bruce, ambassador to Turkey, who shipped his goods back to England to decorate his home, thereby setting off the still-ongoing controversy over the sculptures' rightful owners. The "Elgin marbles" eventually ended up in the British Museum where they are a marvel to see, and Greece has yet to succeed in getting them back.

In 1834 Athens became the capital of the Kingdom of Greece following the war of independence from the Ottomans. It grew to become a modern city of nearly a million people by the time we saw it 1956.

The afternoon of the second day we split up and agreed to meet for dinner at a restaurant near our modest hotel. John and Marianne were already there when I arrived. Holding up a glass John said, "You've got to try this stuff. It's great. I've already ordered you some."

"What is it?"

"It's called *ouzo*. It's an aperitif. Go on, try it, but just take a little bit at first."

"Have you tried it, Marianne?" I asked.

"Yes. It's not my favorite drink, but not bad."

I took a sip and found the drink pretty strong. It had a licorice taste. Then Marianne said, "John, add some water to show him what happens."

I was amazed to see the *ouzo*, a clear liquid, turn milky. However, the taste didn't change. I found it interestingly different, but a little bit went a long way. We learned that it's made from grape stems and aniseed. The Greeks love it.

The restaurant was a small, lively place, with just the proprietor in his grease-spattered apron doing the cooking. His son took the orders. Neither spoke much English nor could we understand the menu, so in order to select what we wanted, we were shown to the smoky kitchen bursting with cooking sounds and aromas. We decided to splurge a bit, since up until then we had eaten mostly in very inexpensive restaurants and cooked some of our own meals. For an appetizer we shared a dish of *dolmades*, stuffed grape leaves. Then we had a fish soup called *psarosoup*a, followed by a salad and *moussaka*, which is baked eggplant, minced meat and potatoes with a cheese sauce on top. For dessert Marianne and I tried a rice pudding called *rizogala*, while John had *pagota*, an ice cream specialty of the house.

I also wanted to try *retsina*, the Greek wine flavored with pine resin that acts as a preservative. No one really knows when the resin originally got added, but it probably goes back to ancient times. It's a favorite for many people. I didn't much like the astringent taste, but we were told that the drink was especially refreshing on a hot day.

The next morning we headed back north toward Thessaloniki and Istanbul. So far our little Beetle had performed admirably. A bit crowded, but with frequent stops to stretch our legs we had little to complain about. We were pretty much on schedule, having allotted ourselves two weeks from Munich to Istanbul.

Paved roads made driving in Greece a pleasure. We had to be cautious, however, going on winding roads over mountain passes where there were no guardrails between precipitous drop-offs and us. We were treated by scenic views of snow-capped mountains and vistas along the coast. Many travelers have told of the clear light in Greece, and we, too, found a luminescence of atmosphere that accentuated the contrast of ancient olive trees against the azure of the sea.

———◆◆◆◆◆———

It was midday on October 18 when finally, after more than 2,000 miles, we arrived in Istanbul. Sitting astride the Bosphorus, the narrow body of water that divides Europe and Asia Minor, the city combines both West and East. From what I first saw of Istanbul, with its noisy markets, exotic music blaring from storefronts, and a skyline punctuated by mosques and minarets, I felt that we had left Europe behind. Unlike Athens, the maddening traffic was filled mostly with run-down American cars used as taxis.

If you were coming to Istanbul by boat, you would first pass through the Dardanelles from the Aegean Sea and enter the relatively small Sea of Marmara, which connects to the Bosphorus that bisects the city and runs north into the Black Sea. The western half of the city is further divided by an inlet called the Golden Horn. To get to the eastern side of Istanbul you had to take a ferry; not for another seventeen years would the first bridge be built.

From almost any direction you can see the city's harbor clogged with ships of every description, from small sailing vessels to large steam ships, many of them freighters from ports around the world. In a snapshot of two men unloading fruit from a sailboat, I caught a watermelon in midair as it was being tossed ashore.

Beneath the oldest part of Istanbul lies the original town of Byzantium, which the Greeks settled in the seventh century B.C.E. and named it for their leader, Byzas. The town eventually became absorbed into the Roman Empire in the second century C.E. It was here in 330 that Emperor Constantine dedicated the new capital of the empire and named it Constantinople. While the western half of the empire was in serious decline by the fourth and fifth centuries, the eastern half survived for over 1,000 years until it fell to the Ottoman Turks in 1453.

Within the old part of the city and close to the harbor is the neighborhood called Sultanahmet. It is here that Istanbul's most famous attractions are found. One is the magnificent Aya Sofya, also known as Hagia Sofia, Sancta Sophia, or The Church of Divine Wisdom. Completed by Emperor Justinian in 537, for centuries it was the greatest church in the Christian world until the Turks converted it into a mosque. Its vast interior, massive dome, and exquisite mosaics are an architectural and artistic wonder. It is no longer a mosque and has been a museum since 1935.

It was in the Topkapi Palace Museum that I had my first exposure to the beauty of Islamic art as seen in textiles, carpets, glassware, jewelry, and manuscripts. The museum is perhaps best known around the world as the setting of a popular 1964 film, *Topkapi,* in which an emerald-studded dagger is the object of a theft. The palace complex itself is a huge place where you could spend days wandering its corridors, courtyards, gardens, and the harem, or women's quarters. Built in the fifteenth century, the palace was the residence for the Ottoman sultans for over 400 years. The last sultan lived there until the early 1800s. One first-hand account of life at the palace was by a Polish musician who was held captive for nineteen years in the seventeenth century. In his writings he described the beauty of the palace's architecture and furnishings.

The number of other sights worth visiting in Istanbul seemed almost endless. The city was indeed a treasure house. Its magnificent mosques were our introduction to Islamic architecture, which would be a common thread during much of our trip. And the bazaar was our introduction to shopping eastern style, where haggling is an art form.

To celebrate the success of our trip so far and to say goodbye to Marianne, John and I took her to dinner. Quite by accident we found a lively, smoky restaurant that we learned later was one of the oldest in the city. Turkish cuisine is a mix of centuries-old influences from the Balkans, Greece, the Middle East and Iran. We all ordered roast lamb, cut from an upright skewer, along with a salad and a potato dish. We chose a domestic red wine from the Cappadocia area of Turkey, known for its wineries. With *baklava* for dessert, Marianne chose tea, the country's national drink. John and I preferred Turkish coffee, brewed with sugar and served in small cups. It is almost like syrup. We finished the evening with a glass of *raki*, the Turkish version of *ouzo*.

"We'll miss you, Marianne," John said.

"I'll miss you two very much. This has been a great trip."

"What will you remember most?" I asked.

She thought a moment. "I'll remember the faces of the people in Yugoslavia, my first view of the blue Aegean Sea, the Acropolis in Athens, and here in Istanbul, the Hagia Sophia. And, of course, the good meals we've had."

Marianne reminded us that her boat was scheduled to leave at 9:30 the next morning, headed for Naples. From there she would take the train back to Munich.

"Your voyage through the Greek Islands should be delightful," I said. "We envy you."

"And I envy you two going all the way to India.

It would turn out that John never saw Marianne again. For me it would take thirty-six years, when I visited her and her husband in Regensburg, Germany in 1992. Our paths would cross again after I came to Poland with the Peace Corps five years later.

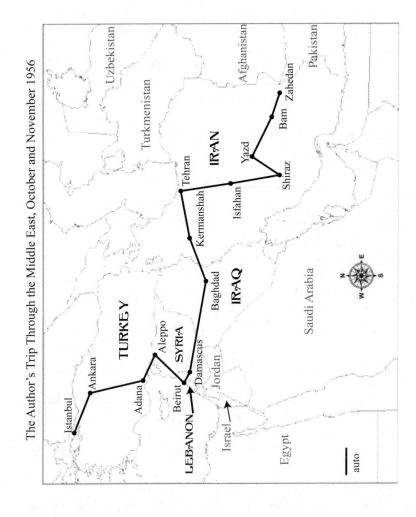

The Author's Trip Through the Middle East, October and November 1956

CHAPTER SIX

Istanbul to Baghdad: October and November 1956

It was now late October. John and I had left Istanbul. He was driving, and I was writing a letter on my small portable typewriter, the 1956 version of a laptop. *We are zooming along the highway about halfway between Ankara and Adana. All around are brown, desiccated hills, but ahead are the Taurus Mountains, snow-capped and rugged, through which we must drive before we reach Syria sometime tomorrow. The stretch of road we are on is not paved, which makes for great clouds of dust, but for the most part the roads in Turkey are very good, mainly due to American money and assistance, so we have made good time all the way from Istanbul yesterday morning. Here in the central part of the country vegetation is sparse, but yesterday we passed through some fine wooded areas, very much like northwestern United States. The drive through the mountains ahead of us will be pretty, too, and with the sun shining every day the weather is still warm enough that we won't be bothered by much snow in the higher altitudes.*

The people here are very friendly and they all seem to like Americans. The large amount of American aid appears to be well appreciated. All over one can see evidence of American money, such as road building equipment and military vehicles. Turkey is very shaky financially, even to the extent that the unofficial rate of exchange for the dollar is three times the official rate.

I go on to describe our stay in Istanbul and how well our trip has gone so far. At that point we had had no major problems. That was about to change, however. Since we didn't keep up with the news everyday, either because we weren't in earshot of an English language newscast or couldn't find a newspaper in English, we didn't fully realize the political turmoil that was building in the Middle East. In the next few days we would have to drastically change our plans. What we didn't know was that Israel, Great Britain and France were about to attack Egypt, setting off a chain of events that would impact the whole region and make travel very risky.

As soon as Israel proclaimed itself a state in 1948, it was attacked by the surrounding Arab countries, leading to a year-long war that Israel won. In spite of the armistice of 1949, tensions continued between Israel and the Arabs, especially the Palestinians. In addition, Israel's relations with Egypt had worsened. In 1949 Egypt closed the Suez Canal to Israeli shipping and refused the United Nations Security Council's order to re-open it. Tensions further escalated in the 1950s as a result of Egypt sponsoring commando raids into Israel from its Arab neighbors and increasing the number of its troops along the Sinai border. Israel in turn led attacks of its own against its borders with Egypt and Syria. While it was known that Egypt was receiving large amounts of arms and military equipment from communist-block countries, the United States had also been a major arms supplier to both Israel and the Arab states. In 1956 Egypt closed the Strait of Tiran, which connects the Gulf of Aqaba with the Red Sea, to Israeli shipping. Israel was convinced that Egypt was preparing for another war.

Parallel to these events, in July of 1956, amid concerns that Egypt had developed too close a relationship with Russia and other communist countries, Britain and the United States withdrew support to help finance building the Aswan Dam on the Nile River. In retaliation, Egypt's President Nasser nationalized the Suez Canal and hoped that profits from the canal would pay for his dam. (The dam was later completed in 1968 with Russian financing.) Nasser's decision riled Britain and France, who had the major financial stake in the canal and had reaped great profits.* They also feared that Egypt could not maintain operation of the canal alone. In addition, Britain had had a military presence in the Canal Zone going back to 1936, though a new agreement with Egypt called for Britain to gradually withdraw its troops, which was in fact accomplished by June of 1956.

---

* Egypt and France were the principal stockholders of the company that built the canal, which was completed in 1869. In 1875 the British government bought out Egypt's shares.

Meanwhile, secret meetings were being held between Israel, Britain and France to plan an attack against Egypt. President Eisenhower was furious when he learned of this plan, but the United States sided with Britain and France to re-establish control of the Suez Canal. The U.S. made clear, however, that it did not advocate using force. By October 13, 1956, while we were still in Greece, the matter was before the United Nations Security Council, where Russia supported Egypt's intention to reject outside control. As we approached the border with Syria, we had only an inkling of what was going on.

—————◆◆❉◆●—————

We arrived in Aleppo, Syria, on October 26. We searched out Aleppo College, which I had learned about through my sister-in-law Muriel Carlton Siddall, whose father, Alfred Carlton, had been its president from 1938 to 1952. The college was founded in the early 1930s by American Congregational and Presbyterian missionaries. Though born in the U.S., Muriel lived in Aleppo with her family until 1945. First we met the dean of the college, who coincidentally had visited Muriel and my brother John in Columbus, Ohio, the previous year.

"Welcome to Aleppo," he said. "You know, this isn't the best time to be a tourist. Things are not politically stable around here these days. Still, you should be able to see some of Aleppo's sights in the next day or so."

The dean introduced us to a young American teacher who said, "I have some free time and would be happy to show you the old bazaar, or *souq* as we say here in the Middle East. There's time to see only a small part of it this afternoon. But tomorrow you can spend more time there on your own. You don't want to miss the Great Mosque. And if you want to indulge yourselves, visit one of the *hammams*, or bath houses."

The next morning, to our consternation, we awoke to find soldiers standing around the college campus and on nearby street corners. A demonstration was going on throughout the city against the French for an incident that had occurred in Algeria, a French colony at that time.

One of the officers who spoke English told us, "You would be advised to leave Aleppo today. It is not safe on the streets. You would be better off leaving Syria and going to Lebanon."

"What do you think?" I asked John. "Should we play it safe or take our chances and stay another day? This is such a fascinating place."

"I agree it's interesting, but what if the demonstration gets out of hand and someone damages our car. Then we're sunk. I think we should leave, like the man says."

Reluctantly we left Aleppo and headed for Beirut on the Mediterranean coast, 200 miles away. We learned the next day that the demonstration in Aleppo had resulted in one person killed, many injured, two French schools burned, and the city put in a state of emergency. It struck us as a bit strange that the first disruption in our trip was due to remote events in Algeria. However, it soon became clear in reading the newspapers that serious events were shaping up close by.

The next four days, October 27 to the 30th, turned out to be crucial. According to the news, something was about to erupt between Israel and Egypt. It also became clear that we had to give up the idea of visiting Israel. However, since things seemed calm enough in Lebanon, we decided to spend a few days and look around.

Lebanon has often been called the "Switzerland of the Middle East." The country was indeed beautiful, with mountains to the east and the blue Mediterranean Sea to the west. Beirut itself had a unique cosmopolitan flare that reflected a European and particularly French atmosphere. We were told that the city had profited more from Middle East oil than many other major cities because Lebanese credit controls and money exchange regulations were less stringent, making it easier for domestic and foreign investment in hotels and real estate. With a more open society in contrast to other Arab cities, Beirut's nightlife was well known in the Middle East, attracting sheiks and sailors alike to its many brothels and nightclubs.

John and I decided to take in a little nightlife of our own. After having supper in a lively, smoky restaurant, we went to a couple of bars to mingle with the local and international crowd. After his third beer John said he was tired and wanted to return to our hotel, a few blocks away. It seemed early to me, so I said I would stay on a while. After I left the bar an hour later, I took a different route back to the hotel and found myself in the red light district. I passed a few darkly lit doorways and then came to one that led to the second floor. I looked up and in a window above a female figure said, "Welcome, come in."

Led by curiosity and libidinous longing, I found myself on the landing at the top of the stairs. To the left was a doorway with strands of beads for a curtain, as I had seen in old films. Though I had never been in a place like this before, somehow it seemed familiar. Inside was a small parlor, and as I entered, the woman in the window came over to greet me. "Please, sit down. France? German? English? "

"No, American."

"Ah, I like Americans." The woman had a heavy accent and it was soon evident that her English was limited. She offered me something to drink. For some reason a cup of tea sounded good. While she was preparing the tea in a tiny kitchen, I looked around. The parlor was furnished with an over-stuffed couch and two matching chairs upholstered in a worn, dark blue fabric. Along the back of the couch was a brightly colored patterned shawl. The only lamp in the room stood on a small table between the chairs and couch, its dim bulb under a frilly shade giving out just enough light to create a calm, even cozy atmosphere. On a table near the window I could see a curl of smoke rising from a stick of incense, its scent mingling with the faint aroma of cigarette smoke and perfume. Surprisingly, I felt relaxed. It was obvious that the woman had a solo practice. I had expected there would be some selection to be made. When she returned with two cups of tea and sat down, I had a momentary sense of dropping in on an old friend, except that the short, dark-haired woman opposite me was wearing a light blue satin robe pulled tight around her waist with a yellow sash, and bright red slippers. Her eyes were outlined in black. I guessed that she was in her early forties, a bit on the plump side, but overall I found her appealing. While we chatted in halting fashion, unbidden thoughts came to mind: *Am I going to stay? John will definitely be surprised when I get back to the hotel. Would I tell anyone else about this? What if someone comes up the stairs?*

As if reading my mind the woman got up and closed the door, shutting out the hanging beads. "Come with me," she said, leading me into her bedroom.

———◆◆◆◆◆———

John gave out a huge laugh. "You what?" The expression on his face was priceless. "Why didn't you tell me you were thinking about that before I left the bar?"

"I didn't know then."

"For Christ's sake, I would have gone with you." He paused and then said, "A guy needs his ashes hauled now and then, you know."

Smiling, I said, "I know, John, I know."

From Beirut we did some sightseeing along the coast in the cities of Tyre and Sidon, remembering that Alexander the Great had come this way. Because we would have to leave sooner than planned, we would miss seeing the ancient cities of Byblos and Baalbek.

The news finally came on October 29 that Israel had attacked Egypt. The next day Britain and France issued an ultimatum that Egypt give up control of the canal. When this demand was rejected, France and Britain joined in the military assault on October 31. In response, President Nasser ordered the sinking of forty ships in the canal, rendering it useless. *

Hearing of Israel's attack, John and I decided we had better leave Lebanon. While it had been clear a few days before that it would be unwise to even attempt a visit to Israel, it was obvious now

---

* The Suez Canal remained closed to shipping until March 1957, when UN salvage teams completed removing the sunken ships. In 1958 the nationalized canal company worked out a financial agreement with its previous shareholders and made its final payment in 1962. The canal was closed again in 1967 during the Six-Day Arab/Israeli War, not to re-open again until 1975. In 1979 a peace treaty between Israel and Egypt gave Israel unrestricted use of the canal.

that going into Jordan was out of the question because the pro-Egyptian government there had declared martial law, essentially closing its borders. This meant that our plan to drive to Baghdad on the paved road from Amman, as the German doctor in Munich advised, had to be abandoned. This left us with only one alternative, to go to Damascus in southern Syria and from there find our way across the desert to Baghdad. We had read that things had calmed down in Aleppo; there was no indication that trouble was brewing in Damascus.

As I read again a letter I wrote home from Beirut, dated October 30, it suggests that while we were not foolhardy, we must have been a bit naïve. We were also lucky.

If you have been reading the same news reports that I have, I can understand that you may be somewhat apprehensive about my presence out here in the Middle East. However, things always sound worse than they really are, but even if that is true we will continue our travels in a more alert frame of mind, for these Arabs have a way of being temperamental about things, and the unexpected could happen at any time. But up to the present moment we have had no first-hand contact with any of the unpleasantness that has taken place in many of these countries, and though we just missed a big riot in Aleppo, our journey has been calm and untroubled . . . . The situation between Israel and the countries around it has become more tense in the last few days. I read today that guards along the Israeli borders with Syria and Jordan have been increased, a sign that is not at all encouraging. The recent election in Jordan, which put in a pro-Egyptian government, and thus an anti-western one, has not helped matters either . . . . Westerners aren't very popular around these parts, and the degree to which President Nasser has come forward as the hero of the Middle East is not to be minimized. He has become the Arab idol. All over one sees his picture on the walls of barber shops, grocery stores, and even in taxi cabs.

But a letter just a few days later had a different tone. *Things have changed so rapidly that for a time we were afraid we may have to cancel our trip from here on. Anticipating attacks by Israel, Syria and Jordan are on alert and have halted air traffic. Jerusalem has been kept in total darkness at night. With Lebanon having a calmer attitude,*

Beirut has become a center for Americans leaving Syria and Jordan. We read of frequent demonstrations against the French and British.

Before we left Beirut, we decided to check in with the American Consulate to see if they might have some useful information. We were told by one of the consular officials, who gave us ten minutes of his time, that the political situation was very volatile in the Middle East and he strongly recommended against going further east. We were advised to return to Turkey where we would be much safer. As we were leaving he smiled and said, "Off the record, I think you should be able to get to Baghdad if you are careful. I wouldn't hang around here any longer, though. You know, you could have picked a better time to make this trip of yours, which, by the way, sounds pretty interesting to me. Good luck."

On November 1, with bombs bursting around the Suez Canal and the Israeli army surging across the Sinai desert, we set off for Damascus, fifty miles east of Beirut.

———◆◈◆———

The founding of Israel as a new country and the impact on its neighbors has a long and tortuous history. The wish for a Jewish state in the Holy Land gained momentum in the 19th century. At that time the region, which included Jerusalem, was a predominately Arab territory in the Ottoman Empire. Beginning in the 1880s, the first significant Jewish immigration began, mostly from Eastern Europe. This did not please the Arabs, who in 1891 petitioned the Ottoman government to prevent Jews from immigrating and buying up land. In 1896 an Austrian journalist by the name of Theodor Herzl published a booklet advocating for a Jewish state. Soon the First Zionist Congress was held in Basel, Switzerland, in 1897. Great Britain was sympathetic to the cause, and its foreign secretary, Arthur Balfour, authored the famous Balfour Declaration in 1917, which endorsed the principle of a Jewish state.

In 1918, with the defeat of the Ottoman Empire following World War I, the League of Nations granted to France and Great Britain mandates (administrative control) of former Ottoman territories in the Middle East. The land was carved up arbitrarily, with France given control over what would be Syria and Lebanon, and Great Britain given control over what would be Iraq and Palestine. When Britain took on its mandate of Palestine, it first divided the territory in two parts, with the Jordan River as the dividing line. To the east was created the Emirate of Transjordan. To the west, the region from the river to the Mediterranean coast, including the Holy Land and Jerusalem, was called Palestine.*

Up until this time Jewish immigration had continued, but it increased dramatically in the 1930s as Jews fled Europe to escape the Nazi concentration camps. Palestinian attacks on Jewish settlements and British army units also increased, which led Britain to attempt greater control over immigration. This was successful during World War II, but became more problematic when increasing numbers of Jewish survivors of the war wanted to immigrate. Weary from the frustration in dealing with the Arab/Jewish conflict, Britain in 1947 turned the problem over to the United Nations, which voted to partition Palestine into two separate territories. In land given to the Jews, the population would still be almost half Arab. Territory allotted to the Palestinians included the Gaza Strip and what later became known as the West Bank. Curiously, these two areas were not connected. Jerusalem would be under international control.

When the British finally withdrew from Palestine in 1948, Israel proclaimed itself a state. Almost immediately, Israel was attacked by forces from Egypt, Syria, Lebanon, Jordan (as it was now called), Iraq and Saudi Arabia. In the war that lasted for over a year, the Arab armies were defeated. The resulting armistice in 1949 allowed Israel to keep much of the territory it had won, including the western part of Jerusalem. However, the Gaza Strip would now be under Egypt's control. The West Bank and the eastern part of Jerusalem that included the Old City with the traditional holy sites would belong to Jordan. Little was left that the Palestinians could call their own. Thousands were now forced

---

* When Syria was a province in the Roman Empire, the southern region was known as Syria Palaestina. It was from this ancient name that the British called the new territory Palestine.

to live as refugees in Israeli-occupied territories or in refugee camps in the surrounding Arab countries.

As John and I passed through the Middle East that fall in 1956, we wanted to understand the conflict between Israel and its Arab neighbors as best we could, but it wasn't easy. In Beirut most of the English-speaking Arabs we encountered angrily denounced Israel. At a restaurant we met an American Jewish couple trying to get into Israel to visit their son.

"Don't believe what the Arabs tell you. It is God's will that we settle this land."

I asked, "How about the Palestinians who have been displaced and forced to live as refugees?"

"Well, that's a problem that needs to be resolved somehow."

At our hotel in Beirut we had lunch with a well-educated Lebanese businessman who told us, "You have to understand the Arabs' hostility toward the British for partitioning Palestine, and toward Israel for taking their land. It's a very complex problem and one that will continue for years. And we don't hear much sympathy from your government for the Palestinians who have been displaced from the land they have lived on for centuries."

It was a big disappointment not to be able to visit Israel and to hear what people there had to say.

———◆•※•◆———

When we arrived at the border between Lebanon and Syria, we were surprised to find friendly soldiers and only a few questions about where we were going. We drove on to Damascus without incident. On the surface, life in the city appeared normal enough. We were unsure whether to stay one or two nights. We found cheap lodging, had lunch in a small restaurant that opened on to the street, bought a map at a tobacco store, and set off to see the sights. We first went to admire the magnificent Umayyad Mosque (completed 706 C.E.), one of Islam's two most treasured early architectural achievements (the other being the Dome of the Rock in Jerusalem, 691 C.E.). The mosque was built on the foundation of a Roman temple and its design reflects the influence of Greek,

Roman and Christian/Byzantine architecture. Byzantine artisans were brought in to create the mosaics used extensively throughout the complex.

Later, as we were walking down a side street, two men came up to us and said politely, "The chief of the security police would like to see you. Please come with us."

We followed them to a small office where the chief, a short, dark-haired, stocky man, greeted us with a firm handshake. "Good afternoon, gentlemen. Could I please see your passports? Ah yes, Americans. Better than being English. What sort of map is that you have?"

We showed it to him and explained we were just sightseeing.

"Of course. However, I would advise you to stay off the streets. When people see you looking at a map, they might think you are our enemy. You can never tell what might happen. If you want to see the city, hire a guide at the travel bureau. Have a nice visit. Goodbye."

Putting our map out of sight we wandered off. We thought a safe place to spend some time would be the U.S. Information Library. We had found similar libraries in other cities to be a good source for news. It would be about a fifteen-minute walk. I felt edgy. Tension had filled the air. We passed shop after shop with radios blaring into the street, while people stood around listening. Then all of a sudden shop keepers came running outside shouting and closing the iron gates over their store windows and doors. It was unnerving not to understand what was going on. No one would tell us anything.

The library was a welcome respite, but they didn't have much information other than security along Syria's border with Israel had been intensified and there was news of a possible attack. When we left the library a couple hours later, the city was again calm, almost subdued. After supper we thought that going to a movie would be a distraction. What should be showing but *The Seven Year Itch,* with Marilyn Monroe and Tom Ewell. Once the film began we were transported back to America. We had gotten halfway into the film to the part where Ewell and Monroe are having a drink in his apartment, and for atmosphere he puts on a record of a Rachmaninov piano concerto. Hearing this, Monroe speaks the classic lines, "Oh, I know. That's what they call classical music. I can tell because there's no vocal." Just then the projector stopped and the lights went out. In the distance we could hear the whine of air raid sirens. After ten anxious minutes, the sirens were quiet. It took another fifteen minutes until the projector started up again.

On the way back to our hotel, we readily agreed that we should leave in the morning for Baghdad. Again we were disappointed not to see more of Damascus, a fascinating place that is considered to be the oldest continuously inhabited city in the world.

———◆◆◆———

In the early morning chill of November 2 we left Damascus. Ahead of us would be a two-day drive across more than 500 hundred miles of desert to Baghdad. We had learned that the Suez crisis had worsened. Israel had routed Egyptian troops and its army had reached the east bank of the Suez Canal. Britain and France had landed forces and demanded that both Egyptian and Israeli troops be withdrawn from the Canal Zone.

The paved road leading out of Damascus extended for some forty miles, where it ended at the Syrian customs point. Up until now we had no difficulty at border crossings. While our passports and visas were always carefully scrutinized, there had been almost no inspection of our luggage or the contents of the car. Today would be different. While one guard took our passports into his barren little office, another started poking around in the back seat of the Volkswagen, opening boxes and looking inside books. He then found the map on which we were marking our trip. He opened it up and then said in a loud, agitated voice "Israel! Israel!" I guessed he wanted us to show him where it was. Unfortunately I did. He took out a ballpoint pen and inked out the name.

"No Israel!" he said.

Beyond the paved road was hard-packed, gravelly sand. But immediately we encountered potholes, making it impossible at first to drive more than twenty-five miles an hour. Sometimes we didn't see them and our little Beetle bounced like a frightened jackrabbit. "Watch out!" I yelled. Too late. We hit a camouflaged hole so hard that the books we had in the well behind the back seat, plus a dozen eggs we had bought that morning, were tossed in the air, making for a sticky mess. In the first two hours we had hardly driven fifty miles. But then the potholes disappeared and off we flew across the dusty, parched earth, cruising steadily between fifty and sixty. Occasionally we came across sand dunes, but we never had to drive through any. A few times we hit loose sand that felt as if we were sliding through water. Fine dust settled all around us, filling every crevice in the car. Even our teeth felt gritty.

We knew from talking with people that trucks often used this route, as did a daily bus between Damascus and Baghdad. We did in fact see two trucks in the distance that day, but no buses. What kept us from getting lost were signposts every half-mile. Sometimes we passed them within a few hundred feet, other times we saw them far off. Our compass also helped to keep us on course.

Besides the trucks we saw very little else. The desert appeared totally barren. Only once did we see any living creature. I was driving and John said, "Look over to the right, way over there by that slight rise."

"What is it? I can't see that clearly. Are they camels?"

"Right. Five camels. And I can see three people walking with them. Can you imagine? Out here in the middle of nowhere?"

Around noontime we stopped to fill up the gas tank and have lunch. (It was only during these two days that we needed to use the extra gas we carried in a jerry can.) Our options were cheese or peanut butter sandwiches, plus a drink of water. The sun was unbearably hot, and with no shade we didn't stay long outside the car.

Sometime in the afternoon we crossed the border into Iraq, and by five o'clock came to the paved road that we had wanted to take from Jordan. Soon we arrived at customs and the security checkpoint. "You are Americans? Welcome, welcome!" It was indeed reassuring to hear this. By sunset we still had at least 200 miles until Baghdad, so we decided to pull off the road not far from a small walled village to make supper and spend the night in the car. We were dirty and exhausted. It had been a long, hot, grueling day.

We had enough water to wash up and heat for soup to go with the delicious Syrian bread we had bought with the eggs that morning. For dessert we had a banana and slice of what could be called a Syrian version of *baklava*. Tonight would be the fourth time that John and I had slept in the car, which we had found not at all uncomfortable. To my way of thinking, it was preferable to sleeping in a tent and avoided being visited by scorpions and other desert residents.

As twilight faded into evening, a soft, cooling breeze kept us company as we were finishing our modest meal.

"You know, we could have stayed longer in Damascus if we had really wanted to," John said.

"Did you want to?" I asked.

"Not really, I guess. But like you said, it was such a fascinating place, with its mosques and the market place. What do they call it?"

"*Souq.*"

"That's right, *souq*. What a great word. Too bad we couldn't have spent more time there."

"Not only that," I said, "but we're missing more of that good Syrian cooking."

"Maybe we should have hired a guide from the travel bureau, like the security chief suggested," John said. "He didn't tell us to leave the city."

"We could have," I said, "but I don't think we would have enjoyed wandering the city even with him, given all the craziness going on yesterday afternoon."

"It was a bit scary," John agreed, "the way they came running out of their shops, shouting and shutting everything up."

"You know," I added, "it occurred to me while I was driving today that except for the police no one seemed to notice us much at all. It was like we were invisible. Maybe we were safer than we thought, but I doubt it."

"I wish we knew what happened today," John said. "The reception on the car radio doesn't pick up much out here. Not in English anyway." *

"And to think we also missed a visit to the ancient city of Petra in Jordan. I've heard that is one fantastic place."

John said, "Well, look at it this way. Given what's been going on, I think we've done all right. We've come more than 7,000 miles without a car accident. Our Beetle hasn't missed a beat. Not only that, we didn't get caught in the middle of a demonstration."

I agreed. It had cost us barely $100 for car expenses, including several oil changes, and neither of us had gotten sick. "And do you realize," I added, "that, so far, you and I haven't had one argument?"

It turned out that John and I were good travel companions. Both of us liked to be organized and plan ahead. Neither of us was demanding or insisted on having things go a certain way, and we rarely disagreed on how to spend our modest resources when it affected both of us. Also, we were both even-tempered enough to tolerate what frustrations we encountered without getting too upset. We were also alike in that neither of us was much of a car mechanic.

Our differences were apparent, however. John was more outspoken than I and more likely to disagree openly with someone.

---

* We eventually learned of the following events: On November 6, Russia threatened to intervene on Egypt's behalf, alerting United States forces worldwide. On November 7, the United Nations worked out a ceasefire and demanded that French and British forces leave Egypt; they eventually complied and had finally withdrawn by December. Israel was also ordered to withdraw and to pull back to its borders as called for in the armistice of 1949. They reluctantly complied and completed withdrawal of their troops by March 1957. United Nations peacekeeping troops had been stationed at the Canal Zone and in the Gaza Strip. The following ten years proved to be the most peaceful between Israel and its neighbors. However, in the 1967 Six-Day War, when Israel captured the Gaza Strip and the West Bank, even more problems were created in its relations with the Palestinians.

Though I could have strong opinions, I often held back expressing them if it meant an argument. Yet I was the one more likely to strike up a conversation with someone at a shop or restaurant; once I had broken the ice, however, John joined in. He had a keen analytical mind, while I was more introspective. I saw John as more sure of himself and predicted he would be highly successful. While we shared an interest in the political events unfolding around us, I didn't have his knowledge or passion for finance and the business world. And he wondered sometimes how I could get excited about something as seemingly insignificant as the intricately carved stone window grills in the mosque in Damascus.

Our backgrounds were also different. John grew up among the well-to-do on the north shore of Long Island, while I was from a small, academic town in northern Ohio. His college years were spent at Williams, an elite school in the northwestern corner of Massachusetts, while I attended socially conscious Oberlin in Ohio. Though John and I had many frank talks about politics, history, growing up, and our time in Munich, neither of us revealed much on a personal level.

◆•◈•◆

Darkness finally came. A new moon was rising on the horizon. Our only company was the empty desert.

"Listen!" I said. "Hear that?"

"Yeah, I heard something, too. What is it?"

"I'm not sure, but it sounds like a flute." It was faint, but definitely a musical sound coming from the small village in the distance. Then there came a muffled drumbeat. "It sounds intriguing. What do you think? Shall we see what it is?"

"Why not?" John replied. "The worst that could happen is that they kidnap us and we end up taking Iraqi wives." In fact the day before we had heard that a Scandinavian couple had disappeared in the desert, most likely captured by a Bedouin tribe.

"Let's go!" I said.

The walled village was a few hundred yards away, less than a ten-minute walk. As we approached we saw the silhouette of two bearded men standing in a doorway. They came toward us and one said, "*Salaam.*"

"Hello, good evening."

"From where?"

"America. We're going to Baghdad."

"Please, please," he said, motioning to us to follow them inside the wall into a large enclosure open to the sky, which was dimly lit with oil lamps. Six men were sitting cross-legged on thick pile carpets. All were barefoot, with their shoes and slippers lined up against a wall. Two men were each smoking a *huqqah* (water pipe, also called a *narghile).*

One man stood up and gestured that we take his place. He then went to where several women were standing in a dark corner, their faces partially veiled, chatting quietly. He said something and one of the women disappeared, soon to return with a plate of sweet cakes similar to *baklava,* a tray of small glasses, and a brass urn, which she gave to the man who set them down in the middle of the circle. The man next to me poured each of us a glass of strong, sweet tea from the urn and then offered more to the others. The plate of cakes was then passed around. We were offered a *huqqah* to smoke, but we declined. Though I was curious, I thought it was safer not to.

By this time my eyes had adjusted to the low light and I could see our hosts more clearly. One was wearing the traditional *kaffiyeh,* a white and black-checkered headdress held in place by a headband, called an *iqal,* giving him a formal appearance. He was younger than the others and may have been a special guest. Another man had on a dark blue *bournous,* a long robe with a hood that fell over his back. Two men wore white, loosely wrapped headscarves.

For the next hour, in the flickering light, while our glasses were refilled and the cakes passed around yet again, we did our best to explain where we had come from and where we were going. The men knew only a few words of English, but understood better the names of cities we mentioned. Still, it was an animated conversation with many hand gestures. The tone of their voices and the expression their faces told us they were surprised we were traveling so far and alone. We could also tell they were as worried as we were about the war going on in Egypt.

"England, France, Israel no good," said an elderly man shaking his head, his face deeply lined. With a faint smile he added, "America? Maybe okay."

Reluctantly we decided it was time to leave. Our hosts stood with us and shook hands, each one saying, "*Salaam.*" I was moved by the hospitality of these Iraqis in receiving two strangers who had appeared uninvited out of the night.

<hr />

The next morning I said, "You know. We never did find out where the music came from last night."

"You're right. I had forgotten all about that."

As we drove toward Baghdad, I imagined a city out of *Arabian Nights,* with exotic images of Shaherazade reclining on silken cushions in a filmy gown, telling a new tale each night to her husband, King Shahryar, so he wouldn't put her to death. Stories of Aladdin, Ali Baba, and Sinbad came to mind, filling my head with scenes of flying carpets, turbaned genies, and sultans in baggy pants surrounded by slinky harem women.

The Baghdad we saw was, of course, nothing of the sort. Except for a few interesting-looking mosques, there was little evidence of anything that could be called exotic or romantic. Baghdad had once been a beautiful city with more than a million people, but that was over a thousand years ago. As I wrote in a letter home, *Baghdad looks very much like a frontier town, with many buildings only half built and streets half paved, though there is evidence of overall planning which looks to the future. . . . Within the last five years the country has acquired a lot of money from the oil fields, but the people don't seem to benefit from the country's wealth, except possibly the taxi drivers who zoom around in shiny new American cars, beeping their horns at every opportunity, making mid-city traffic most unpleasant. . . . Though Baghdad is pretty grubby compared to Beirut, it has more of a genuine Middle Eastern atmosphere. The Baghdadians are extremely friendly, as most Arabs are, and many people still wear the traditional cloak.*

The British influence was clearly visible in Baghdad, with many signs in English and British goods in shops geared to Westerners, especially along al-Rashid, its main street. The British presence goes back as far as the 1700s when the British East India Company began to trade with the Arabs. The English traveler, H.V. Morton, came to Baghdad in 1936, having taken an overnight bus across the desert from Damascus. He described Baghdad as *a mud-colored city on the banks of a mud-colored river. With the slightest wind, powdered mud flies through its streets . . . . The chief architectural decoration is the glazed tile, which is sparingly applied to the cupolas of a few mosques.*

When Isabella Bird, a fifty-nine-year-old widow arrived by boat from England in January 1890, having come up the Tigris River from Basra, she found a bustling city of 120,000. Here is an excerpt from her colorful account: *The weather is splendid, making locomotion a pleasure, and the rough, irregular roadways which at other seasons are deep in foul and choking dust, or in mud and pestilential slime, are now firm and not remarkably dirty . . . In the daytime there is a roar or hum of business, mingled with braying of asses, squeals of belligerent horses, yells of camel-drivers and muleteers, beating of drums, shouts of beggars, ear-splitting snatches of discordant music, and in short a chorus of sounds unfamiliar to Western ears, but the nights are so still that the swirl of the Tigris as it hurries past is distinctly heard. Only the long melancholy call to prayer, or the barking of dogs, breaks the silence which at sunset falls as a pall over Baghdad.*

Founded in 726 C.E. on the Tigris River, Baghdad soon replaced Damascus as the capital of the Arab world. The Islamic culture here reached its peak during the eighth and ninth centuries under Caliph Haroun al-Rashid (ruled 786-809), whose reign is associated with *Arabian Nights*, also known as *The Thousand and One Nights.* *

---

* This collection of stories, originating in several Middle Eastern countries, their authors and dates unknown, was first mentioned by scholars in the ninth century C.E. The first Arab version was translated from the Persian, with some tales set in Baghdad. The first European translation to be published appeared in France in 1717. The most well-known English translation is by Sir Richard Burton, the nineteenth century British writer, linguist and explorer, who published his sixteen-volume edition of *The Thousand Nights and a Night* over three years, beginning in 1885.

Often called the "Golden Age," this period produced great works in literature and science, and it was during this time that scholars began translating classical Greek and Roman works into Arabic, preserving many ancient texts whose translations also found their way to Europe via Spain, where the Arabs ruled for 700 years until 1492. Standing at the crossroad of major trade routes, Baghdad became famous for its palaces, mosques and gardens, and continued to flourish for over 400 years.

Baghdad's decline began in 1258, when it was sacked by the grandson of the Mongol warrior, Genghis Kahn. It was pillaged again in 1401 by Turkish invaders led by Tamerlane. Next came conquests by the Persians followed by the Ottoman Turks, who ruled the region for 300 years beginning in 1638. Over time the past glory of the city vanished, as well as much of the region's ancient network of canals that irrigated the grain fields of Mesopotamia, known as the Fertile Crescent.

Because the Ottoman Empire sided with Germany in World War I, Britain invaded the area in 1917 to protect its oil interests. After the war Britain was given a mandate over the region, beginning in 1920. Through the efforts of the British government and its colonial secretary, Winston Churchill, plus advice from T.E. Lawrence (the famous Lawrence of Arabia), the region gained independence from the Ottomans. In 1921 a treaty with Britain created the Kingdom of Iraq by combining the three provinces of Basra, Baghdad and Mosul, with the city of Baghdad as its capital. Written into the treaty was the requirement that the government be democratic. The first parliament met in 1925. Iraq became a member of the League of Nations in 1932 and a republic in 1958. The country's subsequent chaotic political history is too complex to discuss here, but as I write in 2005, the current war in Iraq continues to claim far too many lives with no end in sight in what, in my opinion, has been a major disaster in United States foreign policy.

An unexpected surprise was meeting up with two of my college classmates, Harry Hunsicker and Jack Noble, at the YMCA where we were staying. I had received a letter from Harry several months before, telling me of his and Jack's proposed trip, similar to ours it turned out. Not knowing their exact timetable, I never considered that we would meet up along the way. But there they were, having tea on the veranda of the Y when we pulled in. They had entered Iraq on the paved road from Jordan, and to their good fortune, just before the Suez crisis exploded, had visited the ancient city of Petra. They told us it was one of the best sites they had seen. There was limited time to share our stories since they departed the next day, heading off toward Iran and Afghanistan. Harry and I had known each other since high school and took a trip together out west when we were eighteen.

What we found most interesting in Baghdad was its *souq*, or bazaar, a mammoth labyrinth of crowded, noisy passageways enclosed by high-windowed walls that were roofed over by bricked arches, where getting lost was part of the adventure. Shops were often clustered depending on the goods they sold. Near one entrance were stalls selling glistening copper trays, pitchers, pots and pans, some dangling out front to catch your eye. Further along were several shops selling painted ceramic ware. In one tiny stall was an assortment of blue and white plates, bowls and cups, which to my eye were probably made in China. The smell of leather caught my attention nearby where belts, handbags, boots and shoes were sold, some items being made on the premises. Around a sharp corner were shops selling gold and silver jewelry, and further on wool hats, silk robes, shawls, and other articles of clothing. Several merchants specialized in beautiful woven wool carpets, which, a turbaned man told us, came from all over the Middle East. Amid dust and the smell of straw and animal excrement we could have bargained for a clucking chicken or a bleating sheep, while nearby we could have bought a saddle for a mule or camel. Down a side corridor we came upon a sweaty blacksmith, his grimy face partially obscured by smoke from his fire, pounding a hot piece of steel on his anvil that added ear-splitting sounds to the already constant din around us. Some of his exquisitely fashioned knives and swords were on display.

Eager to make a sale, merchants would often shout from inside their stalls, "Please, you like?" Or they would come out into the passageway and, grinning through their dark beards, touch you lightly on the arm. "You buy? Very nice." We didn't buy much, but by this time we were getting adept at haggling over prices. I found it entertaining to watch how the locals did business, their bargaining accompanied by much hand gesticulation and raucous conversation. There were also small eating places where you could rest and get a scalding cup of viscous, pungent coffee and a pastry drenched in honey. To our amazement, in the middle of the *souq* we ran into a gaunt-looking young Australian wheeling a bicycle, planning, he told us, eventually to end up in London.

Outside the *souq*, it was in the crowded, littered side streets where city life was its most lively with the sounds and smells of this desert city, though a bit more up-to-date than when Isabella Bird visited sixty-five years before. Besides the noise of traffic and merchants calling out for business, many shops had a radio in the doorway blaring brain-rattling Arabic music. The odor of dung was ever present as we passed mules being led through narrow streets, while barefoot children played in front of open storefronts. We spent time in coffee houses, where smoking *huqqahs* was a popular pastime among local men, and in inexpensive restaurants where we were drawn in by the aroma of roasting lamb. The few women we saw wore the traditional Muslim veil and black full-length robe, called a *burqa*. Occasionally a filthy beggar in rags would approach us, but only one pestered us more than a few minutes. On the shore of the Tigris River we met several friendly boys playing in the shallow, muddy water, wearing what looked like striped pajamas.

We had considered visiting the ruins of ancient Babylon fifty miles to the south, but were told that it wasn't worth the effort. However, we did pay a visit to the Archeological Museum, which contained amazing artifacts from ancient Mesopotamia and Babylonia. Of special interest was an exhibit of 4,000-year old pottery and weapons. However, the museum appeared drab and run-down. Driving around the outskirts of Baghdad we saw the landscape dotted with green fields irrigated by water from the Tigris River, relieving the parched monotony of the surrounding desert. Oases of gardens with orange and pomegranate trees within the city could be found behind mud brick walls where the more affluent lived out of view. Date palms, the Iraqi national tree, provided about the only shade from the unrelenting sun.

On our last evening, as quiet was slowly descending upon the city, we were having a meal in a restaurant with a view of the sun setting over the Tigris River, the fading light blending with a mild breeze. We got to talking about the Suez crisis and how distant we now felt from the political turmoil we had faced only a few days before.

"What bothers me most," I said, "is not so much about Egypt and the Suez Canal, but what will happen between the Palestinians and Israel."

"I know," John replied. "Israel is fighting for its survival, and as long as it has a superior army, it's going to win out over its enemies."

CHAPTER SEVEN

Baghdad to Bombay: November and December 1956

In my next letter home I wrote: *After a two-day ride over rough, unpaved roads, plus a dust storm in Iraq, we arrived in Tehran, the capital of Iran, on November 9. Much of the trip was through mountainous country, which was a great change from the flat lowlands along the Tigris and Euphrates Rivers, but still the earth is virtually treeless.*

It would turn out that traveling through Iran would be the most difficult leg of our journey. It is a large country, about three times the size of France, which meant that we ended up driving more than 1,500 miles over rough roads between Tehran in the north and the border with Pakistan to the southeast.

The morning we set out from Baghdad was typically cool and sunny. In fact we had seen hardly a cloud in the sky since we left Greece, and not a drop of rain since Austria. We couldn't have picked a better time of the year to travel. (With hindsight now, I realize how miserable our adventure could have been if we had traveled in a rainy season.) The road to Tehran headed northeast, and soon in the distance we could see the Zagros Mountains that run southeasterly for hundreds of miles along the western border of Iran, beginning in Azerbaijan in the north and continuing on south as far as the Persian Gulf. At some places the range is 125 miles wide and has little vegetation except in river valleys. Its inhabitants are mostly nomads. Our route would take us through one of the lower passes of this range, slowly gaining altitude, so that by the time we arrived in Tehran, we were at about 4,000 feet above sea level.

While we were still in Iraq a fierce dust storm obliterated the sky, making it impossible to see more than a few feet ahead. At several points we had to pull over and let the wind and dust howl around us. Fortunately, there was little traffic, though a few huge trucks roared by, their headlights barely making a dent in the semi-darkness. After two hours we abruptly came to the other side of the storm, and though it continued to be windy, we were now on higher ground and away from the sandy lowlands.

The first city we passed through in Iran was Kermanshah, famous for its carpet weaving. At this point we had covered about 200 miles, with almost 300 miles yet to go to Tehran. Though rarely paved, the roads were generally well graded, but often we had to drive through stretches with ruts and gullies that pounded the car's suspension. Then, around noon, from the driver's seat I said, "Something's wrong with the front end."

"What do you mean?" John asked with an edge to his voice.

"I'm not sure, but the front right wheel feels funny."

"Like what exactly?"

"Like something's loose. I can feel it in the steering wheel."

"Any guesses?"

"I'm not sure. Maybe we have another flat."

"We should stop and check it. Pull over when you see a safe place off the road."

When we looked under the car we could see that the top of the right shock absorber shaft had sheared off, rendering it useless.

"We can still drive the car, can't we?" John asked.

"Sure. But we'll have to slow down a bit and we'll feel every little bump on the road."

The first thing we did after arriving in Tehran was to get the shock absorber fixed. Volkswagen agencies could be found in every major city; we had already visited several along the way for oil changes and tune-ups. We always received excellent service, and the employees who spoke German or English enjoyed hearing about our trip.

Iran is a region that has seen many invading armies down through the centuries. It was the conquering Arabs, however, that most dramatically changed the cultural and religious landscape when they introduced Islam in the seventh century C.E. Though the Arabs were deposed after 600 years by other invaders, such as Genghis Khan in 1194 and Tamerlane in 1380, Islam remained the dominant religion. John and I were aware of its presence every time we heard a *muezzin* call the faithful to prayer from a minaret, or when we observed men facing Mecca as they prayed on their hands and knees, often on the street. We were fortunate to be able to visit inside a few mosques, each a vast, cool, and dimly lit interior under a huge dome and decorated with colorful ceramic tiles inside and out. (The word mosque comes from the Arabic *masjid*, meaning "place of prostration.") We were told that there were still many places where one risked his life if he entered a mosque uninvited.

We found Tehran to be a huge, sprawling city, more modern than Baghdad, with tree-lined boulevards, less dust, and a much more temperate climate. Its main streets were clogged with buses, taxis, donkey-drawn carts, and old American automobiles. Vendors were everywhere hawking their wares. Tehran is less than 100 miles from the Caspian Sea that lies to the north. The Elburz mountain range runs east and west between Tehran and the sea, appearing to rise up at the city's edge.

For our three days in Tehran we stayed with an American missionary couple, John and Ruth Elder, whose two sons, Joseph and David, were students at Oberlin at the same time I was there. For thirty years Dr. Elder had been the general secretary of the Presbyterian Mission. Their spacious, two-storied home, situated within a large walled compound among other mission buildings, was always open to guests and served as a kind of bed and breakfast for travelers passing through. Three other guests were there as well, a French engineering student on his way to Afghanistan, and a retired British clergyman and his wife who were making their first visit to the Middle East. As was the custom, all of us were asked to help with daily housekeeping chores. I recall mealtimes being full of lively conversation about history, politics and the work of the mission.

The British traveler, Isabella Bird, described the Tehran she saw in 1890 as an unattractive city of about 100,000 inhabitants with *few elements of beauty or grandeur in its situation, even though the triumphant barbarism of the desert sweeps up to its gates.* * She mentioned visiting the Presbyterian Mission, with its church,

---

* In the 1920s, urban renewal took the form of tearing down the ancient walls and demolishing sections of the older city to make way for wide boulevards.

hospital and school, located in the European quarter of the city. During her stay in Tehran, Bird met many of its residents, both Persian and European, and even briefly met the shah on a tour of the shah's palace. She had harsh words for what she saw as the increasing influence of the West that was infiltrating the Persian culture, especially the influx of European and American goods found in shops. She was also critical of the demeaning way Persian women were treated.

Bird's account of her trip to Persia (as it was known until 1934), was published in 1891. It reveals a woman who was not only a keen observer and a skilled writer, but also an almost fearless traveler. She went mostly by mule and horseback, spending several months in Persia and later Kurdistan, accompanied by a small retinue that included a local guide and a couple of servants. She described one of her servants, Hadji, an Arab she hired in Baghdad who spoke six languages, as *big and wild-looking, wearing a turban, a long knife, and a revolver in his girdle.* He turned out to be not only of little help but dishonest, so Bird sent him home after several weeks.

Her trip from Baghdad to Tehran took a route similar to ours, but while we drove it in two days, it took her over two months. For this leg of her journey she was accompanied by a British army surveyor who, unknown to her, was also on a secret mission to gather information about Russian influence in Persia. They started out in January and had to endure drenching rain, bitter cold, and blinding snowstorms as they crossed the mountains. Bird and her group sometimes found lodging in primitive village hostels, but more often they stayed in crowded, smelly, and muddy caravansaries, walled compounds where travelers and their animals could be protected from bandits. Any semblance of comfort was provided by a tent and a fold-up cot that she brought with her. In spite of the hardships, she was rewarded by unending hospitality wherever she went. John and I, too, always felt welcomed, but in our VW we rode in relative luxury.

In the National Museum in Tehran we found a vast collection of beautiful ceramic ware, glazed tiles, glass vases, copper vessels, carpets, textiles, and illuminated manuscripts. Many artifacts were from ancient sites. What is most striking about Islamic art, as one art historian put it, "is the exuberant use of color." Though secular Islamic art allows for the human figure to be depicted, Islam prohibits the use of figural representation in religious art. As a result, artists developed highly intricate decorative patterns using geometric and floral designs, patterns that are often referred to as arabesques. Decoration also includes calligraphy. Combining color and design, the Persians created art of compelling beauty.

A common theme in Islamic art is the depiction of a walled garden, which for Persians represents paradise on earth. In fact, the word paradise in English comes from the Persian word *pairidaeza,* meaning enclosed park. This theme is seen over and over again in woven carpets, paintings, ceramic tile decoration, and in palace architecture, which always includes an extensive garden with pools and fountains.

I was especially fascinated by Persian carpets. Woven with wool, cotton or silk, these highly prized carpets were among the earliest exports to the West because of their aesthetic appeal and the fact that they could be easily transported by travelers. They were known in Europe as early as the 1500s, and were so admired that they were often displayed on tables or hung on walls rather than used as floor coverings. Examples of these carpets are often depicted in paintings by seventeenth century Italian and Dutch artists.

After my return from Poland, I was interested to learn that there is a style of silk carpets known as "Polonaise," a term first used in 1878 that referred to a Persian carpet found in Poland. Foreign royalty, especially in Europe, often commissioned Persian carpets, and a document dated 1602 shows that the King of Poland sent an Armenian merchant to Persia to buy silk rugs. At the king's request his coat of arms was woven into the design, for which he had to pay extra.

On the last morning of our stay, John came to breakfast dressed up. He felt a coat and tie were necessary for a business meeting. In the absence of a papermaking company, this appointment was with the vice-president of a jointly owned British and Iranian factory that made office equipment. I was always impressed with the companies John had on his list, though it turned out that some no longer existed.

While John went to his meeting, I wandered the city looking for a souvenir to take home. I finally found a store that sold a variety of artwork and spent an hour talking with the owner, a white-haired, middle-aged man who had once studied for a year in Paris and spoke quite good English. With his help I bought two small paintings, one showing a scene of a royal hunt, and the other depicting a turbaned personage riding a camel accompanied by a small retinue, all in colorful, exotic dress. Though the paintings were no doubt antiques, they weren't of the highest quality. Still, I was pleased to have found something I could afford.

------◆+◆⋈◆+●------

We left Tehran on November 12. Ahead of us was more than a week of hard driving before we reached the border with Pakistan. Within that time we wanted to visit two important cities, Isfahan and Shiraz, plus the ancient ruins of Persepolis. We estimated we could easily reach Isfahan, about 230 miles to the south, well before nightfall. We didn't make it.

The day started off auspiciously enough. We had stopped in Qum, seventy-five miles south of Tehran, to see the shrine of Fatima, its golden dome gleaming in the morning sunlight. Fatima was a ninth century saint and the sister of Reza, the eighth spiritual leader of Islam after Muhammad. She died young and was much revered in her short lifetime. The shrine is one of the most popular in Iran and draws thousands of pilgrims each year.

What happened just south of Qum caught us completely by surprise. Suddenly the car's windshield shattered into a thousand pieces, a victim, we assumed, of the constant vibration from the washboard roads. Fortunately it was safety glass, so it remained intact, though we couldn't see through it.

"What do we do now?" John said.

"Well, we can't go anywhere like this," I replied. "How do you propose we get the windshield out?"

"Easy. Just like this."

John pointed the car as far to the edge of the road as he could. Then with both of our feet up against the windshield, on the count of three we pushed. The glass easily popped out and clattered onto the hood on its way to the ditch. Tiny shards also littered the floor at our feet, but otherwise it was a successful operation.

We turned around and drove back to Tehran, the wind whistling around our ears. The service manager at the Volkswagen agency was surprised to see us again, but he took us right in. Within an hour we had a new windshield and were back on the road. Amazingly, this was the last mishap we had with the car for the rest of the trip.

We passed through Qum again and headed further south. The barren landscape stretched in every direction, broken here and there by large rock outcroppings and by the Zagros Mountains in the distance to the west. The arid climate made it difficult to do much farming, except near oases, but sheepherding survived in some areas. We passed few people along the road, usually farmers in mule-drawn carts who lived in a nearby village. Once we passed a train of camels lumbering along in their swaying fashion, accompanied by the soft tinkling sound of their bells.

The only vehicular traffic was an infrequent truck, a few intercity busses, and an occasional automobile, all kicking up clouds of dust. By late afternoon we stopped near a village to get a meal and spend the night in the car.

In almost every village we could find a restaurant. Some were extremely modest, but we could count on a hot meal of lamb or chicken that was roasted or cooked in yogurt, with rice and a vegetable. Dessert usually included fresh local fruit, delicious sticky pastries, and sweet, pungent tea. Often the kitchen and dining area were combined, so it was easy to view what the chef was cooking and make our selections.

Finding a safe spot to overnight was always a gamble. For protection we preferred being near a village rather than isolated in the middle of nowhere. We were perhaps naively trusting, but we never felt in danger. I don't recall that we ever considered carrying a weapon. The absence of running water was the main problem; having a shower entered the realm of pure fantasy. Yet we were able to heat enough water on our small gas stove to wash and shave each morning. We always made our own breakfast, some combination of bread, honey, fried eggs, fruit, and tea.

Curious villagers sometimes paid us a visit. I was always frustrated that I wasn't able to talk with any of them. I remember a bearded man who brought a few leather belts and woolen caps he hoped to sell. Another time two scruffy, barefoot boys came to look inside the car. Women never emerged from behind closed doors. Most of the rural people we encountered were dreadfully poor, but there was no disguising their friendliness.

———◆•◆◆•◆———

We could see Isfahan from a distance, its skyline of domes and minarets glistening in the mid-day sun. The city was built around an oasis along an ancient trade route, and with additional water from the Zayandeh River, the city had tree-lined avenues and lush gardens. We spent the rest of the day here amid the friendly, bustling atmosphere, taking respite in one of its many teahouses, viewing the river from one of the city's historic bridges that dated back to the twelfth century, and wandering through the bazaar. It was a busy, crowded city where, for the first time, we saw almost no foreign tourists.

Isfahan has an immense rectangular-shaped central plaza, called a *maidan*. Comprising twenty acres, it is seven times the size of the Piazza de San Marco in Venice and twice the size of Red Square in Moscow. It was built at the end of the sixteenth century by Shah Abbas I, who moved the capital of Persia to Isfahan in 1590. He ruled from 1588 to 1629 and is credited with a renaissance in art and architecture, making Isfahan one of the most beautiful cities in the East. He brought in artisans from many countries, including 300 potters from China. There are many published accounts by visitors to Isfahan during Abbas's reign, mostly Europeans, including ambassadors, diplomats, merchants, jewelers, adventurers, and Catholic missionaries. One person has said that "Isfahan is the quintessence of Iran," and a long-ago Persian poet is often quoted as saying, "Isfahan is half the world."

We walked first to the southern end of the *maidan* to see the magnificent Royal Mosque (*Masjid-e-Shah*), another of Abbas's great achievements. It was completed in 1638 after twenty-six years of construction. We had seen mosques of every description, but this was one of the most beautiful. Before entering, we gazed up at its huge dome rising 150 feet above. Covered with thousands of ceramic tiles that created intricate white and beige floral designs on a turquoise background, the dome was a dazzling sight. We entered the mosque through an elaborately decorated portal in blue and white tiles, itself over ninety feet high. Two minarets, also clad in brightly colored tile, flanked the portal, and through this gateway we came to a large courtyard surrounded by a variety of alcoves, smaller chambers, and semi-domed spaces called *iwans*. Two more minarets stood at the entrance to the mosque itself, which is positioned at a 45-degree angle so that it faces Mecca. Blue and white tiles, similar to those in the portal, decorated the courtyard and continued into the mosque's sanctuary, creating the impression that the dome was almost floating over the vast inner space of pastel blue.

We walked from the Royal Mosque to the bazaar at the opposite end of the *maidan*. The bazaar's entrance was another huge blue-tiled gate. The bazaar zigzagged through the city for almost a mile and connected to the former main square with its eleventh century mosque. On the eastern side of the *maidan* we came to the entrance of the former palace complex whose gardens, with their canals and fountains, were no longer as lush as in former times. Across from this gateway there was the entrance to a smaller but no less exquisitely tiled mosque. Around the *maidan* was a two-storied, blue-tiled, arcaded wall, where there were shops, teahouses and restaurants. Within the *maidan* itself, where royalty once played polo centuries before, a scattering of merchants were selling their wares, while mules wandered about. I was awed by the whole scene.

It was evident, however, that the city's luster had vastly faded since the grand days of Abbas I, 300 years before. It had never fully recovered after the Afghans invaded and ruled the country for a time in the eighteenth century. It had become a city of dusty streets, pestering vendors, toothless beggars, and the ever-present odor of mules and camels.

We decided to stay the night in Isfahan and found an inexpensive hotel with cold running water. Before looking for a restaurant to have supper, we stocked up on bread, eggs and fresh fruit that we would need for the next several days. By chance in one of the shops we met a merchant from India who was on a buying trip, looking for bargains in textiles. He was delighted when we told him we were on our way to India.

"I am most pleased to meet you gentlemen," he said in his clipped Indian accent. "Please be my guest for dinner. I know a nice restaurant nearby."

We enthusiastically accepted his invitation. We had many questions to ask. We inquired about the roads. Our host laughed and said, "I have no idea. No one drives an automobile between here and India, at least no one I know. There may be a few commercial vehicles that travel from here to Pakistan. Adventurers like yourselves are probably the only ones to make such a journey."

"How did you arrive here?" we asked.

"Oh, I came by air to Tehran. From there I took a bus. Not a bad trip actually. Better than some I've taken in the Middle East."

We also asked about the climate and customs. "The weather is delightful now and you will find India a colorful place, especially how the people dress. Very different from this country. But you may be overwhelmed by its dense population. Like here in Iran, though, you will be welcomed every where you go."

The ancient ruins of Persepolis lie about 250 miles south of Isfahan and forty miles north of Shiraz. It is still a magnificent site. Darius the Great began its construction in 512 B.C.E., but it would take another 150 years to be completed. At that time the Persian Empire extended from Egypt and Greece to the Indus River in India (now present-day Pakistan). Persepolis was built as an opulent residence and reception palace. It was originally called Parsa, but we know it by the name given to it in 330 B.C.E. by the invading Greeks under Alexander the Great, meaning "City of the Persians."

The complex of buildings was constructed on a vast stone terrace. The largest structure was the Apadana, or audience hall, that could accommodate over 10,000 people. Originally the roof was supported by seventy-two stone columns, but only thirteen remain standing. The second largest building was the Throne Hall, also called the Hall of One Hundred Columns. In addition were many other buildings, including the Treasury and palaces for Darius and his son, Xerxes.

What have survived almost intact, preserved by the dry climate, are many of the bas-relief stone carvings that line the grand entrance stairway and hallways throughout the complex. They are amazing in their clarity. Some of my best photographs were taken in the late afternoon when the sun cast shadows that vividly revealed the sculptures' images. My pictures show various scenes depicting life at Persepolis, including a royal figure walking under an umbrella held by a servant, a hunt showing a lion attacking a horse, and a parade of envoys bringing tribute. Close-ups show in minute detail the way men styled their hair and beards in short, tight curls.

When Alexander the Great plundered Persepolis in 330 B.C.E., it was one of his most prized conquests. What led him to set fire to the palace is not known. One story is that he was drunk when he gave the order; another is that he was egged on by one of the court prostitutes. But destroy Persepolis he did. The Greek historian, Plutarch, wrote that it required 20,000 mules and 5,000 camels to cart away Alexander's booty.

In modern times, the ruins of Persepolis were not discovered until 1620. The Oriental Institute of the University of Chicago began excavating in 1931, but activity was halted during World War II. Since then the Iranian Archeological Service has been working there.

As I wandered among the ruins that late afternoon, it was not hard to imagine what life might have been like during the glory days of Persepolis. At sunset the columns and stone images took on a soft glow that was almost magical. I wanted to spend the night there, but sleeping among the ruins wasn't allowed, as we learned from the bearded, white-haired guard who motioned to us that it was closing time. We had to settle for a spinney of mulberry trees a mile down the road.

———◆·◆·◆———

Early the next morning we drove to Shiraz, less than an hour to the south. Its abundant water supply has made the city famous for its rose gardens, vineyards, and citrus orchards. The city was a jewel that sparkled in the desert. Shiraz is also well known for its two poets, Hafiz and Sa'di, whose tombs, we were told, attract many visitors.

From Shiraz we set out for the border with Pakistan. We had to drive north again, a third of the way back to Isfahan, and then turn east toward the city of Yazd. According to UNESCO, Yazd is one of the oldest cities in the world. We were intrigued by the wind towers on the roofs of houses designed to funnel air to rooms below, an ingenious form of air conditioning. The city was also a center of Zoroastrianism, a pre-Islamic religion founded by the Persian prophet, Zoroaster, in the sixth century B.C.E. In a country where the majority of people are Shi'ite Muslims, Zoroastrianism has still managed to survive in various out-of-the-way places. Actually, it is far more prevalent in India, where its adherents are known as Parsees. Zoroastrians believe that the dead should not be buried or cremated, but instead left on platforms to be picked clean by vultures. We saw a few of these "Towers of Silence" in the distance outside of Yazd. It was a bit eerie.

Yazd was on an ancient trade route that skirts an immense desert. As we continued south toward the cities of Kerman and Bam, the landscape became even bleaker. Yet, in spite of almost no sign of vegetation, we occasionally saw an enclave of nomads who inhabited this desiccated plain. One time a family came by when we had stopped to stretch our legs. The parents and a small boy were leading two mules, one laden with their belongings tied up in blankets, and the other carrying two younger children. I wished I could have talked with them to find out where they had come from, where they were going, and where they would spend the night so far from any village. Faintly smiling from under their head scarves, the parents allowed me to take their photograph, but the two little ones were shy, especially the boy, who put his head down to hide his face just as I clicked the shutter. John and I often remarked how we missed being able to make contact with local people. Accounts I've read by earlier travelers revealed that many of them had the benefit of translators.

It was now November 17, five days since we had left Tehran. Early that day we passed through the small city of Bam on our way south to the frontier city of Zahedan. In a letter home I wrote that *the terrain has became even more desolate than what we have seen up to this time, since the road goes through the Kerman desert in southeastern Iran, where we saw large sand dunes for the first time, and where one is lucky if he sees one car the whole day.*

We had stopped for lunch by the side of the road, which by now had become two tracks in the sand. Our routine for lunch was simple. For some semblance of a table we put my Samsonite suitcase on the ground, on which we laid out our provisions, usually bread, cheese, peanut butter, and fruit. Peanut butter was a reliable source of nourishment and didn't spoil easily. However, it was hard to find, and the last place we were able to buy it was in Beirut. We only had a jar and a half left. Even in the hot weather we often heated water for tea. Pausing a moment between bites and taking in the arid, empty landscape around us, I saw in the distance a cloud of dust on the road we had just traveled.

"Looks like we're about to have company for lunch," I said.

"Hey, you're right. Better get out our best silverware."

Soon a vehicle pulled up behind our car, and when the driver got out we recognized him immediately. This was what I wrote later: *While having lunch we met up with Peter Townsend, the globetrotting former suitor of Princess Margaret. He is driving around the world in a Land Rover, sort of an overgrown jeep-type vehicle made in England, and on this first leg of his journey he is heading for Singapore. We ended up driving together for several hundred miles over the next two days, he leading our caravan through the wind-swept wastes of Persia and into Pakistan. We were glad to have company over this stretch, for if anything had happened to the car, we would have been in a rather precarious position. Our famed companion turned out to be friendly and easy to talk to. He didn't seem his age, which is something over forty. He is now retired from his military duties, and when asked at the border what his occupation was, said it was "independent." Though we talked about many things, ranging from the Suez crisis to his "upset tummy," the subject of his former romance was left alone, so I can't offer any personal information not already seen in the newspapers.*

Captain Townsend joined us for lunch, such as it was, bringing his own tea and crackers, but he ate little because his stomach was giving him trouble. With the sun now overhead, we didn't linger longer than we had to. Off we went, following not too close to the Land Rover to avoid choking on the dust it stirred up. We would be together over two days and nights, which were getting much colder. We had hoped the first night to sleep indoors in the guesthouse at a U.S. "Point Four Program"* compound in Zahedan, but for some reason we weren't allowed in. Townsend got quite angry with the man in charge, who wouldn't back down. We spent a chilly night in our cars. The next morning we had breakfast together and then set off to cross the border into Pakistan.

Townsend had first become well known in England as a flying ace with the British Royal Air Force during World War II. After the war, he was assigned to the royal family as equerry (the officer in charge of horses) to King George VI. It was then that he met Princess Margaret, who was still a teenager. After Margaret's older sister, Elizabeth, became Queen the following year, Townsend was assigned to the position of comptroller in the Queen's household. By this time it was known that Townsend and the princess were romantically involved, distressing the royal household but captivating the public and tabloid newspapers. To discourage the romance because Townsend was divorced, the royal family sent him to Brussels as air attaché to the British Embassy. In 1955 the couple broke up when Margaret could not get approval to marry without giving up all her royal privileges. The following year Townsend embarked on his round-the-world trek.

---

* These foreign aid outposts were established after World War II. The name comes from President Truman's inaugural address in 1950 in which he referred to this aid program as the fourth among his foreign policy objectives.

149

Townsend told us that he found his Land Rover reliable and rugged, but it wasn't built to go over forty-five miles an hour. Compared to our VW, it certainly had a lot more space. Eventually the Land Rover took him to China, Japan, Australia, the United States, Central and South America, Africa, and finally back to Brussels where he lived. His adventure was recounted in his book, *Earth, My Friend*, published in 1959. This is what he wrote of his encounter with John and me:

Bam was an oasis of palm trees and mud huts upon which the sun beat down with a ferocity more reminiscent of the desert. Bam was in fact on the edge of a desert, the Dasht-i-Lut, and here I had the good fortune to fall in with two young Americans. I had heard of them two days earlier and now spotted their Volkswagen. They had come all the way from Oslo and were bound for Delhi, and we agreed to keep in sight of one another's dust trails across the desert. Beyond the desert the road thrust its way among a multitude of little mountains and up towards the Afghan Pass. It was just the kind of country to harbor robbers and bandits and, though fortunately none appeared, it was somewhere in this region that four Americans were later murdered by a notorious gang. [Fortunately, John and I didn't hear about this.]

That evening we met again in Zahedan, the last and quite the dreariest garrison town in Persia. The manager of the "Point Four" (American Aid) rest-house flatly refused us entry, even into the yard, a hostile gesture which my friends not unnaturally resented. Thoroughly disgruntled, we spent a bitterly cold night in our cars. The next day I felt so ill that I had little inclination to argue with the Persian frontier officials; but argue I had to, as the process of leaving Persia was infinitely more difficult than entering it. [Finally] *I was permitted to cross the frontier into Pakistan, which at this point consisted of a heavy chain across the road.*

It was barely a fortnight since the anti-British riots in Pakistan had caused the Ambassador in Tehran to advise me against going on, but here was the Pakistani immigration officer offering me tea. I felt greatly reassured and, after crossing another hundred miles of desert in the dark, came to Dalbandin. A wizened old man emerged from the rest-house and with a reverent little bow he announced: "I cook." I could not have hoped for better news. There was a homeliness about that old rest-house and its aged caretaker that was more than comforting after the last two freezing nights in Persia. After Dalbandin my American friends and I each went our own ways, they to Karachi and I through the mountains of Baluchistan to the garrison town of Quetta.

We found Townsend to be a charming, well-informed companion, who, like us, was happy to have company. He was rather slightly built and good-looking, with prominent features that identified him, at least to my eyes, as typically British. We actually drove with him almost as far as Quetta, the first significant settlement in Pakistan, which was 400 miles from the Iranian border. The road to Karachi turned south just a few miles before Quetta, and that was where we said goodbye. Townsend then headed north into Afghanistan. I probably would never have come across his book had not my parents seen it by chance in a bookstore in England several years later. I wrote to him in 1979 and received a chatty reply. He and his Belgian wife and their three children were living near Paris. He had become a full-time writer and was working on his sixth book. He wrote in his letter, "Can you imagine crossing Iran today, with the Ayatollah on your heels?" He died in 1995 at the age of eighty.

———◆◆◇◆◆———

John wanted to go to Karachi because one of his economics professors at Williams College was teaching there on a Fulbright Scholarship. Our three days in the city included a Thanksgiving meal with the professor and a group of Americans from the embassy. It was a relaxing time that gave us a chance to get clean again and enjoy the balmy breezes that came in from the Arabian Sea.

We had driven nearly 3,000 miles from Tehran. The landscape had gradually changed from desert highland to more arable country at sea level in the Indus River valley. At the border with Pakistan we entered Baluchistan, the least populated province in the country, but once we got closer to Quetta, the human landscape changed dramatically as well. I note in a letter: *We passed through towns and small cities which were swarming with people, and it is difficult to get used to seeing so many thousands of human beings at such a low level of existence.* We found Karachi very much the same, though being Pakistan's largest city it had its modern commercial center and well-to-do business class.

Pakistan came into existence in 1947 when the British government partitioned India into two separate countries and granted them independence, though both were to remain in the British Commonwealth. Pakistan, which would be primarily Muslim, was itself divided, with West Pakistan taking up previous Indian territory, and East Pakistan, now call Bangladesh, created 1,000 miles on the other side of India. Millions of people were displaced, with over five million Muslims moving into Pakistan, and more than three million people, mostly Hindus and Sikhs, moving to India. Though many people speak English, Urdu has been the official language since 1978. In 1959 the capital was moved from Karachi to Islamabad.

We left Karachi on November 25. It was already sweltering by the time we got underway. Ahead was a drive of almost 1,000 miles before we would cross into India way to the north. Glancing at a map there might appear to be a more direct route from Karachi, but a vast desert separates the two countries and there are no good roads. As it was, the major route we took had long bumpy and dusty stretches as it followed the Indus River and its tributaries north through crowded villages and cities with names like Hyderabad, Khairpur, Sadiqabad, Ahmadpur, Multan, and finally Lahore. Along the way we noticed how differently people dressed than in Iran, especially the women, who wore colorful garments and headscarves. From Lahore it would be a short drive across the border with India to the city of Amritsar. We were about to leave the world of Islam, a world in which we had been guests since arriving in Turkey. In entering India dramatic changes awaited us.

◆━◆◀●▶◆━◆

The Author's 11,000-mile Trip Terminates in Delhi, December 1956

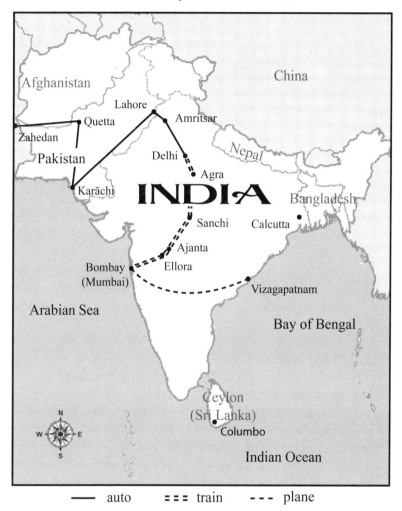

Amritsar, which means "Pool of Nectar," is the holy city of the Sikhs, and the Golden Temple is their holiest shrine. The setting is superb, with the temple and its golden dome surrounded by a pool that reflects the temple from almost every vantage point. To reach the temple one has to walk along a causeway across the pool. Sikhism, founded in the fifteenth century, is a relatively new religion in India. It combines attributes of Islam and Hinduism, both much older religions. A Sikh man is easily recognized by his beard and turban. We were told that a Sikh woman can be identified by the bracelets she wears. Most Sikhs live in the Punjab, the province in northwest India, which is one of the most prosperous. The word Punjab conjures up for me visions of the old India, with maharajahs in bejeweled turbans riding elephants.

The drive from Amritsar to Delhi took most of the day as we had to slow down repeatedly for farmers driving bullock carts, stray cattle crossing our path, or trains of mules too close to the road. It was even slower going through villages with the press of people in the streets mixed in with bicyclists, cows, smoky buses, and decrepit-looking automobiles. However, the countryside was now green, a vast change from the parched earth of the Middle East.

We finally reached Delhi where we inched our way through its deadly traffic and the mass of humanity that contributes to making India the second most populated country in the world. We found a cheap hotel near the train station, and though it was called the Taj Mahal, it held no resemblance to the famous and majestic hotel of the same name in Bombay, where I would have afternoon tea three weeks later. However, our place had the attraction of two monkeys that lived nearby and cavorted outside our window, much to our amusement. Delhi was the last stop in our overland trek. Here John and I would part company. Having driven more than 11,000 miles, we were travel weary and wanted to rest up and take in the local scene in a leisurely fashion.

The second-story window of our hotel looked out on the street below, and from there each click of my camera captured a glimpse into the colorful life of this Indian city—women shoppers dressed in red, blue, or yellow saris, honking taxis, bicycles, and rickshaws, all weaving in and out of traffic. Here and there a cow was lazily chewing its cud between parked cars. Even more fascinating, however, was to roam the streets and observe everyday life from ground level. One of my favorite pictures shows a smiling bearded holy man wearing worn sandals, a soiled purple turban with flowers sticking out, several layers of ragged garments, and an array of necklaces and bracelets. A small group of hangers-on stood by in loyal admiration.

In a letter home I wrote: *Finally I have arrived in India, the colorful land of poverty and plenty, where city streets crawl with spindly-legged vendors and turbaned beggars, where women drift about in diaphanous robes, and where maharajas still rule on princely estates with their elephants and servants and pomegranate trees. It is a country of misery, where many of the 380 million people live close to an animal existence, but it is also a country of splendor, with the Taj Mahal in Agra representing the noble richness of this corner of the world. It is a land with incredible histories and a future of untold potential, and here I am, wandering through this human maze, still not knowing quite what to make of this place of strange sights and noises and smells.*

While I felt overwhelmed at first by the vast number of people and heart-rending poverty, I soon found India totally absorbing and wanted to stay much longer. But with little more than a hundred dollars left, I had to start planning how to get back to the States. John and I decided to remain in Delhi for a week, after which I would make my way by train to Bombay, where I would begin looking for a ship to take me home. In the meantime, John would look for someone to buy his Volkswagen and fly home in style.

The British founded New Delhi in 1911 as the new site for its government and moved the capital from Calcutta after construction was completed in 1931. With its broad avenues, parks, grand public buildings, and upscale stores and restaurants, New Delhi seemed a world apart from Delhi, so we spent little time there. Instead we preferred the congestion and noise of the old city, which was far more interesting. When I wanted some peace and quiet, I took refuge in the local library just a few blocks away from our hotel.

There I could also find all I needed to read about India to help me decide where to stop on my way to Bombay.

In the meantime we took in some of the major sights of Delhi. One was the Red Fort, a massive complex built of red sandstone in the seventeenth century by Shah Jahan, who also built the Taj Mahal. He was one of the Mughal, or Muslim, emperors who ruled from 1527 to 1707. Their influence was centered in northern India; Islam never reached the southern part of the country. Shah Jahan also moved the capital of the Mughal Empire from Agra to Delhi. The Red Fort was famous for its Peacock Throne, made of solid gold with figures of peacocks and decorated with precious stones. But in 1739 an invading Persian king and his army pillaged Delhi and carted the throne off to Tehran. It sits there in a museum. The other main sight was the Jama Mosque, built between 1644 and 1658. It is the largest mosque in India and has a courtyard that can hold 25,000 people.

———◆▸❈◂◆———

The day finally came for John and me to say goodbye. We both agreed that our trip had been a-once-in-a-lifetime experience and were thankful that we accomplished what we set out to do. We promised to keep in touch. We kept that promise, though contact was intermittent over the years. John became successful on Wall Street as an investment analyst, founder of a mutual fund, and radio program host. Early on he ran as a Democrat for the New York State Legislature, but was unsuccessful. He also became a friend and financial advisor to Senator Patrick Moynihan of New York.

Almost all his adult life John lived in New York City, while I ended up living in New England. I remember one visit in the 1960s when my wife and I were in the city and were invited to have lunch with John and his wife at the Stanhope Hotel on Fifth Avenue, not far from the Metropolitan Museum. They were living there temporarily while renovating a brownstone they had bought in the West 80s. Our standards of living were miles apart, as I was recently out of graduate school and supporting a wife and three children on a beginning psychotherapist's salary. Another time many years later (both of us were by then divorced), I was in New York for a conference and called John, who invited me to one of the mid-week dinners he liked to host for friends and associates at his penthouse on Central Park South. He was at the peak of his career, and judging from his guests, well connected in the world of business and finance.

John had acquired sizable wealth and had hoped to leave a generous legacy to his family and alma mater. But late in his career, in 2000, he ran into trouble with the Security and Exchange Commission for what John told me was a "jaywalking offense." The investigation ruined his company and left him practically penniless, he said. I last saw John in the fall of 2002 at Calvary Hospice in the Bronx where he had been admitted with terminal prostate cancer. In spite of his financial ruin and impending death, he was in good spirits. He expressed much appreciation for the support he had received from his children, his former wife, Louise, and friends. We recalled some memorable moments of our trip, and eventually our conversation turned to politics. I was surprised that as a longtime liberal Democrat John supported the impending U.S. invasion of Iraq, which I opposed. I like to think he would have eventually changed his mind. He died on January 31, 2003. He was seventy-two.

John walked with me to the Delhi train station on a bright, sunny morning. The station was jammed with people scurrying here and there. Most were passengers looking for their train; others were baggage handlers and vendors. It was hot and noisy. In the five days I spent traveling the 700 miles to Bombay, every station was crowded, no matter the time of day or night. I had less than thirty minutes before my train left. John and I shook hands and wished each other a safe trip home. In an instant we were both lost in the swirling mass.

———◆◆❋◆●———

I should have arrived sooner. By the time I located my train there were no seats left. Fortunately, I was going only as far as

Agra, which was not much more than a hundred miles. In the three hours it took, I sat on my suitcase. Agra would be the first of three stops on the way to Bombay. I decided to go third class to save money and see how millions of Indians travel. My ticket to Bombay cost all of six dollars. The Indians and Europeans I had met in Delhi were incredulous that I would choose to travel third class. No one but the poor did that, they told me. Besides, I might be robbed or goodness knows what else. The third class wagons had only wooden benches, two along the sides and two down the center, back to back. I was lucky to find space for myself and my suitcase at one end.

Once we were under way, I surveyed the people around me. From their dress, most appeared very poor. Some chatted among themselves, but others sat quietly, their eyes staring blankly. The wheezy breathing and labored coughing of a bearded man nearby caught my attention; I wondered if his ailment was contagious.

With the temperature outside already in the eighties, the air in the car was becoming stifling. A breeze coming in through the open windows brought little relief. Yet along with the breeze, cinders often flew in from the smokestack, sprinkling themselves around with apparently little concern by those on whom the black specks landed.

I stopped in Agra to see the Taj Mahal, probably India's most famous sight. Its beauty almost defies description, so perfect are its proportions. Built of white marble and situated on the banks of the Yamuna River, I first saw it from the end of a long reflecting pool. It is a mausoleum built in the seventeenth century at the height of the Mughal Empire by Shah Jahan to memorialize his second wife, who died in 1631. Her remains, and his as well, are enshrined in the crypt. At first glance the structure might be mistaken for a mosque, with its central dome and decorative minarets. Like many royal building projects, its construction was an international endeavor; one source says that the main architect came from Shiraz, Persia, while artisans as far away as Europe were employed in addition to local laborers. My first view of the Taj Mahal was early in the morning when the sun had not yet dispelled the slight mist rising from the reflecting pool, giving a sense that this stunning creation was almost weightless in the soft, peaceful light.

The second day of my railroad journey took me to see the Buddhist stupas at Sanchi, a day's ride from Agra. This time I was at the station early, pushing and shoving like everyone else to find a seat. As the day before, the car was full by the time we got under way. The conductor blew his whistle and the engine roared into action, belching black smoke and soot. While I found the third class experience fascinating, I didn't look forward to a whole day of not speaking to anyone. I had to be content with my silent observations.

Next to me squatted a turbaned, wizened old man chewing the betel nut (a mild stimulant). Some of its red juice trickled down his chin, while the rest he spit out the open window. I was fortunate to be sitting upwind because I could see that stray drops were finding their way back in.

Across from me sat a mother with two children, a babe in arms and a two-year-old boy sitting bare-bottomed at her filthy, sandaled feet. She was wearing a soiled blue sari; imitation gold and silver bangles adorned her arms. Kohl outlined her eyes, and with the *tika* mark on her forehead, her face had an exotic though deeply worn look. The infant was fussy with a runny nose, which the mother coped with by wiping the nasal discharge with her thumb and forefinger, and then bending down she cleaned the mucus off her fingers by rubbing them on the floor. The child finally fell asleep at its mother's breast. In the meantime, the toddler was given something to drink and chew, and for a while seemed content. But then the inevitable happened. The boy peed on the floor. At first I didn't think it would amount to much as the puddle slowly moved back and forth in whichever direction the car was leaning. But as I watched, the amber pool grew in size, and gaining momentum it started coming in my direction. It was clear I had to do something or my feet would get wet. Like the betel-nut man, I took the universal Indian position by squatting on the bench. Later, a train employee came by with a rag and wiped up the puddle. Through all this, the mother's blank expression never changed. I couldn't help being drawn into this family scene, and like many times before, I felt frustrated that I couldn't ask the mother's name and where she was going.

The Great Stupa at Sanchi is among the oldest Buddhist structures in India, dating back to the third century B.C.E. It was originally part of a monastery complex. A stupa is a religious structure in the form of a large, solid hemisphere, like an upside down bowl, with a relic chamber inside. The stupa was built by creating a huge mound of rubble, facing it with stone, and then applying a coat of white plaster made from lime and powdered seashells. A walkway enclosed by an eleven-foot high stone railing surrounded the stupa. Among the carvings that ornamented the four thirty-five-foot stone gateways were voluptuous female figures, called *yakshis*. One in particular was most striking and the subject of a favorite photograph. An art historian also saw her. *The Sanchi yakshi leans daringly into space with casual abandon, supported by one leg as the other charmingly crosses behind. Her thin, diaphanous garment is noticeable only by its hems, and so she appears nude, which emphasizes her form. The band pulling gently at her abdomen accentuates the suppleness of her flesh. The swelling, arching curves of her body evoke this deity's procreative and bountiful essence.*[*] Modern historians were not aware of this stupa complex until British soldiers discovered it in 1818.

The next day I stopped to see the caves at Ajanta and Ellora. In Ajanta the caves are all Buddhist and date from 200 B.C.E. to 650 C.E. There are twenty-nine caves in all, chiseled into the face of a rock gorge on the Waghore River. It is an impressive setting. The caves contain fifth century paintings and carvings that are amazingly well preserved.

There are thirty-four caves at Ellora that represent three religions, Buddhist, Hindu and Jain. The caves extend for over a mile along a rock face and contain monasteries, chapels, and temples hewn by monks between 600 and 1,000 C.E. Elaborate sculptures carved out of the living rock decorate the caves. One temple is the world's

[*] M. Stokstad, *Art History*. See Bibliography

largest single sculpture, being twice the area of the Parthenon and one and a half times as high. It required more than 7,000 artisans over a period of 150 years to create this masterpiece.

I was captivated by Indian art and wished I could have stayed longer in this fascinating country. But my depleted pocketbook said otherwise. The following day I took my final train ride and arrived in Bombay on December 14. I now had to start looking for a way home.

CHAPTER EIGHT

Bombay to Philadelphia: December 1956 to February 1957

After finding a place to stay in Bombay, I contacted a friend of John's who worked for a Norwegian shipping line. In our brief meeting I was told of a possible job on a ship going to Europe, leaving in January. However, Europe meant that I would still have to cross the Atlantic to get home. The man then said, "If you're interested in looking into a job on an American ship, you need to go to your country's embassy. That's where all ship captains have their documents cleared."

Thanking him, off I went. It didn't take long to find the American Embassy. "You're in luck," said the young consul. "A ship's captain was in yesterday completing his paper work. He mentioned needing two crew members."

"Where would I find him?" I asked.

"Down at the docks. The *SS Rebecca*. The captain's name is Donovan."

"Thanks. I'll go down there right away."

"By the way," the consul said as I was leaving his office, "this is a freighter, not a passenger ship."

"I understand. That's fine with me."

I found the *Rebecca* with little trouble, its name in white across the ship's stern. Below the name was her homeport, New York. The ship looked gigantic, her black hull looming overhead as I came closer. She was tied up along with three other vessels. The deck was crowded with Indian laborers unloading wheat from the main hold. A huge crane, anchored on the dock, swung back and forth as it carried the grain to waiting containers. Several of the ship's crew, shirtless and sweaty in the eighty-degree heat, were scraping rust and painting near the bow. One of them greeted me as I came up the gangplank.

"Hello there. Who are you looking for?"

"I'd like to see Captain Donovan about a job," I answered.

"He's up on the bridge. Follow me."

I was shown to the captain, shirtless and unshaven, sitting at his desk. Unsmiling, he remained seated, but shook my hand and said, "I'm Captain Donovan." I introduced myself and said the man at the American Embassy told me that the ship was missing a couple crew.

"That's right. Where're your papers?"

"Papers? I don't have any papers." I had no idea what he was referring to.

"What do you mean you don't have any papers? What ship were you on before you landed here on the beach?" ("On the beach" is the merchant marine's term for being on shore.)

"I'm not a seaman. I traveled here overland from Europe."

"What? That's a crazy thing to do. Never mind. Look, I'll take you back to the States, but you'll have to work."

"Fine," I said. "I'll do anything."

"Good. I need a wiper and an oiler. You'll probably be a wiper, since you don't have experience. You'll get paid, of course."

It is the custom among the merchant marine to take a seaman stranded on the beach back to the United States as a "workaway," which actually means he doesn't have to work. But as Captain Donovan said, "There'll be no tourists on my ship."

It was arranged that I would meet the *Rebecca* at the port of Vizagapatnam on the east coast of India at the end of the month. There she would be loading up with manganese ore to take back to Philadelphia. It had been my lucky day. I was excited to have a job. Then I wondered, *What does a wiper do?*

In the meantime, I needed to return to the American Embassy to apply for my seaman's papers. After a few more days in Bombay, I took the train south to Miraj to spend Christmas with Eugene and Jo Evans, friends of my parents. Dr. Evans was a physician who had come to India with his wife in the 1920s under the sponsorship of the Presbyterian Board of Foreign Missions. I was looking forward to visiting them, having last seen them in 1949 when they visited my parents and their son, David, a classmate of mine at Oberlin. Dr. Evans was my father's classmate in medical school and they had remained close friends. According to an often-told family tale, Dr. Evans saved my father's life. It was in 1935, when I was five years old. It had been three years since my father had returned from China with my two older brothers and me, our mother having died there. He had been re-married for just a year when he became seriously ill and was hospitalized at the Cleveland Clinic. By coincidence, Dr. and Mrs. Evans were home on leave in Cleveland and visited my father. In recalling this event, Dr. Evans said, "Your father was near death. I was shocked to see him looking so weak and frail."

I remembered, too, when my stepmother took me to the hospital. I can still see my father in bed looking gaunt, his face ashen, his cheeks sunken. I had no awareness that he might not survive. As the story goes, Dr. Evans suggested to the attending physician that the new sulfa drug might be beneficial.

"Your father's physician was a bit reluctant to try it out," Dr. Evans said. "He didn't think it would do much good." He laughed and said, "We all know how wrong he was."

My father fully recovered and I never saw him in bed again until near the end of his life. He died in 1980 at the age of eighty-three.

I described my stay in Miraj in a letter written on Christmas Day, 1956. *Outside my window blooms a poinsettia, across the garden is a huge bougainvillea bush, scarlet against the deep blue sky, and in the shade of a banyan tree lush ferns nod sleepily in the warm afternoon breeze. This is Christmas time in India, a delightful change from the cold weather temperatures at home. I am thoroughly enjoying myself here for a few days, sleeping on a soft bed for a change, stuffing myself with bananas and papayas, and spending relaxing hours chatting with the Evans, visiting the medical center, and meeting their friends. They have a remarkable set-up here, and much good work is being accomplished. Everyone has been extremely hospitable, and the Evans' kindness has been unlimited. They live a modest life, but the compensations are great, and to see the extent to which the work of this group affects the surrounding community has been very rewarding to me.*

I returned to Bombay on December 27 and went to the American Embassy to follow up on getting my seaman's papers. It would turn out that the final paperwork wasn't completed until the captain took me to the American Consulate in Colombo, Ceylon (now Sri Lanka), where the ship first stopped to re-fuel three weeks later.

I still had a few days to do some sightseeing before I had to meet my ship. The only nearby ancient site worth seeing was on the island of Elephanta off the coast of Bombay. There I visited a cave-temple dedicated to the Hindu god, Shiva, carved out of the island's rock. The two most interesting things were the *lingam* shrine, the *lingam* being the phallic symbol of Shiva, and the eleven-foot-tall carved relief that shows Shiva with three heads. The site dates from the sixth century. The brief trip was even more interesting because our tourist boat passed through the bustling, noisy Bombay harbor.

One afternoon I had tea at the Taj Majal, one of the city's famous hotels, built in 1903. I had been invited by a middle-aged American couple I met in Sanchi. The grand, ornate tearoom, with its large, draped windows, had a marvelous old-world charm that I found most delightful. The next day I made the acquaintance of an art store owner, who invited me to his home for a meal with him and his family that included his wife, mother-in-law, and three adolescent children. It was a new experience to eat with my fingers, and at first I felt very self-conscious. This was the only educated, middle-class family I met in India; they were full of questions about my overland trip.

Since domestic air travel was inexpensive, I decided to fly from Bombay to Vizagapatnam. As I made my way to the docks from the airport I was dismayed to find I was getting a sore throat. By the time I came on board the *Rebecca*, I had a fever. A crewmember welcomed me and we went to tell the captain I had arrived. After meeting my roommate I had a light supper and did some unpacking. At least I could look forward to clean sheets and a shower. When I finally crawled into bed, I was feeling miserable.

With the help of several aspirin I slept reasonably well. When I woke up the next morning, however, I ached all over and felt like I was burning up. I managed some breakfast and returned to my room, or fo'c's'le (short for forecastle), as the sailors say. It was about 8:30.

Then came a knock on the door. I opened it and was greeted by, "Good morning. I'm the First. Are you the new wiper?"

"Yes, I am."

"Well, are you ready to work?"

What was I going to say? *Gee, I'm not feeling all that great today. I thought I would just rest up and take it easy. How about tomorrow?* However, since the *Rebecca* was my ticket home, I wasn't about to jeopardize this opportunity. So I said, "Sure."

We shook hands and I introduced myself.

"Follow me," he said. I was following the First Engineer, a slim, sandy-haired man in his forties, who would be my boss. He took me to a small room called the slop chest. "We got old clothes in here left by other crews. The stuff looks pretty beat up, but it's all clean. Find a couple shirts and pairs of pants. Shoes, too, and whatever else you want. I'll meet you back at your fo'c's'le in ten minutes."

I rummaged through the clothes and returned to my room to change. Everything was too big; even the smallest shoes I found were two sizes too large. Where I would be working, however, it didn't much matter what I wore.

I then followed the First to the engine room. So far I had seen very little of the ship, save the bathroom, or head as it was called, the showers, and where we ate. All I knew about a wiper was that he was the ship's janitor. I soon discovered that the wiper had several jobs that no one else would do. When the First opened the engine room door I thought the blast of hot air might singe my hair. We still had twenty feet to go to the ship's bowels, down six or seven steep and narrow metal stairways, where it was hotter still. Some days during our voyage the temperature got to at least 120 degrees, even with large blowers sucking in outside air. In this cavernous space were the ship's vital organs, its pumps, boilers and turbines. Gauges and dials were all under the watchful eyes of the engine room crew.

One of the ships' two large boilers had been shut down for cleaning while we were in port. My first job was to clean the inside. The First showed me where the oil burner unit had been removed, leaving an opening about two feet square. The boiler itself was about twelve feet high, and eight feet wide and deep. Three-inch water pipes lined the inside walls, which when heated produced steam for the turbines that turned the propellers, or screws as they are called.

The First handed me a long electrical cord with a light bulb in the socket on the end, plus what looked like a large putty knife.

"What I want you to do is go inside the boiler and scrape off the carbon that's on the pipes. It'll take you most of the day. Don't forget, you get coffee breaks besides lunch." He explained that they had to do this scraping job every time the ship was in port, otherwise the carbon would build up and make heating the water in the pipes less efficient.

"After you get in I'll pass in this small ladder," he added.

I wriggled myself inside. The light bulb wasn't very bright, which made it spooky. It was also much hotter, and no air was moving. I set to work loosening black, dusty chunks of carbon. I could feel it caking the inside of my nose and probably doing the same to my lungs. I needed something to cover my face. Fortunately, I had a large handkerchief that I could tie over my nose and mouth. Amid the heat and carbon dust, I contemplated my fate. *Would I survive this? Would I pass out and not be found until it was too late? Can my aching body, already being consumed by an unrelenting fever, withstand the task I have been ordered to do? What sort of death notice will appear in my hometown newspaper?* I had never felt so alone in my life.

By sheer determination, I struggled through the day. I tried to keep my mouth closed and breathe through my nose, but sometimes I forgot. My arms got weak as I had to reach the pipes above my head. At lunch, sitting alone because I was covered with soot, I could barely eat. From another table one of the crew looked over at me and said, "Hey, fella, I see you got the prize job. I heard the ship lost one guy inside the boiler a couple years back because it got so hot his brain melted."

When I was done at the end of the day, a shower never felt so good. At supper I was no longer a pariah. I still had little appetite, only an almost unquenchable thirst. I longed for bed and rest.

By some miracle I slept the whole night. When I woke up, my fever had vanished. I felt reborn and ready to take on whatever the *Rebecca* could dish out.

<hr />

The *Rebecca* was scheduled to sail on January 8. That meant I had a week to get acquainted with my shipmates, my job, and the ship itself. I soon learned that my roommate, a short, scrawny fellow, was on parole for having robbed a liquor store in Los Angeles. He was in his thirties, married with four children, the oldest being fourteen. Because of his hometown, he was often called L.A. After I survived my near-fatal first day he said, "How'd ya like that boiler job? Ain't that a pisser though? I had to do it twice."

I first got on his good side by loaning him a little money so he could go ashore one evening. But our relationship became firmly cemented when I agreed to help him write a letter to his parole officer saying he was working fulltime, saving money, and staying out of trouble. Being the other wiper he explained the intricacies of the job, which began each day with cleaning the crew's fo'c's'les and shower stalls from eight to ten each morning. Then it was up to the First to assign specific jobs for the rest of the day. Unlike the rest of the crew, who stood watch four hours on and four off, we wipers worked from eight to five. One job L.A. didn't mention I would learn about in due time.

We shared a small fo'c's'le that had a sink with hot and cold running water, two tiny closets, and a double-decker bunk, with me up top. The only thing missing was a porthole, since ours was an inside cabin. I also remember the small hunting knife that hung in its sheath by his bed. He never told me what it was for, nor did I ask. We got along fine.

Most of the crew I guessed to be in their thirties and forties. I don't remember their first names, though I do recall a few nicknames. One was Turkey, a jovial, corpulent man with a raucous laugh and a gravelly voice, the result of constant smoking. He was a fireman in the engine room, a position that was essentially a dial and gauge watcher. Another was the Animal, a morose, hirsute man who kept to himself and had little to say to anyone. "He's a little wacko, ya know," someone once told me. The thing I remember most is that he took his showers in the dark.

The cook, a talkative outgoing man from Puerto Rico, served up excellent meals. The only complaint I heard anyone make was about his potato salad. The cook couldn't let the comment pass. In his lilting accent he said, "I've been making potato salad since I sat on my grandmother's knee."

One of the deck hands was a boyish-looking young man who I guessed was in his early thirties. His clean-cut looks made him stand out from the rest of the crew, plus the way he talked gave an impression of being better educated. With his blond hair and pleasant smile, he could almost pass for a college sophomore. He seemed like someone I could talk to. Two evenings before we set sail he invited me to accompany him ashore.

"Maybe you'd like to meet a friend of mine," he said.

"Why not? There's not much to do here."

It was a ten-minute walk on a pleasant, balmy evening. In the approaching darkness the lights on the ships along the dock glowed magically. It was surprisingly quiet. My friend seemed a bit overdressed in his white shirt, yellow Bermuda shorts, and loafers with tassels. Soon we were on a street with run-down shops, bars, and cheap restaurants. Around a corner we came to a small house. We entered a hallway that led into a parlor furnished with two worn but comfortable couches and several chairs. Dim light came from two lamps with yellowish shades. Three young women were sitting at a table having a cigarette. I could smell a faint scent of incense. They greeted my companion with smiles.

"We've been waiting for you, Mr. Good-Looking."

One of them got up and embraced him.

"Have you missed me?" he asked, pulling her close and running a hand over her ample bottom. Turning to me and smiling he said, "It's been three whole days."

"And who have we here, another sailorman?"

We joined our hostesses at the table and were served a glass of beer. My friend's sweetheart looked to be in her early twenties, while the other two were not much past adolescence. They made an engaging trio in their short skirts and low-cut blouses, their eyes outlined in black and their cheeks rouged. One was quite pretty.

As we chatted with the girls, I wondered what my friend would have done if his sweetheart had been occupied when we arrived. He told me later that he was her only boyfriend while in port, but I didn't quite believe him. As we were finishing our beers he stood up and said he wanted to spend some private time with his girl. I could stay if I liked. "I can see that you like Suzie there." The two then left, disappearing between two dark red curtains.

"Is your name really Suzie?" I asked.

"No, it's Radha. Would you like to come with me to my room? It won't cost you much."

I was tempted. She was certainly attractive, but when she smiled, her partially decaying teeth spoiled the illusion. Besides, I didn't come prepared.

"Thank you, I think I won't stay. But here's something for the beer."

Radha followed me to the door, and as I walked down the street she called after me, "Won't you change your mind, sailorman?"

●━━◆━━●

It was just past ten on the morning of January 8, 1957. I was taking my coffee break when I heard shouts and whistles on deck. As I stepped into the blazing sunlight, I felt the ship shudder. The *Rebecca* was about to cast off. The deckhands scurried here and there as the deck officer barked orders. From the starboard railing I looked down and could see two tugboats snuggled up to the ship's massive hull. After more whistles and shouts, the *Rebecca* began to slip away from the dock. Guided by the tugboats and a pilot, the ship slowly made its way through the harbor, and then paused briefly to allow the pilot to disembark to a tug below. Now under her own power, the *Rebecca* headed out to the open sea. I was on my way home.

———————◆◆❉◆◆——————

We had been at sea for a week when I had a few uneasy hours. Coming back from lunch, I heard Turkey's raspy voice behind me saying, "Hey there, wiper boy, what's this I hear about you getting the oiler job? Doesn't sound like a good idea to me."

One of the engine room crew had injured his leg and couldn't work. The First came to me that morning and said he wanted me to take the job. I had no reason to object and was to begin my new duties the next day. But when the crew heard about it, some didn't like it. At lunch I began hearing comments.

"We hear you might get the engine room job instead of L.A."

"Doesn't sound fair to me, seein' as how he's been on the ship from the beginning."

"He told us he doesn't like it one bit."

L.A. had said nothing to me. I then heard someone even suggesting I might find myself going overboard in the middle of the night. I decided all this wasn't worth it. I went to the First later in the afternoon and said, "I don't think I'll take the job. The guys don't like me getting it over L.A."

"Awe, that's just talk. They're teasing you."

"Still, I have to live with L.A. If I have any choice in the matter, I'd rather you promote him."

He considered this briefly and said, "All right, if that's what you want."

I felt much relieved. Nothing was ever said again.

———————◆◆❉◆◆——————

Now that I was the only wiper, my daily routine didn't change much from day to day. I was out of bed by six-thirty or seven, had a good breakfast, and was ready for work at eight. After cleaning the crew's fo'c's'les and shower stalls, I took a coffee break at ten. Union rules were strictly followed. I spent the rest of the day below decks, where my clothes became soaked with sweat within five minutes.

My shoes were constantly soggy. Besides the heat, the incessant roar in the engine room was so loud it was impossible to carry on a conversation without shouting. I worked mostly in the engine room itself where I would sweep floors, clean machinery, and haul trash up to deck side. Every afternoon there was garbage from the galley to be dumped over the side, never giving a thought to pollution. I also had other jobs like cleaning up the paint room, where I spent most of a week getting rid of used paint cans, scraping paint off shelves, and trying to restore some order to what had been a total mess. The First was pleased, but said, "It sure took you one hell of a long time. I thought you'd be done in a couple days." Though I had a friendly relationship with the First, it was clear that the rule of no fraternizing between officers and crew was strictly observed. I never met the other officers nor saw where they lived in the upper deck.

The one job I really hated came at four o'clock every afternoon. It was called "blowing the tubes." The task I had of cleaning carbon off the pipes inside of the boiler while we were in port was now done with steam. On the rear of each of the two boilers were, as I recall, six steam valves, which when turned, sprayed steam into the boilers to loosen the carbon. A long chain was attached to turn each valve. A few chains could be reached from the floor, but to get to the others I had to climb the steep metal stairs in the narrow space that separated the rear of the two boilers and the bulkhead.

The First showed me how to do it. Trying to make himself heard above the din in the engine room, he yelled in my ear, "These valves aren't in great shape. Some leak and they can be noisy." The job didn't look too bad.

My opportunity came the next day. I pulled the first chain, but the valve didn't want to move. My sweaty hands kept slipping. On the third try, I finally got the valve to turn. I knew I had to keep pulling until the valve made a complete revolution. It took all my strength until the valve finally shut off. The second valve turned more easily, but it leaked, spraying a small stream of steam as it rotated. I was soaking wet with sweat. I wasn't prepared for what the next valve had to offer. As I pulled the chain, escaping steam let out an ear-piercing shriek that nearly floored me. Pulling my cap on tighter I put my head down to avoid the spray. My arms ached. Slowly the valve turned. It finally shut off after two more pulls. I was so hot and exhausted I was afraid I might pass out. Realizing that I had nine more to do, I wondered what would be left of me. I took a deep breath and summoned forth as much fortitude as I could. I encountered one more badly leaking valve, and with another I had to literally hang on the chain before it moved. Every one of the valves seemed to have a peculiar way of testing me. It took over twenty minutes to do both boilers. When I was finally done I sat on the hot, narrow stairs feeling utterly depleted. I thought to myself, *This is one tough way to get myself home.* The job became a little less difficult once I began wearing a pair of gloves, but each day I dreaded the approach of four o'clock.

<hr />

My workday ended at five. After a shower, I went to supper. I loved meal times. In spite of the heat I had a huge appetite. In one of my letters I recount that *I fill up on fried eggs, pancakes, cereal, fruit, roast beef, southern-fried chicken, mashed potatoes, rice, vegetables, fresh bread, hot rolls, apple pie, chocolate cake, milk and coffee.* Leftovers and snacks were also available in the refrigerator. The cook, working alone, came up with delicious delights. A cook usually has a helper, considered the most menial position on the ship, but there was no helper on the *Rebecca.* Instead it was I, as wiper, who had the distinction of being the lowest man on the totem pole. I didn't care in the least.

I also enjoyed mealtimes because of the stories I heard about other crews and other ships. Stories about nasty captains, storms, fights, unfaithful wives, dear-john letters, going ashore, getting laid, contracting gonorrhea, getting drunk and being left on the beach. Turkey was one of the best storytellers, gesticulating with his beefy hands and wheezing in his loud, husky voice. It was generally agreed that, while perhaps not exceptional, the *Rebecca* had a good crew. Someone once said, "You know, we ain't got such a bad crew here at all. Better than most I've worked with." And looking at me he said, "And we're lucky you're the only new guy we got since we left Seattle three months ago."

Hong Kong was a popular port for female companionship and tailor-made clothes. One day L.A. said, "I want to show ya the suit I got made while we were there." Taking it from his closet he proudly held it up for me to admire. I had never seen a robin's-egg blue suit before. "Ain't that somethin', though? Only fifty bucks. Fits me perfect, too."

I also heard stories about the *Rebecca*. Perhaps rumors are more apt. One was that while she was loading up in some foreign port the weight of the cargo caused the ship to settle on a huge rock, poking a hole in her bottom. It was repaired by filling the hole with cement. Supposedly the Rebecca would be going to dry dock after this voyage to get it fixed. However, some of the crew questioned how seaworthy the cement plug was because they thought it might pop out during rough weather.

Another story was that because of manganese ore in the hold, its relatively small volume left a lot of empty space.

"Ya know what that means, don't ya?"

"No, what?"

"It means that in heavy seas, if the ship pitches too much, the cargo might shift."

"So? And then what?"

"Well, it's obvious, ain't it? The ship could heel right over on its side."

Fortunately, the seas had been calm so far.

———◆➤✕◀◆———

One evening after supper I was sitting topside with one of the deck hands near the forward hatch. Overhead the yellowish-orange booms and superstructure glowed in the setting sun. "So what do you think of this seaman's life?" he asked.

"Not bad," I replied. "But I don't think I would like being at sea for so long."

"You get used to it. Ever been on a freighter before?"

"No, I haven't. What kind of ship is the *Rebecca* anyway?"

"She's a Liberty ship. I forget why, but they're still referred to as ugly ducklings."

I learned later that this description originated with President Roosevelt, a former navy man, who reportedly used that term because he didn't think Liberty ships were much to look at. Measuring 441 feet long and 56 feet wide, over 2,000 were built during World War II to carry troops and cargo. However, because they were slow and easy targets for submarine attack, many were later replaced by the larger and faster vessels known as Victory ships. The First told me that the *Rebecca* continued in service after the war, ferrying goods and servicemen's wives to Korea during that conflict. "We had a good time," he said with a grin.

The weather continued warm and sunny, the sea calm. I still hadn't seen a drop of rain in over three months. In one of my last letters I wrote: *It is at the end of the day, during the twilight hours, when all is quiet save for the dull rumble of the engines, that the most enjoyable moments unfold. As the sun is lost from sight, sometimes setting fire to the sky, sometimes disappearing behind a distant squall, the air becomes sweeter and the breezes softer. With the coming darkness the tired body relaxes and the mind wanders. At this time I often stand on the bow of the ship, for from here I feel most acutely the surging of the ship through the vast waters as I watch the ever-changing color of the sky, and I find myself thinking over and over, soon I'll be home.*

——◆✦❈✦●——

Because the Suez Canal was closed, the *Rebecca* had to take the long way home. It would turn out to be a five-week voyage. From Vizagapatnam on the Bay of Bengal we sailed south into the Indian Ocean, passed Madagascar off the coast of Africa, and continued around the Cape of Good Hope. We then sailed northwest across the Atlantic, skirted the northern edge of Brazil and Venezuela, and finally came up along the east coast of the United States. It was necessary to stop three times for refueling, or "bunkering." The first stop was in Colombo, Ceylon, the second in Cape Town, South Africa, and the last in Port of Spain, Trinidad. Except for the brief time I went with the captain to get my seaman's papers in Colombo, no one was allowed ashore. When we were anchored in port, vendors rowed out to the ship, hoping to entice the crew to buy local trinkets. Because drinking wasn't allowed, I was surprised to see rum come aboard when we were in Trinidad. I heard later that some of the crew had started to secretly imbibe.

The *Rebecca's* route also meant we crossed the equator twice. Following the maritime tradition associated with crossing the equator, the crew celebrated. I don't remember the ceremony, but I do recall the day that some of the crew dressed up in white shirts and shorts, with white pith helmets to match. The photograph I have shows six of them lined up on deck. Four are standing in the background, one of whom is Turkey with a cigarette dangling from the middle of his mouth and his big belly hanging over his belt. Two are kneeling in the foreground, the cook and Mr. Good-Looking with a curved pipe in his mouth. Between them they are holding a large, homemade sign that reads: *69ᵗʰ Vizag Lancers,* a variation, I assume, of the famous Indian *Bengal Lancers.*

It was now early February and we had left Trinidad behind. The voyage was in its final week. Each day the temperature decreased a few degrees. Clouds began appearing, then wind gusts followed by rain showers. One night the ship's pitching woke me up, the first sign of rough seas and blustery weather. As the *Rebecca* laboriously plowed through the sea, ever larger waves crashed over the bow and against the side. A series of photographs record several huge waves splashing up as far as the bridge. It was exciting to feel the ship come alive in the turbulent sea. By the time we passed Cape Hatteras off the coast of North Carolina, the storm had abated and the temperature had dropped to forty degrees.

It was cold but the wind calm the day the *Rebecca* slowly made her way up the Delaware River to Philadelphia. We stopped to pick up a river pilot to guide us in, and then with the aid of a tugboat, he settled the *Rebecca* into her berth. It was February 15, 1957.

This was my last working day, and the last time I had to blow the tubes. I had taken my shower and finished getting dressed when Mr. Good-Looking stopped by my fo'c's'le and asked if I wanted to go ashore to have dinner. I accepted his invitation; we ended up at *Bookbinder's,* one of Philadelphia's famous restaurants. It was busy when we arrived and I remember my friend handing the maitre d' a five-dollar bill to find us a table, a gesture I thought a bit overdone. His choice of the restaurant was excellent, however. The next morning I caught a glimpse of him going down the gangplank accompanied by two men.

"What's that about?" I inquired.

"They're the FBI."

"What happened?"

"This time? It was passing bad checks in Mexico."

"What do you mean 'this time'?"

"I guess he didn't tell you much, did he? He's served time in several places, mostly in Pennsylvania. Sleazy financial stuff, mostly. Nothing violent."

"He sure fooled me."

"He's fooled a lot of people."

By late morning I had been paid off and was free to leave. I found the First coming from the engine room. We shook hands. "It's been a great trip," I said. "Thanks for everything."

"Glad to have you aboard. Good luck."

"Is the captain around?"

"He's up in his office busy with paperwork. I'll tell him you said goodbye."

"Please do."

Before I started packing, I made a reservation for a flight late in the afternoon to Cleveland and telephoned my family. I hadn't seen them in two and a half years. I would arrive home with more than four hundred dollars in my pocket and memories to last a lifetime.

PART III

CHAPTER NINE

Świdnica, Poland: February to June 1998

It was a cold, gray day in early February 1998. The second semester of my first year teaching was under way. After a mild January that surprised all of Europe, the weather had changed and brought a dusting of snow and freezing temperatures. Inside my classroom the temperature was chilly as well. To save on coal bills, our director rarely heated the top floor of the school, which meant that my students often had to wear their jackets or extra sweaters to keep warm. Some had on gloves or mittens. Occasionally we had access to a portable propane heater on wheels, like the one in my apartment that kept me warm on cold evenings. But even then, no one beyond the second row felt any heat.

In spite of the chill, I was having an unexpectedly good day. My students seemed more attentive; and even IIIB, my problem class the first semester, had been less talkative that morning. The second semester had clearly started out to be more satisfying. By this time my students and I were no longer strangers to each other, and I was no longer a totally inexperienced teacher. In addition, I was more assertive about marking names of troublesome students in the *dziennik* (grade book) or giving the students' names to their homeroom teacher (called the *wychowawca*, pronounced vee-ho-Vav-sa).

I had also discovered that music was a way to connect with many students. One day Paweł from IIIB came up to me after class. "I have a cassette you might like to hear. It's one of my favorites. Especially the song, 'Wish You Were Here.'"

"I would be delighted. May I keep it for a few days?"

"Yes, of course."

What he gave me was a cassette by the British group Blackmore's Night called *Shadow of the Moon*. The song Paweł recommended, "Wish You Were Here," had a lilting melodic line, first with a guitar, then a female vocal followed by soft harmony from back-up strings. I was drawn to it as well. The following week I brought in my cassette player and asked Paweł's permission to play it after our lesson was done. They loved it. I eventually found that the song also appealed to my other classes. Soon some students knew the words by heart. "Wish you were here. Me, oh, my countryman, wish you were here. I wish you were here, don't you know the snow is getting colder and I miss you like hell, and I'm feeling blue. I've got feelings for you, do you still feel the same? From the first time I laid my eyes on you I felt joy of living, I saw heaven in your eyes…I wish you were here…."

Having made this successful connection, sometime later I decided to introduce some songs I liked. I chose Simon and Garfunkel's "Bridge Over Troubled Water," and anticipated an outpouring of feeling. To my dismay the piece fell flat. Almost everyone's face was blank. Later I took Paweł aside. "Why didn't they like it?"

"Much too slow," he said. "It doesn't have enough, I don't know what the word is. Just doesn't have it." I was disappointed. After that, when it came to popular music, I let the students decide what we would listen to.

———◆◆◆◆◆———

Now in the early afternoon I was looking into the faces of my students from IIID. It was a class of almost all girls who, though they could be too chatty at times, were bright, polite, and conscientious. Only a couple of students gave me anything close to heartburn.

It turned out that today would also be another lesson for me in flexibility. Fortunately, it came about in a less jarring way than what I had gone through with IIIB the previous fall. This afternoon we had spent the first half of the hour on passive verb forms, reading aloud from our textbook. We started out learning about how Coca-Cola is enjoyed around the world and how the first bottling plant was opened in Dallas in 1895. When we finished I said, "Kinga, please remind us how the passive is formed." I knew I wasn't putting her on the spot. She always knew the answer when asked.

"It is formed with the auxiliary verb 'to be' plus the past participle."

"Excellent. Thank you. Any questions?"

Then I said, "Let's read this next short section." This piece was about how nylon was invented in the early 1930s and was used to make parachutes and ladies' stockings. *Today nylon is found in many things like carpets, ropes, seat belts, and computers.* After we were done I said, "Now we'll turn to page fifty-six in the workbook for further practice."

Above the sound of shuffling books I heard a quiet voice in the third row say, "This is boring." It was Sylwia speaking, not to anyone directly, but more to herself as though thinking out loud. With just the tips of her fingers peeking out from the sleeves of her blue-gray sweater, trying to keep warm, she looked surprised and her face flushed a little when I said to the class, "Did you hear Sylwia's comment?"

"No, we didn't," said someone from the back of the room.

"I did," said Magda who sat near the front. Raising her voice so everyone could hear, she said. "I agree with Sylwia. Doing these exercises would be too boring."

"Sylwia, would you like to say more?" I asked. She was an excellent student and not one to complain. It was worth hearing what she had to say.

"Well, we learned all this last year. Our lesson today was a good review. But I don't think we need more practice from the workbook."

"Do you agree?" I asked the class.

"Yes, we do."

I paused a moment to consider my response. "I have an idea. Have any of you ever talked with your parents or other relatives about what it was like for them to be in school?" A few hands went up. I nodded in Agnieszka's direction.

"My father told me once that if a student misbehaved, the teacher could hit him."

Magda chimed in, "My aunt told my sister they had to wear uniforms in school."

I said, "I imagine things were very different when Poland was a communist country. What I would like you to do is interview someone in your family. It could be a parent, an aunt or uncle, a grandparent. Then write it up, but no more than two or three pages. You'll have a week to finish it. One more thing. Include three examples of passive verb forms." There were a few questions. Then to their relief I added, "I'll cancel the grammar test I scheduled for next week."

This was also the class in which I first introduced singing. One day after we had finished our lesson I asked, "Do any of you like to sing?"

Several hands went up. "We sometimes sing in French class."

"Well, today I just happened to bring the words to a song. If you like it you can all learn it. It's quite easy." When I said I would sing it for them first, I saw astonished expressions on several faces.

Sylwia laughed and said, "We've never had a teacher sing in class before."

"Well, there's always the first time," I replied. "Are you ready? Here goes." I think they were also surprised that I could actually sing and clapped when I finished. Though they would learn other songs, "Oh! Susanna" remained their favorite. Kinga and Beata were among the most ardent fans, their clear voices helping to carry along the more inhibited girls.

I had made enough copies for the whole class and had them write the words in their notebooks. I used the copies in other classes as well. I eventually had a set of words to several songs. The two American songbooks I had brought with me and used the previous summer with my chorus during our training proved to be a great asset. This first year I made use of music mainly as something fun to do after lessons and to practice pronunciation. It wasn't until the next year that I began to combine singing and grammar lessons.

The bell rang and as the students began leaving, Sylwia came by my desk and said, smiling, "I liked your singing."

I started my diary when I first received news in April 1997 that I was going to Poland in June. I recorded my entries in my laptop computer, which I had just bought. By the end of my two years I had written over fifty pages, but I didn't read any of it again until four years after returning home.

In one of my diary entries in the beginning of the second semester I wrote: *My first week back at school has gone fairly well. I actually enjoyed a few classes.* Another entry ended with: *I realize that I can't run a perfect class*, which reflected the fact that I was having more realistic expectations of myself. However, it wasn't until April that I wrote: *I have felt relaxed during these last few days, like I almost have a normal life.*

———◆·◆·◆·◆———

I slowly began to make new friends in addition to Urszula and her family. The first time I met Ashraf Benyamin was following his conducting the Świdnica Chamber Orchestra in a concert the previous autumn. I was introduced by a Polish-Dutch couple with whom I was acquainted. Ashraf appeared to be in his thirties, with black hair and dark complexion, and spoke excellent English, but with a non-Polish accent.

"Please join us for some after-concert refreshment," he said.

I happily accepted the invitation and on the way to the restaurant I said, "I know you're not Polish. Where are you from?"

"I am Egyptian. From Cairo. I used to be a violinist in the Cairo Symphony Orchestra."

I eventually became good enough friends with Ashraf and his Polish girlfriend, Wioletta, with whom he lived, that I could stop by for a visit on short notice. They lived in a small, crowded apartment with a tiny, yapping dog, about a fifteen-minute walk from my school. On my first visit I asked Ashraf how he got from Cairo to Świdnica.

"I really wanted to be a conductor, so I came to Poland in the late 1980s to study conducting at Poznań University. It has an excellent music school, one of the best in Poland as far as I'm concerned."

"That was still during the communist era, wasn't it?"

"Yes, and the cost of living was much less then," he said. "I was able to live on the equivalent of not much more than $1,000 a year. Couldn't do that now, I imagine." Later he told me that he also received financial help from his brother, a physician in Cairo.

He eventually found his way to Świdnica as conductor of the Chamber Orchestra. "I've been here three years now. But my relationship with the city fathers is strained."

"What do you mean?"

"Well, there is sometimes friction between us. I'm not sure they will hire me again for next year."

During my first year Ashraf conducted several more concerts, which always meant a pleasant gathering of friends and musicians at a restaurant afterwards.

One time I invited Ashraf and Wioletta out to dinner for a birthday celebration at the Park Hotel down the street from my school. They were curious about my apartment, so afterwards I invited them to see it. It was unusual for me to have visitors because I felt that my modest place wasn't suitable for entertaining. As we walked up the steps to the school's entrance, I took out my bulky key ring. Unlocking one of the two heavy wooden front doors required two keys. Once inside there were more steps leading up to the first floor hallway, now dimly illuminated by the faint early evening light. As we began the long climb to the fourth floor, Wioletta said, "I went to school here. It hasn't changed very much. But it was never this quiet then."

Wioletta was fluent in English and worked for a local company that manufactured railroad cars that had been recently bought by an American firm. She was highly valued as a translator and had once accompanied a group of managers to a meeting at the company's headquarters in Portland, Oregon.

When we reached the fourth floor landing, I said, "Behind that door straight ahead is my classroom. My apartment is down the hall here to the right. I'll have to unlock the gate first."

As we walked down the long hall I said, indicating the doors on the left, "One of the teachers here told me once that when the school was a Russian Army officers' club, they sometimes had prostitutes in these rooms." I grinned and added, "No longer, obviously."

I unlocked my apartment door and followed my guests through the narrow entryway with the shower stall and into the kitchen/dining area, and then into my combination living and sleeping space. My two rooms were rather small, only about fifteen feet long and ten feet wide. As my guests looked round, I put water on for tea. Wioletta was drawn to my bookcase, filled mostly with books left by my predecessor. She found one by the Czech author, Milan Kundera, called *The Unbearable Lightness of Being.* "Could I borrow this? I've heard he's a good writer."

"Yes, he is," I agreed. "Please take it. I recently read it and liked it very much."

Looking out the window Ashraf said, "You certainly have a fine view of your neighbors' rooftops." Then noticing my laptop he said, "Are you connected to e-mail yet? No? Perhaps I can help you. I know someone who works at *Zeto*, our Internet provider."

We had our tea sitting at the kitchen table. I asked Wioletta if she would help me translate into Polish a letter I was working on. I was planning to send it to several museum directors in Wrocław, informing them that I would be available, for no fee, to help edit material they might have in English, such as labels or brochures. This was one of several activities I was involved in to fulfill the Peace Corps requirement of having community-oriented projects outside the classroom. To give us time for this, we were not scheduled to teach on Fridays.

"Of course," she said, and reminded me that I had helped her a couple months previously with a document her employer asked her to prepare in English.

I couldn't help wondering what Ashraf and Wioletta really thought of my garret-like lodging. After taking another sip of tea, Ashraf leaned back and looked around once again at my sparsely furnished rooms. "What's it like living way up here in this small place all by yourself?"

◆━◆✕◆━◆

A newspaper article about me led to another friendship. One day in March I got a note from the school secretary that a Dr. Wioletta Bawolska, a local physician, had called requesting English lessons. I contacted her and a meeting was set up for 10:00 Saturday morning at the Park Hotel, a short walk from my school. The hotel was a recently renovated large house that sat among a row of formerly grand, older homes, some looking a bit forlorn, which, like the school, faced the park across the street. I was familiar with the hotel's bar and small restaurant because I occasionally went there for a light supper on weekends.

I arrived early, and as I sat waiting, I imagined the doctor to be a short, middle-aged woman with a formal manner and signs of graying hair. When she walked in, I couldn't have been more surprised. The doctor was tall and slender with long, blond hair, wearing a white blouse, black slacks, and a silver necklace with matching earrings. I guessed she was in her mid- thirties. She could easily have passed for a film star. After we introduced ourselves she said, "I read about you in the newspaper. I didn't know we had an American living in Świdnica."

"As far as I know, I'm the only one."

What I anticipated would be a brief meeting over a cup of coffee extended into a pleasant two-hour chat. She was curious to know about how I came to Świdnica as a Peace Corps volunteer and was surprised when I told her I lived at the school down the street. She told me about her parents and younger sister living in Chicago, about her grandmother and other relatives who still were living near Świdnica, and about how she decided to become a physician. She lived in a small town nearby, in the house her parents still owned. Her office, however, was in Świdnica. She specialized in obstetrics and gynecology.

"You may be interested to know that my father was also a physician and practiced the same specialty."

"Really? That's quite a . . . I can't think of the word."

"Coincidence."

"Is that it? See?" she said smiling. "I've learned a new word already."

"I think your English is quite good."

"Thank you," she replied, "but I want to improve before I visit my family in Chicago later this year."

"How often would you like to meet?" I asked.

"I'm not sure. Maybe once a week, or every two weeks. I have a busy practice, so it would depend. I could also help you with your Polish."

"That would be great," I replied.

As our conversation was winding down Wioletta said, "I was thinking that since you don't have a car, I could show you some of the sights around Świdnica. There are some interesting old castles we could visit for example."

"I would enjoy that very much."

Over the next few months, we did in fact visit some castles. A particularly interesting one not far from Świdnica attracted many visitors and was a favorite site for weddings, if one could afford the steep rental fee. Some of the other castles we saw were ruins, while others had been brought back to life as hotels. In May we visited a well-known arboretum when the rhododendrons were in bloom, a colorful setting for close-up portrait photography. In between castles and other historic sites, she took me to a few out-of-the-way restaurants that I never would have found on my own. Besides the pleasure of our rides in the countryside, her cheerful manner and ready laugh made for pleasant company. I tried not to think of us as more than good friends, but being squired around by this attractive woman fed a flimsy fantasy that something else might develop. It never became clear if she was interested in more than our English conversations. The only clue she ever gave came on one of our drives. Out of the blue she said, "You're more interesting than most of my friends, because all they want to do is sit at home and do nothing."

The first time Wioletta invited me to her home for dinner, I was surprised to hear the music of Glenn Miller and the songs of Frank Sinatra coming from her stereo. This was music I grew up with and I was pleased that she liked it, too. The house she lived in, which her parents had built, sat in a country setting along with several other homes, each with a good-sized lawn. Over time I met several of her friends and relatives here.

Wioletta told me early on that she was married but had been separated from her husband for several months. I wondered if she would find someone else. This question was eventually answered as a man began to appear on the scene. Her new friend, Jurek, had a distinctive look with his closely cropped black hair, a two-day-old beard, and dark glasses. He was a friendly, outgoing man who worked as a pharmacist. I wondered how his presence would change the arrangement that Wioletta and I had. In fact very little changed. Wioletta and I continued our jaunts in the country, though now she was driving me around in Jurek's car, a white 1988 Dodge, an ex-police vehicle that he had shipped over from California for reasons that I never really understood.

From the time I arrived in Świdnica the previous fall, I was diligent in my efforts to improve my Polish. However, I felt frustrated at every turn. Though every now and then the pieces fell into place, constructing even simple sentences required mental gymnastics. My first private tutor was a retired schoolteacher who was recommended by my Peace Corps predecessor. What I found most useful was having her help me translate into Polish something I had written in English. One of the first exercises we worked on was an account of my visit to a cemetery on All Souls Day, November 1. The day is a national holiday in Poland when everyone honors the memory of deceased family members. There was a large cemetery not far from my school, and all day long people streamed by carrying cut flowers, potted plants, and candles. Some people would spend much of the day there, bringing folding chairs to sit on around the family grave. I made my visit after dark. Even a half-mile away I could see a warm light hovering in the sky. A throng of other visitors kept me company as I walked the long driveway through a wooded area that led from the street. The scene at the cemetery, spread out over several acres, was awe-inspiring. Along every path mourners were gathered around grave sites filled with flowers and flickering votive candles, their illuminated faces glowing in the chilly night air, their murmuring voices the only sounds to be heard.

The sessions with my tutor ended after two months, however, because she didn't want to sign the form I had to send to the Peace Corps office in Warsaw for reimbursement. She didn't think the arrangement was confidential enough and was afraid that if someone in the Polish government found out, she would have to pay income tax. My reassurances after checking with Warsaw were not convincing. I was disappointed. Nevertheless, our meetings had been congenial and she helped me begin a systematic approach to continue learning Polish on my own.

It took me several weeks before I found my second tutor, a young woman who was a part-time reporter for one of the local newspapers and a student at the university in Wrocław. Unfortunately, she proved to be unreliable, often canceling sessions or not showing up. However, one positive consequence was that she wrote the article about me that my new physician friend had seen in the newspaper. Several days after the article was published, one of my students brought a copy to class. Amid much excitement she read it out loud while others helped her translate into English. She and her friends were thrilled to see that in my interview I had specifically mentioned their class.

I wouldn't find my next tutor until the summer.

———◆◆×◆●———

While I was making new friends in Świdnica, I was keeping in touch with my Peace Corps friends. Paula and I saw each other again during semester break when our group of Peace Corps volunteers gathered in early February for five days of language study in Sopot, a city in northern Poland on the Baltic Sea. Sopot is not far from Gdańsk, a centuries-old port whose architecture is very much like Amsterdam and other northern coastal cities. Known as Danzig when it was part of Germany, Gdańsk became famous for the shipyard strikes against the communist regime led by Lech Wałęsa in the 1980s. Paula, Shirley, Jenni, Jon and I visited the city on a cold and dreary afternoon. Since wandering the streets wasn't much fun given the weather, the warmth inside the city's shops appealed to me more. I was especially drawn to the jewelry stores that specialized in amber, a fossil resin found mostly near the Baltic Sea. I was surprised to learn that the amber trade goes back even to Roman times. I bought several lovely amber and silver bracelets as gifts.

In March I got a call from Paula while I was taking a break in the teachers' room. "Hey! How are ya?"

"I'm fine."

"How about coming with Jenni, Ruth and me for a weekend in Poznań?"

"Sounds like fun. When were you thinking?"

"In two weeks. We've made reservations in a youth hostel. It'll be cheap."

The hostel part turned out to be the only drawback to an otherwise pleasant weekend. It was cheap all right, but having to sleep in the same room with four male strangers didn't appeal to me. Like many other young volunteers, Paula and her friends sought out youth hostels when they traveled, mainly to save money. I much preferred the privacy of inexpensive hotels. This was my second trip to Poznań; the first time was on my way home from Sopot six weeks before. Poznań is a thriving city and has an excellent university and art museum. I was particularly interested in the museum's collection of nineteenth century Polish artists, about whom I wanted to learn more.

During the second semester Paula and I exchanged visits to each other's school. The small town of Złoczew where she taught was several hours by bus from Świdnica. Her apartment was part of the school's complex and much roomier than mine. I don't remember the exact layout, but she had it attractively furnished and said she was very comfortable there. She was also happy with her Polish colleagues and had become good friends with one teacher and her husband.

On the weekend that Paula came to visit me, we met in Wrocław on a Friday at the Architecture Museum, which had accepted my offer to help edit materials it had translated into English. When Paula arrived I was working on a series of labels that had been printed out from the museum's computer. Some required only minimal editing, while quite a few had to be rewritten to make the best sense. The museum was housed in a retired Gothic church and was a great space to install particularly large displays.

While I finished up, Paula wandered around. When she returned she remarked, "I really like this place. There is also an interesting exhibit on the restoration of the Peace Church in Świdnica. What's that about?"

"It's a unique seventeenth century Protestant church and Świdnica's most famous tourist attraction. A lot of money from the Lutheran Church in Germany is helping to finance the restoration. We'll visit it over the weekend."

We arrived in Świdnica late that afternoon after an hour's bus ride from Wrocław. On the way from the bus station Paula said, "You live in a real city. There's obviously a lot more to do here than where I am."

When we got to my apartment and Paula saw my living/sleeping room, she blurted out, "Jeez, Larry, your place looks more like a dorm room than your home. You need to fix it up better."

I was taken aback, not really knowing to what she was referring. I had to admit, however, that for someone so particular about his domestic surroundings, I had put little effort into "fixing up" my apartment. I never felt completely at home there, seeing it, I guess, as a temporary way station. Yet I didn't see how I could arrange things much differently, especially since there was no closet space. Where else could I store my two suitcases and vacuum cleaner except in one corner? What else could I do but lean the ironing board and spare mattress against the wall opposite the bookcase?

"Do you have any suggestions?" I asked.

"Give me time to think about it. I'll come up with something."

After we came back from supper she said, "You hardly have room to turn around in here for one thing. For another, the stuff in that huge bookcase could stand some rearranging." She paused. "But I got to tell ya, the clothesline you got strung up there doesn't, in my opinion, add diddly squat, as my uncle used to say, to the aesthetics of this room."

I laughed. "The young woman who lived here before left it."

"I don't care if it was left by the Pope. I couldn't live with it for even a day."

That night, after we had turned the lights out, I started chuckling quietly.

From the mattress on the floor, Paula said, "What are you laughing about up there?

"Just my clothesline."

With a little laugh of her own Paula said, "What you need around here is a woman's touch."

After Paula left that weekend I remember sitting on my couch trying to think of changes I could make to the bookcase that took up more than half of the wall space. It was a large piece of furniture, painted black, with three separate sections. The center unit had two glass doors. Over the next several days I removed the instructional aids and related texts that my predecessor had left and donated them to the school library. This left space to more artfully display the remaining books and small art objects I had acquired. Then I took photographs and mailed them to Paula. "That's a good start," she wrote a couple of weeks later.

I never did take the clothesline down.

———◆◆◆———

Anna Bielawska invited me to Easter dinner, an occasion which ranks high among feast days in Poland. I first met Anna, who taught English in another high school, the previous fall. She had asked me to be one of three judges at her school's annual English competition. We had since become friends. I also got to know her husband, Stanisław, who taught Polish at my school. The Bielawskis* lived in an apartment with high ceilings and large windows facing the street, where the ornate, though faded, façades of apartment buildings still reflected late nineteenth century grandeur.

---

* When a woman's last name in Polish is used alone, it has the feminine ending "a." A man's name has the masculine ending "i." When they are mentioned together, the masculine ending is used.

When I arrived for Easter dinner, Anna greeted me at the door. "Welcome. Come in and meet my children and guests."

I followed her into the spacious dining room, where she introduced me to her daughter and son, both in their early twenties. I then met her elderly parents who lived there. Anna told me later that they were among the first Poles to settle in Świdnica after World War II. They had previously lived in the eastern part of Poland that is now Ukraine and had to leave when Stalin appropriated the region. Other guests included Anna's brother, his wife, and their two adolescent children.

I was amazed by the amount of food. An array of dishes sat on the dining room table and on the upright piano nearby. In addition, at each end of the table was a bottle of Bison Vodka, a special Polish brand that contains a blade of grass from the fields in northeastern Poland where the indigenous bison graze. As we took our places, Stanisław poured each adult a small glass of vodka; Anna poured juice for the younger guests. Holding up his glass, he offered a toast. We all joined in saying, "*Na zdrowie!*"

The meal began with borscht (beet soup), creamed herring, and devilled eggs stuffed with mushrooms. The main dishes were sliced ham, white sausage, and fried chicken. Besides a salad of potatoes, green peas, hardboiled eggs and carrots in a mayonnaise sauce, there was fruit encased in a golden gelatin mold. Accompaniments included pickles, horseradish, and mustard, plus dark bread, rolls and butter.

"What do you think of our Polish food?" asked Anna's son, who was sitting on my right.

"Excellent, delicious," I said. "Your custom of having so many different kinds of food at one meal is new to me."

"Easter is a very special time. This is one way we celebrate."

"Do you also celebrate by going to church?" I asked.

"Some members of my family attend, but like many of my friends, I have less interest."

From across the table his sister asked about life in the States, and which part of the country I came from. "I want to live in America for a year after I finish my university studies," she said.

"I may go to Chicago, where a friend of mine lives. I've heard that Chicago has the largest Polish population outside of Warsaw."

An hour had passed when Anna interrupted everyone's conversation. "There will be a pause while we take away these plates to make room for dessert."

Meanwhile, Stanisław replenished our vodka glasses. It took almost another hour to make our way through homemade pastries and poppy seed cake, along with a choice of tea or coffee.

As the meal came to an end, I said to Anna, "This has been a very special occasion for me. Thank you for inviting me."

"It has been our pleasure to have a guest join us all the way from America."

◆◆⋇◆●

Though I had made friends and kept busy with my classroom duties, I still felt isolated. Since I didn't speak the language well, it was as if I lived inside an invisible membrane that prevented normal interaction, except, of course, with my English-speaking colleagues and friends. I experienced it every day in the teachers' room, the post office, and the grocery store. It even began in my apartment. Though I had a radio, short-wave reception was unreliable, which made it difficult to hear BBC newscasts. The television carried just one Polish channel. I remember well how cut off I felt from the rest of the world when Princess Diana was killed in Paris in September of 1997, soon after I arrived in Świdnica. I had to rely on my students to give me news updates. While the Peace Corps office in Warsaw sent the European edition of *Newsweek* to all volunteers and was very much appreciated, by the time it arrived the news was already more than a week old.

As for television entertainment, for a few hours each day there were old American movies. Instead of Polish subtitles, the volume of the soundtrack in English was lowered (but still slightly audible), and a male voice, droning in Polish, spoke for all the actors. I found this both odd and unsatisfying, so I rarely watched.

Then, in late spring, my contact with the outside world opened up. The school director finally agreed to have my television connected to a cable service. I offered to pay for it, but he declined. I now had eighteen channels, several of which broadcast programs from other countries including France, England, Germany, Italy, and the Czech Republic. Though one channel had the European edition of NBC, I couldn't get CNN.

Also, I decided to buy a cell phone. The phone in my room was an extension of the school's number, and though I was able to call out in the evening or on weekends, I was unreachable once the secretary went home. Now friends could contact me after school hours.

Finally, I got connected to e-mail. Ashraf went with me to *Zeto,* the local Internet provider, and introduced me to his friend there who helped me get it all working. The next step was to buy a telephone line to connect my laptop to my phone. Since they were in different rooms, it required forty feet of wire because it had to run along the baseboard on both sides of the dividing wall. I stopped in a small electronics store to buy the wire, and when the owner learned that I was a Peace Corps teacher, he gave it to me gratis. I never told anyone at school that I was hooked up. Since I didn't spend much time on the Internet, I doubt that my usage increased the school's phone bill by much.

With or without these amenities, I never forgot the fact that in comparison to most Peace Corps assignments throughout the world, my living situation might have been described as luxurious.

◆◆✕◆◆

The second semester came to a close much more rapidly than I anticipated. With mid-June fast approaching, it felt as if all of a sudden I had tests to give, grades to turn in, and year-end Peace Corps reports to write. In addition, I had to prepare material for a summer project that was required of all volunteers. In my case I had signed up to be a teacher at a ten-day English camp organized by one of my Peace Corps colleagues. I would need to leave Świdnica two days after the last day of classes. I also had to get ready for visitors from home who were due to arrive soon after I returned.

I was doing errands downtown at the *Rynek* on a warm afternoon. Clouds were moving in over the city. Rain was in the offing. I had just been to the bank to withdraw some cash and was on my way to a travel agency to get information about travel to Russia, where I was thinking of going later in the summer. Suddenly the sky darkened and almost immediately there was a downpour. I was only a few paces from a bookstore and dashed inside just in time to avoid a drenching. While I waited for the rain to stop, I decided to browse in the children's department thinking I might find something easy in Polish to read. Then I heard a voice say, "Good afternoon."

I turned around. "Well, good afternoon." It was Sylwia Dąbrowska from IIID, the student who had voiced her class's boredom, but who had also said she liked my singing. "What brings you here?" I asked.

"I was about to get rained on."

"Me, too."

"What are you looking for?" she asked.

"Something simple to read in Polish. Maybe a children's book."

"I have some at home I could loan you."

"I would be delighted." We chatted for a few minutes. She was definitely looking forward to summer vacation. She wasn't sure what she would do to keep busy, but said that she was looking into a part-time job with a newspaper. Many young people in Poland don't work in the summer, partly because jobs are hard to find, plus the culture doesn't seem to expect it of them.

I asked, "Would you be willing to come with me to the travel agency across the street? I want to find out if they have group trips to Russia. You can help translate. Do you remember my mentioning this in class?" I had been surprised by the students' reactions. Some had worried looks on their faces and told me that I shouldn't go because they thought it was not safe or the Russian mafia might get me. This reflected Poland's long-standing distrust of the Russians.

"Yes, I remember. My friends and I are concerned about you. But I'll come with you."

The travel agency told us they didn't sponsor trips to Russia, and didn't think any other agency did either. I would pursue it anyway, though I wouldn't have time until I came back from the English camp.

"When you return," Sylwia said, "call me on your new cell phone and we can go to the other travel agencies. In the meantime, I'll look for some easy books in Polish to loan you." She paused a moment. "I have something else I wanted to say, but it can wait."

CHAPTER TEN

English Camp in Poland: June 1998

I awoke earlier than usual on the morning of June 20. It was just two days since the last class of the second semester. I was still frazzled after finally getting grades turned in and then having to write up lesson plans for the English camp. I had a fitful night's sleep thinking about what loose ends I might be overlooking. During breakfast I went over the list of things I had to do before leaving town that morning. Ahead of me was a full day of travel to the north of Poland where I would meet the four Peace Corps colleagues I would be teaching with for ten days. I knew them to be bright and personable, and I was looking forward to seeing them. However, I was feeling a little anxious because they were decades younger, all in their twenties. I wondered if the age gap would be a problem, since we would be living and working closely together. The next ten days would be very different from when we were all in training the previous summer.

After breakfast, I tidied up my apartment and was eager to get going. With my luggage in hand I walked to the bus station, took a bus to Wrocław, an hour's ride, and from there boarded a mid-morning train. I was headed for Czersk, over two hundred miles away.

I always enjoyed riding the train. It was inexpensive, relaxing, and provided a changing view of Poland's countryside of lush green fields and patches of dense forests. Seeing farmers working the land brought back memories of the summer when I worked on a small farm in Ohio at the age of seventeen. I recalled the sweet morning air while pumping water at the well before breakfast, the barn's familiar aroma and comforting warmth, the cows feeding contentedly at their troughs, the muffled chug-a-chug of the milking machine, the tractor's steady rhythm while cultivating row upon row of corn, and the golden acres of wheat waiting for the combine to do its work.

As a teacher I carried a document that allowed me to travel half price, so I always went first class. While fancy or luxurious would not describe any Polish train I ever rode on, they were usually clean and most of the time punctual. The rail system was extensive and serviced many out-of-the-way places. My half-price document came to me through the school director, but I think it originated with the Ministry of Education. Unfortunately, and for reasons that were never fully explained, I didn't receive this document my second year. A colleague told me that the school had to contribute financially and that the director probably decided the school couldn't afford it. The next year I traveled second class.

I finally arrived in Czersk late in the warm afternoon. Waiting for me were Carlee Cole and Aaron Ramsey.

"It's great to see you two," I said. "How are you?"

"We're fine," said Carlee. "How was your trip?"

"It went okay, but a long day. Two changes and a layover in Poznań."

Carlee's teaching assignment was in Czersk, a small town whose main attraction was a medieval castle. Petite and energetic, she was the primary organizer of the camp and had found facilities located on a nearby lake. Her apartment was not at her school, but in a quiet residential neighborhood where she shared a house with her landlady. Waiting for us there were Jennifer Maxson and Eric McConkie, who like Aaron and I, had traveled some distance that day. I knew Jenni the best since she was a good friend of Paula's and I had seen her more frequently. Opening her front door, Carlee called, "We're back. Larry's here."

Eric and Jenni welcomed me with smiles. "There he is, Mr. Music Man himself," said Eric with his usual ebullience. "Come in. Drinks are about to be served."

Jenni added, "And supper will be ready soon. We've been working on it while you were gone."

An inviting aroma was coming from the kitchen, and I could see that the table was already set. The plan was to stay overnight at Carlee's place and then go to the campsite the next morning. That would give us time to review the plans and schedules we had worked out and go over each of our responsibilities. While settling in, which meant finding space on Carlee's living room floor, we all told stories of feeling frantic as we rushed to finish up our second semester and get ready for camp. Expressions such as "You wouldn't believe" punctuated the conversation. Soon it was time for supper, which began with a Polish-style vegetable soup, followed by American-style spaghetti with a meat and tomato sauce, dark Polish bread, and a salad. Wine from Bulgaria and beer from Poland complemented our meal.

While we ate, Carlee brought us up to date. She had put a tremendous amount of work into recruiting the students, finding the site, raising money through grants, and getting the project approved by the Peace Corps office in Warsaw. "We have fifty students signed up. Twenty-five are coming from my school and the surrounding area. With help from my colleague, Marina, who is Russian, the other twenty-five students are coming from Kaliningrad, Russia."

"Is that far from here?" I asked.

"Not really. It's just over the northern border. It's the capital of a small area that's separated from the rest of Russia and sandwiched between Poland and Lithuania."

Eric said, "I think it used to be called Königsberg in the old days when it was a German city."

Carlee added, "In fact it was Marina's idea to recruit Russian students, hoping that this experience might help in some way to improve relations between the two countries."

"How old are these kids?" Aaron asked.

"As far as I can tell, they range from fourteen to nineteen."

Jenni laughed. "We're going to have our hands full." We all agreed.

After doing the dishes we relaxed, chatted, and finished the bottle of wine. I learned that Carlee had grown up in Florida and had just graduated from college in North Carolina. Jenni, in her late twenties, also came from North Carolina, where she had been working before joining the Peace Corps. Aaron was a recent college graduate from Oregon. I don't recall Eric mentioning where he was from.

Though we shared great hopes for this cultural exchange, we were naturally a bit apprehensive about the next ten days. Yet I remember that there was an unmistakable sense of optimism and enthusiasm in the air. I could tell by the way things went that first evening that the five of us would get along just fine.

———◆◆✕◆●———

The next morning two of Carlee's male colleagues drove us in two vans to the campsite on Lake Wiele, about twenty minutes away. Near the main entrance were the administrative office, cabins for its staff, a recreation building, and the dining hall. Scattered throughout several sparsely wooded acres, closer to the lake, were clusters of cabins and tent sites. We had exclusive use of a specific area with cabins. It looked like an ideal setting, with the lake in front and a denser wooded area behind.

We spent much of the first day checking in the students, meeting the adult women chaperons, and helping everyone find their cabins. Each cabin had two floors. In ours, all five of us would sleep upstairs in cramped quarters under the slanted roof. With five bunks, two small tables and three wooden chairs, there wasn't much room to spare. The only hanger I could find was a nail in the wall above my bunk. I was lucky to have my bunk at the far end near one of the two windows. We could stand up straight only in the middle of the room, at the peak where the sloping rafters were joined. Sometimes we entertained ourselves by reading aloud the graffiti that covered the walls and ceiling, most likely written by adolescents. The four Russian chaperons slept on the first floor, and the Polish chaperons were in a nearby cabin.

Once everyone was accounted for, we gathered in the rustic dining hall, a cavernous wooden structure with exposed beams, where we formally welcomed everyone. After supper we announced the next day's schedule and ended with singing, first a few songs in English, followed by the Polish and Russian students each singing a song in their own language.

At last we wished everyone a good night. As we were leaving, two Polish girls came up to us and said, "Can we walk with you? We don't know the way back to our cabin."

"You certainly can. I'm sure one of us will remember the way."

"Who has the flashlight?"

It was a cool, clear evening with a light breeze coming off the lake. We showed the girls to their cabin. I wondered to myself if this was their first time sleeping away from home.

——◆◆◆◆◆——

We followed pretty much the same routine each day. Everyone gathered for breakfast at eight o'clock. Beginning at 9:30, we had scheduled three fifty-minute classes that lasted until 1:00 P.M. We had the use of the local elementary school, which was a ten-minute walk from camp. The school, though not new, was an attractive building with plenty of light from the classroom windows. The first hour of instruction was a grammar lesson, followed by conversation, with the third hour an elective, such as music, art, literature and poetry. I taught the music class. Their favorite song turned out to be "She'll Be Comin' Round the Mountain."

After lunch the students had free time, and then beginning at three o'clock there were outside activities such as swimming, boating, games, and hiking. I was soon initiated into Dizzy Dizzy, a game Jenni organized one afternoon. I resisted at first. "I'm just here to watch," I said

"Come on! We need one more on the red team."

With two teams of eight, the object was to run ten yards toward a stake in the ground, go around it three times, then run, or try to run, back to the starting point and tag the next runner. As I attempted my return run, I recall clearly the sense of utter helplessness as I veered this way and that, much to the delight of the students. I never saw Jenni laugh so hard. After that I referred to the game as the looking-stupid club.

We were relieved to see that our young campers were making new friends. We tried hard to keep track of them to make sure no one was being left out or not mixing in. I was glad to see that Roman and Vadim, two initially shy Russian boys, were getting along well. Roman told me that he was surprised how respectfully he was treated in class, because he rarely experienced that in his school, especially with his male instructors. His friend, Vadim, learned to play Scrabble so well from Jenni and Eric that he ended up beating almost everyone.

At breakfast one day, Aaron, Eric and I were talking about the previous evening's talent show. "The singing groups were really good, I thought," said Eric. "Especially the five Russian girls who harmonized when they came to the chorus of their song. Really nice."

"Yes, they were," I said. "And Aaron, you did a great impersonation of Louis Armstrong's 'It's a Wonderful World.' The kids loved it."

"Thanks. Everyone seemed to have a great time."

"See the two Russian girls at the far table?" I said, nodding to where they were sitting with their heads together, whispering and laughing."

"Do you mean Anya and Tanya?"

"Yes."

"What about them?"

"Well, they seem to hang around together much of the time."

"Maybe that's because they're older than many of the other students."

"I'm sure that's one reason. But I can't help thinking that they're up to no good."

Eric and Aaron laughed. "What does that mean?"

"I'm not sure. They just have a mischievous look about them."

Eric looked at Aaron and said, "I guess we'll just have to keep an eye on them."

———◆✦◆———

The overall theme of the camp was learning how democracy works. Our goal was to have each cabin vote on a representative, and then the representatives, with our help, would draft a constitution. Eventually an election would be held for camp president and vice president. Toward the end of the first week Carlee expressed concern. "The kids are dragging their feet on this."

Eric said, "I agree, but how can we get them more interested?"

"I think we should announce a deadline for cabin representatives by tomorrow evening," Jenni suggested.

Aaron added, "And all of us should talk it up in our classes."

Within two days each of the cabins had a representative, and together they met with Carlee and Eric to begin writing a constitution. The next day at supper we were delightfully surprised when Irada, an eighteen-year-old Russian girl, stood up. Speaking excellent English she said, "I have something to say. I have decided to run for president of our camp. Who among you will be brave and run against me?"

Irada's announcement created much excitement. By the next day one of the Polish boys put his name on the ballot. In the end Irada emerged the winner. She took the election process seriously and revealed a strong competitive streak. I told her later that I predicted she would be the first woman president of Azerbaijan, where she had grown up. In spite of her outward confidence, however, she was open about her self-doubts and had difficulty accepting compliments. In this setting, though, she appeared to be a natural leader and made many new Polish friends. I corresponded with her for a while afterwards and sent her a photograph I had taken of her. As far as I know, it may still be sitting on her family's bookshelf where she said her parents displayed it. Irada faded from view, but then an e-mail announced that she had married a young Australian businessman and was waiting for her visa to be approved so she could join him. As much as I could tell from the e-mail, she sounded happy.

Another camper I kept in touch with was Kasia (nickname for Katarzyna), an excellent student from Carlee's school. As with Irada, one connecting link was a photograph I took of her. I found the picture so appealing that I included an enlargement in an exhibit several years later of candid close-up portraits of people from eight different countries whom I had encountered in my travels. These images became almost like friends, though Kasia is one of only two whose name I know.

As a Catholic, Kasia's religion was important to her. Later in the summer she wrote that she had been one of the many pilgrims who made the annual trek in August to Częstochowa, the city with the Black Madonna. After graduating from her high school the next year, Kasia went on to the university in Poznań to study linguistics and literature. In addition to English ("In class this week we read poems of Emily Dickinson, who is from your city."), she was becoming fluent in Spanish and spent two summers in Spain. Later, in 2001, she wrote:

I must say a few words about a true American tragedy which happened on Tuesday, September 11th. I, my family, and all Poles are still shocked. We really feel sorry for all Americans and we pray for those who lost their lives in this horrible catastrophe. While I was watching news on that day, I thought it was a movie, but in a movie there is always a hero who saves our planet at the last moment. But in real life no one saved people in World Trade Center. Now fighting terrorism is our duty. I only hope that it won't be a beginning of a third world war.

One afternoon I was talking with Carlee and Jenni outside our cabin when one of the campers came up to us and said, "Alina has a problem."

"What's that?"

"Here she comes."

Alina, one of the older Polish girls, came slowly down her cabin stairs with the help of two friends. I had chatted with her the previous evening at the bonfire where, besides singing and storytelling, we introduced the art of roasting marshmallows. Alina became our most enthusiastic marshmallow fan. Now, with her arms in the air, she was holding up the bottom part of her pullover, obscuring her head.

"What is it, Alina?" Carlee asked.

A pained, quiet voice spoke something we couldn't quite hear.

"Please say it again," Jenni said.

At first we didn't believe what we were hearing. "Are you saying that your eyelid is caught in your zipper?"

"Yes."

Carlee, Jenni and I looked at each other as though to say, *What do we do now?*

"Are you in much pain?" I asked.

"It's not too bad, but my arms are getting tired."

We got her two camp mates to hold up the pullover. I then gently pulled down one side and could see that the zipper had indeed caught a small section of her eyelid. "Do you want me to unzip it?" I asked. "It would hurt."

"I don't think so," she said.

Carlee told Alina that we needed a few minutes to discuss what to do. We finally decided that the first step would be to cut out a piece of Alina's pullover around her eye. That way she could take it off and at least rest her arms.

"Are you willing for us to do this?" Carlee asked.

"Yes," said Alina.

Someone found a pair of scissors and gave them to Carlee. "I really don't want to do this," she said, and handed the scissors to Jenni.

Jenni shook her head and passed the scissors to me. "Here, you perform the operation."

I explained to Alina that I first had to make a hole in her pullover before I could do any cutting. This meant poking the end of one scissor blade through the fabric. While other hands pulled it gently as far from her face as possible, I began to cut. As I slowly made headway I asked, "How are you doing in there, Alina?"

"I'm all right."

With the sharp tips of the scissors only inches from her face, I carefully made each cut. I paused when I arrived at her zipper. Getting through it was tougher going and extra hands were required to minimize tugging at her eyelid.

"Ouch!" she said once.

"Sorry."

Only a couple inches to go. Finally I made the last snip. Off came the pullover. Alina was pale and gratefully received a hug from Carlee. But I couldn't help thinking that she looked a bit comical with a small piece of cloth dangling from her eyelid.

In the meantime, someone had found the camp physician and offered to take Alina to see him. She returned within the hour, her pretty face now fully visible. She had a sore red eye for two days, but otherwise there were no complications. That weekend she asked permission to go home for an afternoon to get some things; her sister would pick her up.

"Are you bringing back another pullover?" Carlee asked.
"Yes, but one with only buttons!"

———◆—▶◀—◆———

At lunch on the next to the last day, the five of us lingered while most everyone else had left the dining hall. "Would you all agree that things have worked out pretty well?" I asked.
"Yes."
"Definitely."
"Better than some of us anticipated, actually."
I added, "I want to thank all of you for a great ten days. And I want to say to you, Carlee, the prime mover and yet the youngest of us, that at your age of twenty-two I wouldn't have been able to do what you've done here in a million years."
"I don't know if I would agree with that, but thank you. Don't forget, though, whatever I've done, this wouldn't have happened in a million years without all of you."

———◆—▶◀—◆———

On the last day, there were hugs and tears throughout the camp. Saying goodbye was difficult for everyone. Seeing Anya and Tanya for the last time, I was reminded that I had been wrong about them in the beginning. Besides being conscientious students, they were a delight to be around and both had made many friends. I received a note from each of them, which I read again on the train going home. They wrote in part:

When I saw you at the first time I've understood that you are of the same kind and understandable people in the whole world . . . . I want to tell you great thank for you are on the earth, for lessons which we had together, especially for your music lessons. You have a wonderful voice! . . . . Great thank for your words, which you have told me. I'll be missing you so much. Love, Tanya from Kaliningrad. P.S. Maybe you'll find any mistakes. Sorry for them.

I don't want to leave this camp. I don't want to leave such friends. I just want to thank you for your kindness, your comprehension and your concern for us. . . . I just want you to be happy and want nothing to interfere with feasibility as your plans for the future and your dreams. Good luck! From Russian girl, Anya.

CHAPTER ELEVEN
Visitors from Home: July 1998

After I returned to Świdnica from camp, I had only a few days
before the arrival of guests from America. My brother and sister-
in-law, John and Muriel, and a friend, Betsy, were coming for a
week's visit. The plan was to meet them in Prague on July 7. After
a couple days of sightseeing, we would rent a car and drive first to
Świdnica and then on to other sights in Poland.

Before I left for Prague, I called Sylwia and arranged to meet
the next day at the Piast Hotel,* just off the *Rynek*. On the phone
she had told me, "They have a nice lounge where we could have a
cup of tea. I want to hear all about your English camp."

"See you tomorrow. Two o'clock."

It had been a week of warm, sunny weather. With low humidity
and gentle breezes, there was a sweetness to the air. I took my
time walking downtown, enjoying the leafy shade as I passed
through the park across the street from the school, and delighting
in the flowers blooming in the small courtyard gardens in front of
apartment buildings closer to town. The hotel was located in a row
of attached, gray stucco buildings on one of the streets branching
out from the *Rynek*. The restaurant was not busy, so I was able to
choose a table next to one of the large, curtained windows. I had
been here several times previously and found it a comfortable place.
Sylwia soon appeared. She looked especially attractive wearing a
blue blouse, beige skirt, and a bracelet on each wrist. I wasn't used
to seeing my students wearing anything other than jeans or slacks.
We shook hands. "Isn't this a lovely day?" she said. "Maybe we
could take a walk later."

---

* Piast comes from the name of a dynasty in early Polish history. The last
king of that dynasty was Kazimierz the Great, who ruled in the fourteenth
century. Among his legacies was a law in 1346 that gave protection to Jews
from persecution, which led to Poland having the largest Jewish population
in Europe. Also, in 1364, he founded the first Polish university in Kraków,
the second oldest in central Europe after the university in Prague.

"That would be fine, but first we're going to the other travel agencies. Remember?"

"Yes. Do you still want to go to Russia?" She sounded a bit hesitant to ask.

"Definitely. I'm curious about what the country is like, and I really want to see Moscow and St. Petersburg. I'll probably never be as close again to Russia as I am here in Poland."

She smiled and nodded slightly. "I can see that your mind is made up. Oh, I have something for you." Reaching into her bag she took out two books. "I brought them from home. I think they are easy to read."

"Thank you." One of the books had a colorfully illustrated cover showing a woodland scene with a handsome youth bowing to a pretty maiden. I thought it was probably a fairytale.

We chatted for an hour over a dish of ice cream (a favorite among Poles) and a cup of Lipton tea with a wedge of lemon. I gave a brief report on English camp. Sylwia could hardly believe the story of the zipper and the eyelid, and was intrigued by my account of the twenty-five Russian students from Kaliningrad. "You would have enjoyed getting to know them," I said.

"I'm sure I would. It sounds like you had a good time."

"I did. I met a lot of interesting people, and I was pleased to see how well the Polish and Russian students got along. I think they made some long-lasting friendships."

"Do you remember my telling you at the bookstore I had something else to say to you?"

"Yes, of course."

"I was thinking that though your Polish is improving, maybe you'd like extra practice. I could help you if you like."

"Really? That's a very nice offer. I'd be delighted." I thought it unusual that she would want to spend time during her summer vacation correcting my Polish.

"You could also help me with my English."

"I could, but you speak very well already. I'm impressed with how fluent you and many of your classmates are. You wouldn't find many high school students in America speaking a foreign language as well."

"Thank you. We begin very early in school to study another language. I've heard that this is not so in America. We have much preparation before we get to the *Lyceum*, and I think our English teachers there are very good. We also learned a lot from the Peace Corps teacher before you. All of us have had much practice."

Sylwia was now working part-time as a reporter for a local newspaper, and her schedule varied from week to week. She suggested I call after my American guests had departed, and we would set up a time for a Polish conversation session.

We then made the rounds of the three other travel agencies in town, none of which offered a packaged tour to Russia. Sylwia said, "You've told me that you've traveled a lot by yourself. Maybe you will have just as good a time going on your own."

"Yes, I think you're right. But I'll need to get more information about a visa and air flights, which probably means going to Warsaw. I'll look into that in a couple of weeks.

"I still have time this afternoon. Shall we take a walk? I have a suggestion. You've probably been there. Just like in New York City, it's called Central Park."

On July 7 I took the train to Prague. As the crow flies, the distance between the two cities is less than a hundred and fifty miles, but the Karkonosze mountain range that separates Poland and the Czech Republic to the south is a formidable barrier that makes a direct route impossible. The weather was pleasantly warm the morning I left and continued throughout the day. The train was late, so I didn't arrive until 7:30 P.M. I changed some currency at the station, and because taxis were expensive, unlike in Świdnica, I decided to walk to the Ambassador Hotel in the city center.

I had been in Prague briefly six months before at the end of my trip to Italy and Germany during Christmas break. For the one night I was there I stayed in an out-of-the-way hotel that required two streetcar changes. That evening I was able to get a last-minute ticket to Mozart's opera, *The Magic Flute,* in a beautiful eighteenth century Baroque theater where, I was told by a young Italian couple next to me, some of the movie *Amadeus* was filmed.

I arrived at the hotel after a fifteen-minute walk. There to greet me were John, Muriel and Betsy. They had arrived earlier in the afternoon, which gave them a chance to rest up after their flights. Though John and Muriel had started out in Columbus, Ohio, and Betsy from Boston, they were able to schedule their flights to arrive within a half hour of each other.

It was already past dinnertime, so we set out to find a place to eat. Not far from the hotel we found the Mucha Restaurant, named after a Czech artist I had not heard of. (Polish, a related language, also has the name Mucha, which means fly and is pronounced Moo-ha. One of the teachers at my school also had that name.) We all took the recommendation of our English-speaking waitress and ordered a typical Czech dish, which was a kind of goulash with boiled potatoes and salad.

Taking a sip of wine John said, "So, tell us, little brother, how are you surviving over here so far from home?"

Little brother was about to turn sixty-eight in two weeks. John would be seventy-one in August. He was a retired anesthesiologist who, with Muriel, was enjoying traveling and visiting their four children, ten grandchildren, and family members like me.

"I'm doing pretty well, actually. I'm getting the hang of being a teacher, though I'm probably learning more than my students are."

"You haven't changed a bit in the year since we've seen you," said Muriel.

Betsy added, "I was thinking the same thing."

"Well," John said, "we have a busy week ahead of us, don't we. Once we get to Poland, we're looking forward to having someone who speaks the language fluently to show us around."

I laughed. "I can show you around, but don't count on fluency. Polish is the most difficult language I've ever encountered. Some of my young colleagues speak it quite well, but in my case fluency is a fantasy. Still, I know enough so that we won't starve. We're not likely to have many English-speaking waitresses like in this restaurant."

Betsy said, "I'm looking forward to seeing where you live. How long will it take us to drive to Świdnica?"

"All day probably. It will be two-lane roads most of the way."

Betsy and I were long-time concert and movie-going companions. She also liked to travel, which she juggled along with a hectic work schedule as president and CEO of a large social service agency. She had taken off one week for this trip and would return to her office the day after getting home. She had met John in Amherst several years before when he came there to pick me up on our way to England for two weeks; he and I thought it a novel idea for just the two of us to take a trip.

John and I looked a lot alike. Though he was a couple of inches taller, we were both bald and had similar builds. He was more the natural athlete than I, though I was as active in sports as he was in our school days. Growing up we got along well, but because he was three years older, we were in different social circles. Though our older brother, Clair, Jr., and I were born in China where our father was a medical missionary, John was born in Cleveland while our parents were on a year's leave. I was two years old when our family returned to America in 1932 following our mother's death in China. The family soon settled in Oberlin, Ohio, where our father opened his medical practice. John and I were still young boys when he re-married. Seeing John that evening reminded me of those early years.

------◆◆◆◆◆------

In the summer of 1933, Estelle Warner, a voice student at the Oberlin Conservatory of Music, came to see my father as a patient. I was unaware of their developing relationship, but a year later they were married in the home of Estelle's parents. At twenty-two, Estelle was fifteen years younger than my father and only thirteen years older than my brother, Clair, Jr. I had turned four a month before the wedding.

The first memory I have of Estelle is when I realized I wasn't able to call her "mother." I must have tried, but apparently it didn't sound right. I remember talking about it with her in my bedroom one afternoon. No doubt I was influenced by my older brothers, who most likely had already been calling her Estelle. In any case, she accepted my decision. She has been Estelle to my older brothers and me throughout our lives.

The first of my younger siblings was my sister Jane, born on Mother's Day in 1939.

In 1941, the year Japan bombed Pearl Harbor in Hawaii, Estelle had a second child named Ralph, whom we called Ralphy. He had been born with a defective heart, but I was not aware of his condition. I came home one afternoon after school when Estelle was bottle feeding Ralphy in the living room. He was about six months old. I had just gone upstairs to my room, when I heard Estelle cry out, "Call your father! Ralphy is having difficulty breathing! Now he's turning blue! Hurry!"

What I remember next occurred several hours later. I was sitting with my brothers in the library. Our father came in and told us that Ralphy had died, and he wanted us to come upstairs to see him. He led the way as we trailed behind. When we entered my parents' bedroom, I first saw Estelle standing by the window weeping. I felt a pang of anguish because I had never seen her cry before. She was being comforted by one of my father's colleagues, a family friend. Then my brothers and I in turn approached the crib. I looked down and saw Ralphy lying there with closed eyes, his soft face pale in the early evening light, his small shoulders covered with a light blanket. I recall the moment as one more of curiosity than sadness.

Estelle's muffled sobs drew me away and I didn't know what to do next. Then our father ushered us from the room. For weeks afterwards the household was subdued, and for months Estelle would become teary if Ralphy's name was mentioned, something I avoided if at all possible. Two years later, when I was thirteen, my brother Jim was born.

Two of Estelle's characteristics stood out and endured over the years. These were her uncommon good looks and her soprano voice. In growing up I often heard people say how attractive she was, and after hearing her sing in church, they would say what a lovely voice she had. I often heard her sing at home as she accompanied herself at her Steinway piano. There's no doubt that my love of classical music has its roots in those early years, hearing songs of Schubert, Brahms and Schumann. As an adolescent, however, I was more drawn to the popular Big Band music of Harry James, Vaughn Monroe, and Artie Shaw, and the singing of Peggy Lee and Frank Sinatra.

My father, Clair Siddall, was a good-looking man, five feet ten inches tall, slender, with reddish blond hair. Because of his ski jump-nose and receding hairline, it was often said that he looked like a combination of Bob Hope and Fred Astaire. He and Estelle made a handsome couple.

In contrast to Estelle's reserve, my father was outgoing and liked to tell us about growing up a clergyman's son in a large family in Dayton, Ohio, spending summers on his uncle's farm near Findlay, working his way through medical school, and family life in China. My siblings and I learned from him the pleasure of story telling; we always had an audience at dinner time. My father's ease with people and his commitment to serving others made a strong impression on me. He knew in high school that he wanted to be a doctor; I didn't figure out my life path until I was thirty. He told a newspaper reporter at the time of his retirement that going to China as a missionary was very much like going into the Peace Corps today.

My father also had a delightful sense of humor. I remember a time as a youngster when a friend of mine came for supper. We were having meatloaf, and as my father was carving it he asked my guest, with a perfectly straight face, "Would you like a wing or a leg?"

John and I exchanged news of the family. "From letters I've received," I said, "everyone seems to be doing fine. That's always reassuring being so far away."

Turning to Muriel, Betsy asked, "How did you and John meet?"

"We were students at Oberlin. He was a returning navy veteran."

I said, "I was also a student there at the same time. John and Muriel were married while in college, and the next year the three of us were in the same economics class. It was amusing when the professor first took attendance; by the time he got to the third Siddall, he looked a bit puzzled. Also, I'll tell you a funny story in connection with their wedding."

I recounted that at the time I had a summer job as a dishwasher at the Oberlin Inn. Meals were included, and because I ate so much the female cooks called me Garbage Can. I got time off to be an usher in the wedding, which was in the early afternoon in a chapel on the college's campus. The reception afterwards was held downtown at the Inn. I rode with a friend and we parked in front of the movie theater across the street from the Inn. One of the cooks was sitting in an open window on the second floor having a cigarette, and when saw me get out of the car dressed in a tuxedo, she called out, "Hey there, Garbage Can, you sure look sharp!"

They all laughed and John said, "I hadn't thought about that in a long time."

"Would you believe," I added, "I had to wash their reception dishes after I got back to work."

John grinned and looked at his watch. "It's late. We should be getting back to the hotel."

Compared to the modest places in which I was accustomed to staying in Poland, the Ambassador Hotel, which John and Muriel had selected, was classy. It had a spacious lobby with gold trim around the heavily draped windows, a room with an oversized bed, a multi-channel television, and a large, sparkling-clean bathroom with an array of towels and toiletries. Breakfast the next morning, served buffet style and geared to the international traveler, provided what seemed like an unlimited selection of juice, cereal, eggs, sausage, waffles, pancakes, sweet rolls, yogurt, cheese, ham, tea and coffee. Staying there for two nights was a real treat.

During the night a cool front had come through, bringing intermittent rain. In the morning we took in a few sights and paused for photographs on the Charles Bridge* that spans the Vltava River running through the city center. Wandering around Prague, one of Europe's most beautiful cities, was a pleasure. While Baroque-style buildings tend to predominate, a legacy of the Hapsburg rulers in the seventeenth and eighteenth centuries, there are also outstanding examples of Gothic architecture, such as St. Vitus Cathedral, and Romanesque, Renaissance, and Art Nouveau as well. The city survived World War II unscathed because Hitler wanted it preserved for his use, but the communist regime that ruled following the war left Prague with its share of drab apartment buildings similar to what one can see in Poland and other former communist-bloc countries.

The next day, after another sumptuous breakfast, we set off in a rented German *Opel* for Poland. In spite of the many crazy drivers on the road, I felt safe with John driving. We arrived in Świdnica

---

* Named after Charles IV, who became king of Bohemia in 1346 and Holy Roman Emperor in 1355.

in the late afternoon. I had reserved rooms for my guests at the Park Hotel, which provided attractive and comfortable lodging. After supper in the hotel dining room, I invited my guests to see my apartment.

Looking around, John said, "This is a bit more modest than what you're used to living in, but you probably didn't expect it to be much different, did you?"

"Not really. It's fine. I don't need more than what I have here."

Muriel and Betsy exchanged glances, as if to say, *I don't think I would choose to live here for two years.*

The next morning we walked into town to see the Peace Church (*Kościoł Pokoju,* pronounced something like Kost-you-po-Koy-you), the one Paula had asked about at the museum in Wrocław. On the way we passed through the *Rynek,* where I pointed out my bank on the corner of the same street leading to the Piast Hotel, a centuries-old fountain in the square itself, and the colorfully restored façades of the town houses facing the square. The sun, already high overhead, cast a soothing warmth over the city. The Peace Church was another five-minute walk, situated within an extensive walled area. The church's unusual architecture immediately caught my guests' attention.

The church was built in the mid seventeenth century and takes its name from the Treaty of Westphalia in 1648 that ended the Thirty Years War. In the preceding century, the Protestant Reformation had come to this region, but by war's end, Catholicism had returned and the Protestant clergy were forced to leave the city. The treaty also meant that Świdnica and the surrounding area known as Lower Silesia, were now annexed by the Austrian Empire. In order for the Protestants to have a place of worship, special permission had to be granted by the Catholic Hapsburg Emperor. Permission came in 1652 and the church's cornerstone was laid in 1656. There were strict conditions, however. The church had to be built outside the city, it could not be constructed of brick or stone, it could not have a bell tower, and it had to be completed within one year.

What we were seeing from the outside was a large edifice in the form of a Greek cross constructed of exposed, dark, heavy wooden beams filled in between with straw, sticks and clay covered with white stucco. The result was reminiscent of the Elizabethan Tudor style of architecture. It is the largest timber-built religious building in Europe. Two similar churches were built in the region, but only one of them survives. The richly decorated interior included Biblical scenes painted on the ceiling and two tiers of dark-wood galleries. Dominating one end of the sanctuary was a huge Baroque-style altar.

Pointing to the rows of pews and the galleries, I said, "Can you believe that this church could seat over 3,000 people? But now, except for the concerts that are often held here, only about fifty people worship here on a Sunday morning."

Muriel asked, "Do you attend services?"

"Yes, occasionally. I understand a little bit, and I've written down the Lord's Prayer in Polish that I copied from the hymnbook. I don't like singing their hymns much. To my ear many of them seem almost tuneless. Also, I find it a bit odd that they sit down for hymns and stand for prayers."

Betsy wondered if I sang in the choir. "There is no choir. One reason, I'm sure, is the small congregation. Also, my impression is that there is less interest in choral singing here in Poland than in Germany, for example. I don't know if the Catholic churches have choirs that sing regularly or not."

John asked, "Why all the scaffolding?"

"Much of the gallery space is unsound, and overall there's a lot that needs repair. The work will take years. A good deal of the money for restoration comes from Germany. It's amazing that, even though it's built of wood, the church has survived for over 300 years. Officially this congregation belongs to the Evangelical-Augsburg Parish. I've been told that many of the frequent visitors are German tourists."

In reply to Betsy's inquiry about the large ornate organ, I pointed and said, "See those two angels? They used to move when the organ was played, but no longer. Because the organ eventually required frequent repair, they built a smaller one a hundred years later. If you turn around, you can see it high above the altar. Both are in working order now and are also sometimes played during chamber music concerts."

We looked around further and then I suggested that we listen to the recording in English available to visitors; there were also versions in Polish and German. I had heard it before, and because it was difficult to understand, I mentioned that I was thinking of getting permission from the pastor to make a new recording.* Glancing at my watch I added, "It's getting close to lunch time. I know a scenic place in the country."

I had in mind Książ, a castle about a twenty-minute drive from Świdnica. I had been there earlier that spring with my physician friend, Wioletta. The car park was some distance from the castle, almost a quarter of a mile, which meant a leisurely walk through a stand of large, old trees. From several vantage points we could see the castle up ahead perched on a rocky cliff overlooking a river and wooded ravine. It was a magnificent setting. Once up close, we could see from the variation in architecture that the castle had been added onto over a period of several centuries. It now had over 400 rooms.

After a self-guided tour we decided to have lunch in one the castle's cafés. "I'll treat you," I said, "in honor of your first visit to Poland."

We returned to Świdnica by mid-afternoon and at my suggestion took the bus to Wrocław, which I mentioned was the former German city of Breslau. "Driving takes less time, but this way we don't have to worry about traffic and finding a place to park. Be prepared to be jostled when getting on the bus. People don't line up here. Shoving and pushing are normal behavior."

As we strolled around Wrocław's central square under the warm late-afternoon sun, Betsy said, "This is an impressive scene."

"Yes, it is," I replied. "Besides Kraków, where we are going tomorrow, I think the *Rynek*, where we are standing, is one of the most attractive in Poland. And one of the largest. Look around

---

* In September I did speak to the pastor, who was pleased to have a new recording made. I wrote a script using the original tape and a brochure, plus additional information I gathered as a result of a chance meeting at the church with an art history graduate student from the University of Wrocław who was writing her thesis on the church. I then arranged to make a cassette recording in a professional studio. In 2001 the church was selected by UNESCO to be a World Heritage Site. English-speaking visitors to the Peace Church can still hear my voice today.

and see how beautifully they've restored the buildings facing this huge market place. You can see by all the people walking around how popular it is. Let's wander a bit longer and look for a table in one of the outdoor cafés where we can have a drink and dinner."

◆━◆✕◆━◆

The next day, on the way to Kraków, we stopped at the Auschwitz concentration camp. In 1940, the Nazis selected the small, isolated Polish village of Oświęcim, where there were abandoned army barracks, as the location for the camp and re-named it Auschwitz. It soon became, along with nearby Birkenau, a vast extermination center. Compared to Majdanek, which I had visited the previous summer, Auschwitz was far more extensive and claimed far more lives. In spite of its grimness, the presence of so many tourists diluted for me a sense of despair like I had felt at Majdanek. Nevertheless, our two-hour visit to this gruesome place, where unspeakable crimes had been committed, left us subdued as we drove away.

The Pollera Hotel in Kraków was the most charming I encountered anywhere in Poland. It was on Spitalna Street, not far from the *Rynek* and close to the opera house. As we entered the small lobby, to the right was the reception desk and straight ahead was a wide stairway. At the first landing, where the stairs separate to the right and left, was a large, beautifully illuminated stained glass panel. It was just one of the hotel's unique features. We stayed here for our two nights in Kraków, which is, in my opinion, Poland's most interesting and architecturally appealing city. Fortunately, it was not seriously damaged in World War II. The spacious *Rynek*, in the middle of which stands the centuries-old covered market called the *Sukiennice*, has been the center of city life since medieval times.

It was raining when we arrived in the afternoon. After settling in at the hotel, we walked to the *Rynek* and had dinner at the Hawelka Restaurant.

"This is a really neat spot," John said.

"I thought you'd like it. I found this place last winter when I spent three days here during semester break. This was a pleasant shelter from the cold and snow, plus the good food and old-world atmosphere."

Grateful for the return of the sun the next morning, we headed on foot to the city's famous Wawel Castle and Cathedral. For centuries, until the seat of government moved to Warsaw in 1596, Polish rulers had their headquarters in the castle and worshipped in the cathedral, where many of them are buried. Wawel Cathedral has the same stature in Poland as Westminster Abbey does in London or St. Peter's Basilica in Rome. It was here that Karol Wojtyła served as the Archbishop of Kraków before being elected Pope John Paul II. He once referred to the Cathedral as "the sanctuary of the nation."

On our return to the city center we had lunch in a Ukrainian restaurant located downstairs under decoratively painted arched ceilings. Each of us had a bowl of hearty soup, a green salad, thick slices of bread, a pastry for dessert, and tea, all of which cost less than fifteen dollars for the four of us.

Back at the *Rynek*, we visited St. Mary's Church, another of Kraków's most well known sights. The church dates from the fourteenth century and is said to be one of the best examples of Gothic architecture in Poland. It was rather gloomy inside from soot of burning candles over the centuries, but the restoration going on behind scaffolding had already revealed brightly colored painting on the ceiling. The altar, which was carved by Veit Stoss from Nuremburg in the fifteenth century, is considered an outstanding example of Late Gothic art.

There is also a centuries-old legend connected with the church. It says that in the thirteenth century, when Kraków was about to be attacked by the Tartars, a watchman high in one of the church towers sounded the alarm on his trumpet when he saw the enemy approaching. But an arrow shot through his throat abruptly ended his playing. Today the sound of a trumpeter is heard on the hour from the tower, and the melancholy tune he plays suddenly ends at the moment when the watchman was supposedly hit. This observance is broadcast daily on the radio throughout the country.

To end the day I took my guests to the Princess Czartoryski Museum to see one of its most prized possessions, Leonardo da Vinci's *Lady With an Ermine.* This painting is one of only three female portraits by Leonardo, executed in 1490-91, nearly fifteen years before the *Mona Lisa.* The sitter is the beautiful Cecilia Gallerani, a young Milanese noblewoman and the mistress of Leonardo's patron. She looks to the viewer's right, her fine features framed by her closely drawn brown hair that blends with the almost-black background and the dark color of her dress. Around her exposed neck is a long string of beads. In her lap her slender hand holds an ermine, whose white fur tells us that the season is winter.

The Czartoryski family bought the painting in Italy in 1798. The museum is fortunate to still have possession of it. To protect it from a Russian invasion in the early 1800s, the painting went from one secret hiding place to another in Paris and Dresden. During World War II the painting was stolen, along with hundreds of other art works, by the Nazis and taken to Berlin. It was eventually returned in 1946. During the war, more than 800 objects were lost from the Czartoryski collection alone, and thousands more are still missing from museums throughout Poland.

On the recommendation of a passerby, we had dinner at the *Staropolska Restauracja* (Old Poland Restaurant), situated on a side street off the *Rynek*. It was a lively place where we seemed to be the only non-Poles. The menu reflected the rich variety of Polish cuisine that has been influenced by such countries as Russia, Lithuania, Ukraine, Bohemia (what is now the Czech Republic), Germany, Austria, Italy, and even Turkey. Jewish culture has also made a significant contribution over the centuries. Poles are fond of meat, especially beef and pork. Polish sausage, *kiełbasa*, is known far beyond the country's borders. Bread and soup are considered by many to be essential to a meal.

I ordered for the four of us. After we were served I said, "Here we don't say *Bon appetite!* Instead, we say *Smacznego!*"

We started out with *barszcz czerwony* (red beet soup) with a dollop of sour cream. Our four main courses were breaded veal cutlet, poached trout, roast chicken, and *gałąbki* (cabbage leaves stuffed with chopped meat and rice; it is often referred to in

America as galumpki). In addition we had bread, green salad, and shared a plate of *pierogi*, small dumplings, similar to ravioli, stuffed with cheese or meat, which I especially liked and often had as a meal when I ate out on my own. For dessert we had an assortment of fresh fruit and pastries. It was a grand Polish meal.

I said, "You know, we've been fortunate on this trip to have found such good restaurants. And relatively inexpensive, too. The bill this evening is only about thirty dollars for all this delicious food."

Our last day and two nights were spent in Zakopane (pronounced zah-ko-Pah-ney), situated south of Kraków in the Tatra Mountains on the border between Poland and Slovakia. Popular for its winter skiing and summer hiking, the town has a history as an artist colony. Over the years it has also become a magnet for tourists and souvenir shops.

After a quick look around the town's center, we took the funicular railway up to a vantage point overlooking the town and to an easy trail along the foothills that would eventually lead us back to town. Again we were blessed with a warm, sunny day. The views of the valley below and the mountain peaks beyond were spectacular. More than an hour later, as we were beginning our descent, we came to a small settlement of wooden houses next to a field where farmers were harvesting wheat. While the men sliced through the slender stalks with scythes, the women raked them into golden sheaves and piled them in large stacks. It was an idyllic scene, accentuated by the mountains rising up beyond the field and reaching high into the brilliant blue sky. With permission I took several photographs. My favorite is of two sturdy, smiling women standing in front of a hay stack holding their long wooden rakes, clearly proud of their day's labor.

At supper that evening, for a moment I felt sad that I would be saying goodbye to my guests in the morning. While they would be driving back to Prague, I would be on my way to Świdnica. My moment of melancholy quickly passed as I reflected on what a delightful week it had been.

"So, tell me," I asked, taking another sip of beer, "what do you think of my adopted country?"

CHAPTER TWELVE
Moscow and St. Petersburg: August 1998

The plans for my trip to Russia quickly fell into place once I realized that I had to go to the Russian travel agency, Intourist, in Warsaw. One of their English-speaking Polish staff helped me with plane and train tickets, hotel reservations, and a visa for eighty-five dollars cash, almost double what it would have cost if I had applied to the Russian Embassy myself, but less paperwork and much quicker. It would be a ten-day visit, flying to Moscow from Warsaw on August 18, and returning from St. Petersburg on August 27. Since getting to Warsaw from Świdnica took at least seven hours, I would have to stay over the night before my departure and the night after my return. I had already been to Warsaw several times for Peace Corps business, such as getting my mid-term medical and dental checkup, and I always stayed at the Sokrates Hotel, a very un-fancy place owned by the University of Warsaw, not far from the Peace Corps Headquarters. A night's stay cost thirty dollars, including breakfast.

Until my departure I had three weeks to learn the Russian alphabet and some phrases. Russian is a Slavic language similar to Polish, and my students who were studying Russian told me it was not difficult to learn. I also had time to visit friends whom I hadn't seen since the end of the semester. When I called Urszula she said, "Please come for *kolacja* (supper) tomorrow." She and her family, looking robust and tan, had just returned from a vacation in northeastern Poland, a popular area in the summer because of its many lakes. She was delighted to hear of my plans. "I am so pleased that you will be visiting my ancestral home. I am sorry that you won't see the countryside. After our meal I can help you with the Russian phrases you are working on."

A few days later I had a message on my cell phone to call my physician friend, Wioletta. We agreed to meet the next morning. She looked tired and a bit pale. It turned out she had been up most of the night with three deliveries. Yet she was eager to hear about the visitors I had from America. Then I surprised her with my latest travel plans. She said with a slight scowl, "You're going to Russia? Really? Are you sure it's safe?"

The following week Sylwia and I got together again at the Piast Hotel. "You look different somehow," I said.

"Oh, I had my hair cut. Do you like it?"

"It's very becoming."

"What does that mean?"

"Ah, there's a new word for you. It means you look nice."

Sylwia was patient when I tried out my Polish. "It takes most foreigners a long time to learn this language," she said. "You will just have to stay here an extra year or two. But first you must get to Russia and back."

◆→◆×◆←◆

It was also during this time that I met my new tutor. I was downtown on a warm, sunny Saturday afternoon, joining the crowds celebrating Świdnica Day, a fair that was held a couple times a year on the *Rynek,* with food stalls, balloons, games, rides, and loud music. The restaurants with outside seating were jam-packed, mostly with patrons drinking beer. I had brought my camera and was looking for interesting faces to photograph. My best shots were mostly of children, young ones dressed in bonnets and older ones eating ice cream.

By chance I met up with Ashraf, the conductor. He asked if I had found a tutor yet. "You haven't? I know someone you might consider. In fact she's here in this crowd somewhere with friends." He took a moment to look around. "There she is."

I recognized Anita Odachowska at once. "Hello," she said smiling. "We know each other already, don't we." Anita had taught Polish part-time at my school, but we had very little contact. "Ashraf says you are looking for a tutor."

"I am. Would you be interested?"

"Yes. I could be available for an hour or two a week. But we should get more acquainted first, since we never really did at school. Let's find a place to have a drink."

We found an empty table in one of the outdoor cafés and each ordered a beer. She said, "I know one of your students, Sylwia Dąbrowska."

"Really? How?"

"She's working part-time at my newspaper as a reporter. Very nice person and does excellent work. We've become quite friendly."

"Well, that's a coincidence. She's told me a little about her job. She enjoys it very much."

Anita and I were able to meet twice before my trip. She lived with her partner, Artur, in a small, first floor apartment; they were planning to be married in the fall. Short, slender and attractive, I guessed she was in her twenties. She had been a student at the school where I taught and was a graduate of the University of Wrocław. She was now working full-time for a local newspaper as a reporter and editor. It was soon evident that Anita was not only an excellent teacher, but fluent in English. In addition to practicing conversation, I asked Anita to help me write in Polish something I had written in English. At the end of our second meeting she said, "I'll look forward to hearing about your trip to Russia. That will be something interesting for you to write about."

<hr />

My flight on July 18, 1998, from Warsaw to Moscow on the Polish airline LOT, took less than two hours. From the air there was not much to see but green landscape stretching for hundreds of miles. I was excited about this trip, though I couldn't completely ignore the concerns expressed by my students and others. I also knew something of the violence that Russia had periodically visited upon Poland.

One event that most Poles can tell you about is how the Russian army allowed the Nazis to destroy the city of Warsaw. At the time of the Warsaw Uprising in 1944, the force of civilians and the underground army believed that even though they had only light weapons, they could defeat the occupying German army because they outnumbered them. They were also convinced that help would come from United States and British airlifts, and from the Russian army, which by this time had advanced as far as the outskirts of Warsaw and were encamped on the other side of the Wisła River. Not only did the Russians not intervene, but they prevented the Allies from flying over its air space or landing at its airbases. As a result Allied planes, primarily British, flew dangerous missions from Italy to make airdrops. The Nazis finally put down the uprising after sixty-three days. A furious Hitler ordered the rest of Warsaw's inner city systematically dynamited. With such widespread devastation and thousands of its citizens dead, Warsaw now posed no threat to the Russians who would soon occupy the city.*

After the war, as Russia imposed its communist regime on Poland, it was ruthless in its treatment of political dissidents, many of whom were shipped off to labor camps in Siberia. It is ironic that while the Allies liberated Western Europe in 1945, Eastern Europe was subjected to another fifty years of oppression.

Another tragic period in Poland's history that involved Russia goes back to the eighteenth century. It began in Prussia, which had long coveted Poland's access to the Baltic Sea. In 1772 Frederick the Great of Prussia convinced Austria and Russia to support him in conspiring against Poland. As a result, thirty percent of Poland was divided up between the three countries. This was called the First Partition.

The Second Partition came in 1793, following the failed resistance against Russia led by Tadeusz Kościuszko, the former American Revolutionary War hero and advisor to General George Washington. This led to additional territory being appropriated and the dissolution of Poland's 1791 constitution, which had particularly galled Catherine the Great of Russia because it went contrary to her autocratic style of rule.

Kościuszko led another unsuccessful rebellion against Russia, resulting in the Third Partition in 1795. This time all Polish lands were swallowed up by Prussia, Austria and Russia; Poland literally disappeared from the map for the next 123 years. How the Polish culture survived during these years is an amazing story. It was not

---

* Norman Davies has written a detailed account of the uprising in *Rising '44: The Battle for Warsaw*, 2004. See Bibliography.

until the end of World War I in 1918 that Poland's sovereignty was restored. However, this lasted only until 1939, when Germany's invasion of Poland began World War II.

The Polish people had every reason to be wary of the Russians. However, for now, I focused instead on the Russia that was home to great literature, music, and a sense of the romantic.

------◆━◆━◆━◆━◆------

Upon landing I was surprised that Moscow's new-looking airport appeared small for a city of nine million people. I had no difficulty getting through customs, where I found that my hotel voucher was as essential as my passport and visa. I exchanged some American dollars for rubles and then looked for the correct bus directly outside the airport's entrance. I wasn't sure which one to take, but a friendly security guard pointed it out. Twenty minutes later the bus stopped at the end of a metro line. It was a thirty-minute ride to the city center. I wanted to get near Red Square and my hotel, but I didn't know at which station to get off. I decided to ask for help from the couple next to me. I showed them the name of my hotel with its address and then pointed to the metro map above our seats. They thought a moment and shook their heads. They asked the person next to them, but he didn't know either. Then two people across the aisle got interested and consulted with my seatmates. Finally, after much lively chatter and gesticulation, they pointed to the stop on the map. The couple then indicated that they would stay with me until I got off. This friendly gesture was the first of many I encountered.

The subway system in Moscow, whose construction began in the 1930s, is impressive. It is fast and efficient, and is distinctive for the art and architecture in its stations. Many are constructed of marble and decorated in bas-reliefs, frescoes, and mosaics. Each station has a different theme, many being political. I saw a few stations that even had glittering chandeliers. Some of the first stations were built far underground so they could serve as air raid shelters. It's a long ride down on some of the escalators, each watched over by uniformed women.

From the metro stop it was a ten-minute walk to Red Square. I noticed right away how clean the streets were. I even saw a woman street sweeper pick up a cigarette butt. As I entered the square through the Resurrection Gate, immediately to my left was the colorful Chapel of the Iverian Virgin, built in the eighteenth century to contain a famous icon. Painted in red and gold with two square-looking towers topped by golden finials, it was my introduction to Moscow's exotic architecture.

St. Basil's Cathedral, the famous sixteenth century church with multi-colored, onion-shaped domes, was at the far end of the immense square. The red brick wall of the Kremlin was to the right. To the left was the ornate GUM State Department Store (Gosudarstvenny Universalny Magazin). It was a cavernous building, whose brightly lit interior I discovered the next day, had over 1,000 stores on several floors where one could buy goods from all over the world. Several open elevated walkways provided great views. Until recent decades the store was open only to foreign shoppers.

I continued through the square towards St. Basil's and eventually reached the Russian Hotel off to the left, another ten-minute walk. The friendly English-speaking receptionist, dressed in a tailored, light-brown suit, took my hotel voucher and passport, and checked me in. The hotel was a huge place, quite new, with over 3,000 rooms. I had a comfortable room with a high ceiling and polished dark woodwork on the eighth floor. Down the hall, sitting behind a counter, was the floor attendant, an unsmiling woman in a white-collared, dark blue dress with whom I left my key when I went out. Near her station was a small area with a few tables and chairs where you could get drinks and snacks. Breakfast was in the spacious, light-filled restaurant on the twenty-first floor with a terrific view of Red Square and three golden-domed cathedrals inside the Kremlin wall. Figuring out the circuitous way to the restaurant took several tries and required a change of elevators.

One morning at breakfast I met a young Italian couple who were visiting art students. "What brings you to Moscow?" I asked.

"We are studying Russian church architecture. Have you been to the churches inside the Kremlin wall?"

"Not yet, but I can see them from here," pointing out the window. "I plan to visit them later this morning."

"You don't want to miss them."

Every day several men in dark suits and white shirts stood at the restaurant entryway. While the hostess who greeted guests had something to do, the function of these men was not apparent. I saw this phenomenon repeated many times at restaurants and stores. The only thing I could think of was the mafia that my students had warned me about, but these men didn't appear all that sinister. I assumed they provided security.

Founded in the twelfth century, Moscow had a population of over 100,000 by the 1500s, making it one of the world's largest cities. The Kremlin, which means stronghold, was first built of wood around 1150; a white stone structure replaced it two hundred years later. A new period of construction took place from 1475 to 1516 and produced many of the buildings still in use today. I was disappointed that I wasn't able to see the rooms in the Kremlin from which Ivan the Terrible and Stalin ruled the country.

The Pushkin Fine Arts Museum was just around the corner from the Kremlin. It is especially noted for its fine collection of Impressionist and Post-Impressionist paintings. Many of the museum's older European paintings were appropriated from private collections after the revolution of 1917. As I left the museum through one of its side doors, I passed one of the guards outside having a cigarette break. He was a good subject for a photograph. I got out my camera and approached him with a friendly smile. He turned out to be a willing subject. The photograph shows him looking very official in his gray uniform with three silver bars on its epaulettes, a silver emblem on his gray cap, and a museum badge pinned over his left breast pocket. He's perhaps in his thirties. I detect a hint of humor in his expression as he clenches a cigarette holder firmly in his mouth.

On the way back to the Russian Hotel, I took several more close-up photographs. One shows two smiling military officers in crisp uniforms, who surprised me by interrupting their hurried strides long enough to be photographed. Another was of a young boy sitting on a park bench with his parents. Dressed in a multicolored jacket and cap, he is eating ice cream from a paper cup. Further along in the park I came upon a mother and her three daughters feeding birds. In a wordless conversation, the mother and I had the girls pose. In my photograph, the youngest looks about five and wears a large white bow in her hair, a common sight in Russia. Her sisters are about ten and twelve. From their expressions they are delighted to have their photograph taken.

Since it was August, neither the Bolshoi Ballet nor a symphony orchestra performed. I wondered what I could find for entertainment. The first evening I was having a drink in the crowded hotel lounge, which was nothing more than a bar and several tables at one end of the immense lobby. Sitting at one table were two solidly built prostitutes, looking more like nightclub bouncers than someone to have sex with. Ignoring their glances, I chatted with the bartender, a rotund, bearded man with flushed cheeks. He spoke a bit of English and suggested I try the operetta theater, and wrote down the address.

The next morning I went to see about a ticket. Several people were waiting in line at the box office. I asked if anyone spoke English. A stylishly attired, middle-aged woman said she did.

"Could you tell me about this evening's performance?" I asked.

"This is a popular Russian operetta. The male lead is famous in our country. Everyone knows the music. I think you will enjoy it."

The audience that evening had dressed up for the occasion and I could feel their excitement. When the famous singer first appeared on stage, he had a long wait before the cheering and applauding subsided. The response was no less enthusiastic for the female lead. Almost every aria and dance routine brought prolonged applause, and the dialogue produced unending laughter. Everyone was clearly having a good time. I was impressed with the elaborate, colorful set design that included huge swaths of billowy, bright-red fabric that hung as a backdrop. The ticket-line lady had given me good advice. It was a delightful evening.

The next day I took a twenty-dollar three-hour bus tour of the city. Before getting on the bus at Red Square, I met an American couple traveling with their college-student daughter, and asked if one of them would take my photograph. It shows me squinting a bit in the strong light, standing in the middle of the square with the cream colored GUM Department Store in the background.

Near the university I noticed that one of the large, wedding-cake-style buildings was similar to the Palace of Culture in downtown Warsaw. Many of these post-war buildings struck me as unimaginative compared to the older, eastern styles of architecture that I found much more appealing. It was during this stop that I saw a woman offering to sell a handmade doll. I was impressed with the fine needlework and gladly paid the modest price of ten dollars. It would be a gift for my granddaughter.

There were far fewer restaurants than I expected for such a large city, and the ones where I ate must have been too expensive for the average citizen. In one place recommended by my guidebook, the menu on my table was exchanged for one in English with higher prices, so I decided to leave. I wondered what the bill would have been if I had stayed, because at a more modest place nearby I had to pay nearly twenty dollars for just soup, salad, and tea. That evening I ate at a restaurant where I had a brief conversation with the young hostess who had recently studied for a year in Houston. She was the only Russian I met who had been to the States.

On the last afternoon I took the metro to the outskirts to see what Moscow looked like away from the city center. Among drab high-rise apartment buildings and littered streets, people were busily and noisily doing business in outdoor markets and enjoying beer in sidewalk cafés. Life seemed more real here away from the tourist sites.

———◆◈◆———

My train to St. Petersburg left just before midnight. I had bought a ticket for a first class sleeper car for the eight-hour trip. Railroad cars in Russia are larger than in Europe and run on wider gauge track, a decision by one of the tsars who wanted the railway system built on a grander scale than in Europe. My first class accommodation was close to luxury and not expensive. It had the advantage over second class of having just two bunks, both on floor level. A female conductor showed me to my compartment, where to my surprise a woman occupied one of the beds. She was under the covers but still awake.

"Do you speak English?" I asked.

"Of course," she answered in a heavy accent.

Our conversation was brief because she soon fell asleep as I was getting settled. The compartment had dark wood paneling, and on the table between the beds were a small bouquet of flowers, two bottles of water, and two boxes containing our breakfast. After getting my things arranged, I went down the corridor to the washroom. The train departed promptly at 11:56 P.M. I crawled into bed, turned out the light, and waited for sleep. It took a while because the air conditioning wasn't working well and I wasn't used to a rocking bed. I finally drifted off.

By the time I awoke, my companion, who looked to be in her fifties, was already up and having breakfast. She stepped into the corridor while I quickly dressed. After washing up and shaving in the washroom, I joined her in our morning repast. She looked tired, but pendant earrings and a bright green scarf brought color to her face. She wasn't very talkative, but did tell me she was a lawyer in St. Petersburg. I commented that the night before we had hardly said hello before she fell asleep.

She smiled slightly and said, "I had been visiting my beloved in Moscow for two days. I see him only twice a year."

At 8:30 the train pulled into St. Petersburg station. My compartment mate looked at her watch, picked up her suitcase, said goodbye, and swiftly disappeared down the corridor. She never did tell me her name.

◆━◆━✕━◆━◆

St. Petersburg was very different from Moscow. The city didn't exist until the eighteenth century. Peter the Great founded it in 1703 on land bordering the Gulf of Finland, previously belonging to Sweden. With the exception of several cathedrals, the city didn't have the exotic architectural flavor that Moscow did. Because of its canals, St. Petersburg is sometimes called the "Venice of the North." However, the unique atmosphere one finds in Venice, where canals are its thoroughfares and where it is easy to get lost wandering its narrow, winding streets, was not evident in St. Petersburg. Yet, beauty could be found in the many bridges that crossed the canals.

My hotel was seedy by comparison to my lodgings in Moscow. In my small room on the sixth floor, the bathroom had a shower, but no stall, so practically everything got wet. I ended up just using the waist-high faucet that intermittently discharged smelly brown water. The slow, creaky elevator could be used only for going up. The hotel wasn't conveniently located near the city center, so I had to figure out how to negotiate the bus system.

Breakfast was limited to bread and butter, slices of meat or cheese, sometimes a small glass of diluted juice, maybe a hardboiled egg or a section of tomato. The tea or coffee never got beyond tepid. One morning they served what looked like a plate of lentils covered with brown gravy with pieces of liver floating on top. It tasted worse than it looked. I managed two bites.

Eating in restaurants provided more felicitous moments. As in Moscow, I found few inexpensive places that served decent food. I decided to have lunch early one afternoon in a restaurant below ground level where they seemed to be short of light bulbs. There were few other patrons. My waitress was an attractive young woman who, when not attending to me, chatted with the other two waitresses. None of them spoke English, but after my meal I persuaded them to pose together for a photograph. After I returned to Świdnica and showed my photographs to Urszula, she said, "I told you that you would see pretty girls in Russia. Have you thought of sending them copies?" I liked the idea, and since I had the restaurant's address Urszula wrote a note for me in Russian and addressed an envelope. I never received a reply.

On the way back to my hotel, I visited one of St. Petersburg's most elaborately decorated churches. As I stood gazing around under its vast dome, a guard motioned for me to take my hands out of my pockets. I was surprised but immediately complied. I assume it meant a sign of disrespect. The incident reminded me of the time during my first week of teaching, when I asked a class to tell me some of the customs in Poland I should know about. A girl responded, "It's not polite for a man to speak to a woman with his hands in his pockets." I then realized I was standing in front of the class with one hand in my pocket.

━━━━◆◆◆◆◆━━━━

Wandering through the Hermitage was an amazing experience. It holds such a gigantic collection of art in its 300 rooms that to see it all would take months. The paintings alone number more than 16,000. The museum complex is made up of five buildings, the largest of which is the ornate Winter Palace, residence of the Russian tsars until the revolution of 1917. Catherine the Great commissioned its construction on the banks of the Neva River beginning in 1754; it took eight years to complete. In 1764 she acquired a large collection of Western European paintings from a wealthy German merchant (Catherine herself was a German princess) and founded a museum for the royal court; she built the Small Hermitage just to house this collection. Over time the museum expanded into other buildings as other collections were acquired. Later renamed The Imperial Museum of the New Hermitage, it opened to the public in 1852. The Winter Palace was seriously damaged during World War II. The story of efforts to dismantle and protect the museum's immense collection is one of personal heroism and sacrifice. Today, no trace of the war years is visible. The main staircase inside the entrance is itself almost worth the price of admission. Built of white marble, the wide stairs ascend from two sides. Along the wall above where the stairs join are slender, light-blue columns, on top of which are gold flowery capitals that lend their support to a richly decorated ceiling. This opulent entryway is a fitting introduction to the fabulous art that awaits the visitor.

Peter the Great, who ruled before Catherine, built a summer palace twenty miles from St. Petersburg. I went there by a hydrofoil that speeds down the Neva River. The palace rivals Versailles in size, splendor and beauty. The mansion that Peter originally built is not the grand palace that you see today. It was during the reign of his daughter, Elizabeth Petrovna, that Peterhof (the name means Peter's court in Dutch) as we know it was constructed between 1747 and 1756.

The palace's ornate design and sumptuous use of gold leaf in its decoration, especially in the grand staircase and ballroom, were breathtaking. The palace's vast gardens and more than 100 fountains were also marvelous creations. One fountain that especially caught my attention was more playful than artful. From a variety of openings flush with the ground, water intermittently shot up, invariably soaking an unsuspecting child, or sometimes an adult, trying to guess when it was safe to walk across. As I strolled through this beautiful park, I realized that for a country with so many economic problems, Russia certainly had invested heavily in maintaining its major sights.

Though not as famous or as extensive as the Hermitage, the Russian Museum is home to a vast collection of artifacts that illustrates the history of Russian painting, sculpture, and the decorative and folk arts, spanning almost a thousand years. Among my favorite galleries was the museum's collection of religious icons that have long been a tradition in the Eastern Orthodox Church. The museum has over 6,000 of these icons. I was drawn to the beautiful images for the richness of color and the haunting faces.

Though I missed a ballet performance in Moscow, I saw *Swan Lake* in the beautiful Hermitage Theater. Since photography without flash was permitted, I got several good pictures with the aid of a zoom lens. The next evening, in a much smaller theater, I went to a highly entertaining performance of Russian folk dancing and singing. I was amazed by the colorful costumes, powerful voices, and athletic dancing. During intermission I talked with a few of the English-speaking tourists. I recall a gray-haired, good-looking American businessman from St. Louis. "Yes, sir, this is the first trip abroad for me and the missus. We're with a small group. A highlight tour, you know. London, Paris, Rome, Moscow, now here. Great time. But I got some questions about this country. I keep hearing their economy is a bit shaky right now. If you ask me, these Russians could use a bit of our American know-how. Am I enjoying the show this evening? You bet! It's terrific! Aren't those female dancers gorgeous, though?"

———◆◆▶◀◆———

When I think back on my trip, I keep seeing the street artist I encountered outside the Winter Palace. She and other artists were sketching passersby for a modest fee. I stood watching her as she deftly brought to life her subject's features. After she had completed her work, she saw me, smiled, and motioned for me to take a seat. I politely declined, but then gestured that I would like to take her photograph. With a little coaxing, she agreed. In the picture she is wearing an open pink cotton jacket, under which is a wool sweater zipped up half way, and under that a knitted, light brown pullover. She looks to be in her fifties. Her deep blue eyes, partially shaded by the beige broad-brimmed hat that is tied under her chin, look directly at the viewer. She is unsmiling, but her gaze and round face suggest contentment. I wonder what her life is like. Does she support herself as an artist on the street? I wish I knew who she was, so I could tell her that her dignified image has been seen by many admirers in a photography exhibit half way around the world.

———◆◆▶◀◆———

When I returned to Świdnica, I found a note from my colleague, Grażyna, inviting me for a visit. I hadn't seen her all summer. She lived in a quiet residential neighborhood of single homes, a fifteen-minute walk from my school. Her gray, stucco-sided house had a small front yard with lawn and flowers enclosed by a low brick wall, similar to the other houses on the street. I rang the doorbell.

Grażyna soon opened the door. "Please come in," she said, smiling.

We shook hands. "I was delighted to get your note," I said. "It's been a while since we've seen each other."

"Yes, it has been. I want to hear about how you spent your summer."

I followed Grażyna to the living room, which looked out on the back yard. A tree I couldn't identify provided shade for a small patio. "Please have a seat on the couch. I've made tea to go with some Polish pastries. I remember that you especially like *pączki*."

I laughed. "Yes I do. They're my favorite." Looking around, I said, "Your house is very nice."

"Thank you. I'm sorry you won't be able to meet the rest of my family. They aren't here at the moment." She sat down opposite me. On the coffee table between us was a teapot and a plate of pastries.

As Grażyna poured the tea, she said, "So, tell me about your summer."

I told her about the English camp, visitors from the States, and my ten days in Russia. "I just returned a couple of days ago."

With surprise in her voice, Grażyna said, "You went to Russia? What was it like? Was it safe?"

"Oh yes. I found the people very friendly. Unfortunately, I could speak with only a few people who knew some English. No one understood my Polish. I especially enjoyed visiting the art museums."

"And you went by yourself?"

"Yes. It worked out fine. I had a great time."

"Well, you're quite adventuresome."

"I took a lot of photographs. I'll bring them to the teachers' room after I get the film developed."

"I'll look forward to that." She paused as she poured more tea. "I also wanted to tell you about your second year. Instead of being the only teacher of grammar for third-year students, you will have several classes from the second and third years and concentrate on speaking and writing. The other English instructors and I will teach the grammar."

It had been exactly a year since we had first met in my apartment, and I recalled the anxiety of not feeling prepared. Her message this year was good news.

"That sounds fine with me." I felt as though a weight had been lifted.

"School begins next Monday," Grażyna reminded me. "Let me know how things go."

CHAPTER THIRTEEN

Świdnica, Poland: September 1998 to January 1999

A golden afternoon light filled my classroom. Standing by the large bank of windows, I could see that the leaves of the neighborhood trees were fringed in yellows and browns. Autumn was on its way, yet there was still time to enjoy September's warmth. I was taking a brief pause between classes. I felt relaxed—it had been a good day and a good beginning to the first semester.

It was soon apparent that my second year of teaching would be less difficult than the first. As Grażyna had told me just a few days before classes began, I would share the load with my colleagues who would teach the grammar, while I focused on speaking and writing. The new arrangement gave me more freedom in class. It was a great relief.

While the number of students assigned to me almost doubled in the second year, from 110 third year students to 210 second and third year students, the total teaching hours remained the same because I saw some of my classes just once a week. Mercifully, my classes were divided in half, so that I didn't have more than sixteen students at one time. Though I was essentially free to do what I wanted, I tried to coordinate my lessons to reinforce the grammar my students were working on in their classes with Grażyna, Krystyna, and the new teacher, Ania.

After spending the first week getting acquainted and having the students write brief accounts of how they spent the summer, I began a review of verb forms and adjectives by introducing an exercise that turned out to be popular.

"All right class, this morning we're going to write a fairy tale together." A ripple of excitement ran through the room. "As you can see, I've written the main characters on the board." Pointing to each one, I had the class read them out loud together. *King, queen, princess, duke, stable boy.* "You may want to add more. I've also written the first sentence, 'Once upon a time there lived a wicked old king.' Now, each of you will have a chance to add a sentence. Let's start with you, Magda. Please come to the board and write the next sentence. Remember, class, in this exercise we will be using the simple past tense."

Magda, a dark-haired girl with glasses, always wore a small gold crucifix on a thin black ribbon around her neck. She was a good student, but I could tell by her expression that she was reluctant to be the first to come forward.

"Magda, don't be shy," I said. "We'll help you if you need it."

With encouragement from those around her she slowly walked to the board and picked up a piece of chalk. She read the sentence on the board to herself, then turned to me.

"Can I write anything?" she asked.

"Yes, anything."

She then wrote, *The queen was very beautiful, but very sad*, and read it out loud at my request.

"Excellent," I said. "Now pick one of the boys in the class to come up next."

She surveyed her classmates, some squirming in their seats, and finally settled on Piotr, a handsome blond boy sitting in the last row. I knew them to be close friends and he, too, was a good student. He lumbered to the blackboard with his usual awkward gait. He stood thinking for a moment, and then, with suggestions from a few of his friends, wrote: *The wicked king had little money and wanted his daughter, the princess, to marry the rich duke.*

The story soon unfolded as the class got involved and were eager to see its outcome. A few of the more confident students began volunteering. It didn't take long before the princess, who hated her father and didn't want to marry the duke, planned to run away with the stable boy, whom she met with secretly in the forest. But the duke, on his way to the castle, was brutally attacked and killed by enemy warriors, whose leader, a rival of the king, fell in love with the queen. The final outcome was uncertain when the bell rang.

As this exercise was repeated in other classes, sometimes with different characters, I was impressed with the students' imagination in telling a story and the excitement they showed in creating something of their own. I was surprised at first, though, by how bloodthirsty some of the younger boys could be when battles were fought and killings took place. These exercises also permitted the students to talk in class, relieving me of having to monitor their chattering like little birds.

Another lesson I enjoyed teaching was an introduction to art appreciation. I hoped that I could convey to the students some of my own enthusiasm for art history that began when I lived in Munich in the 1950s and had remained a life-long interest.

"Good afternoon, class. Today we are going to learn about how to look at works of art." I could see both frowns and smiles on their faces. "Let's begin by listing some of your favorite artists on the board. One artist for each of you. Andrzej, would you like to start? Edyta, you're next, so start thinking."

Within a short time the class had written at least twenty names on the board. I remember that Picasso was the best known. After completing their list, I asked if they could identify the artists' home countries. This wasn't so easy. There was lively discussion over this because they couldn't agree on several of the artists.

It seemed that so far I had their attention. Interest picked up when I showed them pictures by two Pre-Raphaelite artists from an illustrated calendar published for an exhibition of nineteenth century Victorian British artists at the National Gallery in Washington, D.C.

"How many of you have heard of Ophelia in Shakespeare's *Hamlet*?" Several hands went up.

The picture I showed them, completed in 1851 by the British artist, John Everett Millais, depicts Ophelia, rejected by Hamlet and half mad after the death of her father, Polonius, as she is floating almost submerged down a stream in which she will shortly drown.

"Notice the flowers along the bank, Ophelia's beautiful dress, and how she is staring blankly toward the sky."

I picked up the second painting. "This next work, *Beata Beatrix*, was painted in 1864 by Dante Gabriel Rossetti and shows the artist's beloved in a trance at the moment between life and death. There is a lot of symbolism in this painting that we will talk about later."

I then held up the two paintings together. "The same young woman is the model here. You might be interested to know that her name is Elizabeth Siddal." I wrote it on the board and explained that her family name was spelled the same as mine, but that she changed it after meeting Rossetti, whom she later married. I added, "Sadly, she died from a drug overdose at thirty-two." Many in the class were surprised to hear that drug abuse had been a problem that long ago.

Naturally they asked, "Are you a relative?" I am not.*

I developed a list of questions for the students to consider when looking at a work of art, questions that asked about a painting's main subject, its composition, the artist's use of color, significant details, what the artist is trying to say, and the students' response to the painting. As we discussed each question in turn, I asked a student to write it on the board and everyone to write it in their copybooks. For each question I showed them a different picture from the Victorian exhibition calendar, which we discussed in detail. Since we could cover only one or two questions in a period, there was enough material for several class sessions.

For their final exercise, I taped several pictures on the wall that they had not seen, and working alone or in clusters, they were asked to pick one and analyze it using the questions we had discussed. I was pleased at how involved the students got as they wrote down their observations. Using their notes, they then had to write a short report that could be finished at home.

A shy, reserved boy said to me several days later, "I've never been much interested in art, but I think I've changed my mind."

———◆◆◇◆●———

It took me awhile to realize that when lessons went well I was much less self-conscious in the classroom. I think my students sensed when I was more relaxed, and they in turn were more responsive. I was discovering the satisfaction of what it was like to be a real teacher. I found myself looking forward to the next day.

---

* After returning home from Poland I did research on Elizabeth Siddal, and drawn to her story published a paper entitled, "The Sad, Short Life of Elizabeth Siddal. Pre-Raphaelite Model and Artist." See Bibliography.

However, my second year of teaching was not without problems in the classroom. IIIB, like its predecessor the year before, had more than its share of bright students, and likewise, more than its share of attention-seekers who talked too much and could be disruptive, a few even rude at times. Two of the standouts were bright boys who were repeating the grade. As far as I could tell they were failed because they were lazy. I couldn't believe my eyes when I saw them in my class at the beginning of the year. *Oh, no, not again*, I thought.

———————◆♦◆◆———————

Soon after the semester began, Sylwia dropped by my classroom to say hello. She was now in her last year and would not be in any of my classes. I was sitting at my desk grading papers. My door was open, but she knocked. "May I come in, Mister Russian Traveler?" she asked, smiling. She looked tanned from her summer activities.

"Well, hello. Yes, please come in. Here, have a seat," I said, pulling up a chair next to my desk.

"I'm glad you're back safely from your trip. How was it?"

"I had a great time," I replied. "Friendly people. Great museums. Soon I'll have my photographs to show you."

"I'm eager to see them," she said. "I also have some pictures from this summer. Shall we meet sometime soon?"

"How about this Saturday afternoon?" I suggested.

"Yes, that's fine. Two o'clock? At the Piast Hotel?"

Saturday was warm and sunny, and the *Rynek* was bustling as people hurried to finish shopping before the stores closed in mid-afternoon. Sylwia arrived before I did and had found a table. As had become our custom, we each ordered Lipton tea with lemon and a dish of ice cream. We then brought out our photographs. Hers were from a couple of weekend jaunts she had taken with friends and family to nearby lakes for sunning and swimming.

"You're becoming a very good photographer," I said. "Several of these close-ups of people really show interesting details. And this scene of the sailboat silhouetted against the setting sun is excellent. Who's in this picture with you?"

"That's my friend, Kasia. The other two are my younger brother and sister. We're sitting in an outdoor café near where we went swimming."

"You're a handsome group."

"Thank you.

I showed Sylwia some of my photographs. She especially liked the one of the boy eating ice cream on the park bench in Moscow, the street artist in St. Petersburg, and the ones I took of St. Basil's Cathedral. Our conversation then turned to the new school year. Sylwia's classes were going well. In spite of heavy homework assignments, she continued part-time at the newspaper where she had worked during the summer. That was also where my tutor, Anita, worked. They were becoming good friends.

"Well, would you like to speak Polish for awhile?" Sylwia asked. "I have plenty of time this afternoon."

"Yes, I'm ready."

I enjoyed Sylwia's company and I always looked forward to our meetings. She was intelligent, pleasant to be with, and was especially perceptive in her observations about people. Though I became friendly with other students, she was the only one I would keep in touch with after I left Poland.

———◆·✕·◆———

Weekly sessions with my tutor, Anita, which had begun in late summer, were happily working out well. She seemed to sense intuitively how much new material I could absorb. We met in her apartment, where she served tea or juice along with cookies. Though she was encouraging of my efforts, I often felt that I was improving at a snail's pace. I couldn't help compare my time in Poland with my two years in Munich in the 1950s, when I became quite proficient in German. It was little consolation when I reminded myself that learning a language is more difficult when you are older. I had hoped that by this time I would be speaking more fluently.

As we became better acquainted, sometimes I stayed for supper, which was an opportunity to get to know her partner, Artur. He was as large a man as Anita was petite. They shared many interests and both had a delightful sense of humor. Artur didn't speak

English, but knew German from working in Germany. It was a virtual three-ring circus when we were together, with Anita and Artur speaking Polish, Artur and I speaking German, and Anita and I speaking English and Polish. We had a good time eating, drinking, and telling stories.

I was fascinated to hear about life under the communist regime. Anita recalled when food was rationed. "There were long lines to buy almost everything. I remember standing with my mother for over an hour at eight in the morning to buy bread, and then another hour to buy milk. Coffee and fruit, such as bananas, were rarely available. Families were allowed just one piece of chocolate for each child per month. Smokers were allowed ten packs of cigarettes a month, though many people rolled their own with tobacco bought on the black market."

"On the other hand," Artur said, "everyone had a job and a place to live. Many factories let out early in the afternoon. People remember having more time together with their families." He went on to say how travel abroad was restricted and passports were kept in a government office. Even Lech Wałęsa, the trade union leader who was awarded the Nobel Peace Prize in 1983, was denied permission to attend the award ceremonies in Oslo.

"The communist government told us that we had a good life," Artur added, "but no one believed it. Newspapers and television were tightly controlled. As a boy I always looked forward to Sunday mornings because those were the only times cartoons were shown on TV. Otherwise, it was mostly Russian war films." He paused for a moment to reflect. "You told us once, Larry, that you visited Majdanek, the former concentration camp near Lublin. My grandfather was there for eight months."

One time, while Anita and I were having tea after my lesson, she talked about her father, who died as a young man. Recalling him with fondness, she related the following story, which I asked her later to write down.

"I was six when I already could read without my parents' help. One day my father, who was always a reading-book fan, took me to the library and asked the librarian if she could depart from the principle of only enrolling children who are seven and enroll me.

The lady didn't want to believe that I could already read. In Poland children start to read at the age of seven, the first year of school. So she asked nicely if I would read something for her, and I said yes. She handed me the newspaper on her desk and pointed to a headline. But because she had just been reading it, the newspaper was upside down. So I told her that I hadn't learned yet to read upside down. She laughed and turned the paper right side up. I then fluently read the headline and a few sentences in the article. She stopped me and said she would make a special card for me and put it in a special place so that the other librarian would know it was for the little six-year-old girl who could read."

"What a delightful story," I said. "I'm sure your father was very proud. You must miss him very much."

"Yes, I do." We sat in silence for a moment and sipped our tea. "You've mentioned that you were born in China and that you lost your mother there. Would you tell me about her?"

"It's a rather long story. Her name was Annette."

———◆━◆◆◆━◆———

My parents, Clair and Annette Brane Siddall, went to Canton, now called Guangzhou, China, in 1923. This was a year after they were married and my father graduated from medical school. He was fulfilling a dream to be a medical missionary. He felt he could be of more service in a country where disease was widespread and much of the population lived in poverty. He was twenty-six years old. Annette, an attractive woman with auburn hair and just over five feet tall, was twenty-eight. Both were outgoing and made friends easily. One of Annette's sisters once described her to me as fun to be with, having inherited her father's sense of humor. He was a clergyman with the unusual name of Commodore I. B. Brane.

My father was on the medical staff of Canton Hospital and thrived on the myriad medical problems he and his colleagues, American and Chinese, faced every day. My mother adjusted well to the strange new culture, though she had to endure bouts of malaria and dengue fever. Like my father, she learned to speak Chinese. Much of her energy went to raising a family. My oldest brother was born in Canton, while my next oldest brother was born in Cleveland when my parents were on leave.

After my family returned to Canton in 1928, we lived on the campus of Lingnan College. I was born there at home on July 23, 1930.

I have four letters that my mother wrote to her two sisters during this time. The letters are chatty and mostly relate everyday events, including finally getting over one of her "fevers" and entertaining friends. She was also looking forward to coming home in two years.

In the summer of 1932, my parents decided that following Annette's three deliveries, she would have minor gynecological surgery for a perineal repair. It would be done at the small Lingnan hospital. Performing the operation would be the chief surgeon at Canton Hospital, a colleague and close friend of my father's. As a special precaution they had all of the surgical instruments and linens sterilized in the Canton Hospital.

On the last day of June, the operation was performed in about forty-five minutes. My father administered the chloroform anesthesia. On the third day Annette was feeling fine and was brought the short distance home. The next day, although the wound looked clean, she had some fever and her appetite was not good. On July 3rd her fever shot up to 103. She felt exhausted. The surgeon came to examine her and opened the swollen wound. My father made a smear from the infected tissue, and as he looked at it under a microscope he was horrified to see streptococci bacteria. He then knew what had caused my mother's rapid rise in temperature. He also knew that the infection was most likely to be fatal.

In spite of a blood transfusion and intravenous glucose, the following day Annette sank into a stupor with heavy breathing. It was the Fourth of July. My brothers and their friends were asked not to shoot off the firecrackers they had purchased.

My father sat by Annette's bedside for the rest of the day. As darkness descended and joined him in his grief, he tried vainly to get her to respond. In a desperate moment he shouted her name, but there was no recognition. He stayed up with her most of the night. My mother died quietly the next day. She was thirty-seven years old.

The funeral was held the following day in our home. Everyone was in shock. Afterward Annette's casket was taken to Hong Kong, where she was buried in the Happy Valley Cemetery. My father soon realized that he couldn't continue his work in Canton. Knowing that he wouldn't return to China, he decided to have Annette's body disinterred and cremated. Eventually, after we returned to the United States in the fall *of 1932, he buried her ashes in the family plot in a country cemetery two hours from the small Ohio town where I would grow up.*

In a subdued voice Anita asked, "Do you have any memory of your mother?"

"No, I don't. I was only two."

"She was so young."

"Yes. And to think that within two or three years antibiotics would have been available and saved her life."

———•✕•———

Adding to the convivial atmosphere in the teachers' room between classes were the frequent mini-parties. These occasions occurred during the longer mid-morning break. They usually honored someone's name-day, which is based on the feast day of the saint after whom the person is named. (Birthdays aren't celebrated as much as they are in America.) When one of the faculty had a name-day, it was up to her or him to provide the refreshments, usually an assortment of pastries and fruit. The school provided the tea and coffee.

Though I didn't have a name-day, I felt I should take a turn, and decided that my party would mark the beginning of my second year. I set a date in early October.

First, I needed to buy paper plates, cups and napkins. Since I didn't want just plain white ones from the supermarket, I had to search out a specialty shop. I eventually found one that sold the colorful supplies that I was looking for. Then I went to my favorite bakery and ordered the pastries, including a plate of *pączki*. When the day came, I enlisted the help of two girls from one of my classes to go with me to the bakery. Taking a cue from previous parties, I recruited them and two of their friends to set the table and help serve.

When I walked in that morning, I couldn't have been more pleased. Everything was laid out beautifully. My students had done well. As soon as most of the teachers were gathered, I clinked my tea glass to get their attention and then read a few words I had prepared in Polish. "Today is not my birthday nor my name-day, but I want to take this occasion to celebrate the beginning of my second year in Świdnica, and to thank you for accepting me into the school family."

My colleagues responded with warm applause and the party continued until the bell rang. Afterwards, Grażyna said, "You speak Polish very well."

I was pleased by her remark, and in the following months received several similar comments from colleagues. It didn't occur to me until much later, however, that I never heard Grażyna say anything about my teaching. No one else said anything either. In fact, I never received any evaluation. Except for a brief visit early in my first year by my Peace Corps supervisor from Warsaw, none of my colleagues ever entered my classroom. The director came by once, but just to make an announcement. I'm sure he and other teachers heard from my students how I was doing, but none of this, either positive or negative, ever filtered down to me. Though I never knew what my colleagues thought about my teaching, outside of the classroom I definitely felt accepted by them.

I welcomed every opportunity to attend a performance of classical music. I had heard choral concerts and the chamber orchestra in Świdnica, as well as symphony concerts in Wrocław, Kraków, and Warsaw, but one musical experience was especially memorable. It was a cold and rainy November evening when Wioletta, my physician friend, and I were having dinner in a restaurant on the *Rynek* in Wrocław before attending a performance of Verdi's *Requiem*. I had seen little of her over the summer, but in September we resumed our occasional visits and outings into the countryside. A couple of weeks earlier when we were having coffee, I had casually mentioned the Verdi concert and was delighted when she expressed interest in going along. The event was to be performed by members of the city opera company and held in the Maria Magdalena Church, a large Gothic structure not far from the *Rynek*. The opera house was still being restored following damage during World War II.

There was no letup in the rain as we walked to the church in the dark, sidestepping puddles and trying to avoid getting splashed by passing cars. Besides our raincoats, we had only my umbrella for protection. Unfortunately, a section of the fabric had come loose, and as we hurried along it flapped uselessly in the soggy night air. We finally reached the church, and with much relief we entered its large front portal.

The interior was dimly lighted, but an otherwise somber mood was alleviated by large swaths of colorful cloth suspended near the altar and around the windows. Seats were filling up fast. It was soon a packed house. The *Requiem* is a wonderful piece, very dramatic, and calls for a full orchestra, chorus and soloists. Giuseppe Verdi composed this work in 1873 as a memorial to the Italian poet Allesandro Manzoni. In describing the piece, one music critic wrote, "It is a work of universal catastrophe, destruction, terror, and despair; then hope at its most urgent and poignant."[*] I was familiar with the *Requiem,* having heard it performed several times and sung it once as a member of a chorus. But I was unprepared for what we would witness that evening.

I knew something unusual was going to happen when the chorus and soloists came down the aisles in elaborate dress and took their places in the transept. Then, after the music began, they started to move about as they sang. It wasn't long before they were joined by other performers—angels, the devil, goblin-like creatures, and colorfully costumed dancers. At one point, as the music was building to a climax, grotesque-looking figures started rollerblading up and down the aisles. As the end was approaching, the figure of Christ, wearing a loincloth and carrying a cross, slowly entered the sanctuary from the rear, accompanied by robed attendants. For a few moments he was lost from view, and then we could see him hanging from his cross near the altar. His lifeless-appearing body was then lowered and mourners carried him slowly back down the aisle as the music came to its peaceful end.

After a moment of silence, the audience's response was thunderous. No one wanted to leave. It had been a magical experience, one of the most creative and compelling performances I've ever seen or heard anywhere.

---

[*] Quoted by D. Kern Holoman. See Bibliography

As I looked out on my students each day, I was reminded how ethnically similar they were. There was not one dark skin among the sea of white faces. No one spoke with a different accent. No one had a non-Polish last name. Foreigners had not yet begun to immigrate to Poland as they had to countries like Germany and France. How different Świdnica was from the Ohio town of Oberlin where I grew up. African Americans began settling there during the Civil War, when the town became a stop on the Underground Railroad that helped slaves escape to the North.

As a boy I didn't give much thought to who was white and who was black. I was undoubtedly naïve, but as far as I could see, in school we were all pretty much on equal footing, whether in the classroom or on the athletic field. It was only after school that our lives diverged. While some of my pals at school were black, none of my after-school friends were. This was not a conscious choice, but reflected the way we lived. Segregation was obvious, because most of the black families lived in the southeast part of town.

The older brother of one of my friends was able to cross the color line. He had somehow been invited to several gatherings the black kids had at their social hall. After some of us heard that he had learned from them how to jitterbug to the Big Band music that was popular then, we talked him into teaching us. It was only years later that I began to give serious thought to the divide between us.

On a visit to Oberlin in 2006, I looked up one of my African American childhood classmates, a tall, handsome woman, who had returned to Oberlin with her husband in their retirement. She left Oberlin after high school, became a nurse, and married a man who would become the first black engineering manager for IBM. I wanted to know how it was for her growing up in Oberlin, and why she thought we didn't socialize after school. She reminded me that some of the black kids did come to a regular Friday night dance at the Teen Canteen, sponsored by the church I belonged to. But she agreed that blacks and whites didn't mix in parties held in private homes.

As we reminisced about attending elementary school together, she recalled that when she was seven or eight, she often stopped on the way to school to pick up one of her friends, a white girl in our class. One chilly morning she arrived early and had to wait outside. Later she asked why she wasn't invited to come inside. Her friend's response was, "Because my mother said you were colored." This was the first time, she told me, that she realized she was black. She spent a long time after school that day sitting on her grandmother's lap as the world of race was explained to her.

We both remembered that there had been one or two racially mixed marriages among our contemporaries. She also recalled that in high school she and a white boy in our class were attracted to each other. "Nothing was ever overt," she said, "but we had an 'understanding' with our eyes and smiles."

———————

As winter and the holiday season approached, I decided to have a party for my friends at the nearby Park Hotel. This would be a dress-up affair with dinner, followed by music and dancing. I drew up a guest list and set the date for the first Saturday in December.

The Park Hotel had originally been a private home. Built in the early 1900s, it was one of several formerly grand houses along Pionerów Street. It was just a stone's throw from my school and faced the same park. The hotel's separate private dining room was the perfect size for the occasion. When the date arrived I came early to help our waiter set out the wine, beer and soft drinks on a side table. I was pleased to see that the hotel staff had tastefully decorated the room. In one corner was a small Christmas tree, and on the walls hung several wreaths with red ribbons. Adding to the festive atmosphere, the long table was set with a cream-colored tablecloth, dark blue napkins, and two vases of fresh flowers.

My guests included Urszula, her husband Alexander, and their two boys, Marcin and Szymon; Anna and Stanisław Bielawski; Ashraf and his girlfriend; my physician friend, Wioletta, and her partner; and looking almost like sisters, Sylwia and Anita.

Once everyone was seated, I welcomed them and said a short piece in Polish, thanking them for coming and saying how much I appreciated their making me feel at home in Świdnica. Then we all drank a toast.

After dinner we played a mix of generic Christmas songs and American dance music on a CD player provided by the hotel. Throughout the evening I took photographs and later presented everyone with enlarged copies. The party lasted past eleven o'clock, though Urszula sent her boys home earlier in a taxi. As Anita and Sylwia were about to leave, they said they had a pre-Christmas gift for me. It was a book of color photographs of Świdnica, one that I had admired in a bookstore. Each had inscribed it with a short note. I thanked them warmly. It had been a delightful party. I truly felt in the holiday spirit as I walked home in the cold, star-lit night.

—————◆•॥◆•◆—————

I had Christmas dinner with the family of a young woman I was tutoring in English. I had met her early in the fall where I had lunch. She came over to where I was sitting. "Hello, my name is Ewa Łukasiewicz. I heard you are American. Would you be interested in giving me English lessons?"

"Can you sit down for a moment?"

Ewa told me she was married and lived at home temporarily because her husband worked out of town. Both she and her mother taught mathematics in another school. After I agreed to help her with English, I gladly accepted her suggestion that we meet at her home, and in return for lessons, I would join the family for *kolacja* (supper). And so began a pleasant relationship.

Every Wednesday I arrived at five o'clock for Ewa's lesson. The family's attractive home was among a row of newly built townhouses in a development that was a fifteen-minute walk from my school. Since Ewa's parents, Hanna and Ryszard, didn't speak English, mealtime conversation was in Polish. Ewa helped me out if I ran into trouble. They all were good-natured about my mistakes. They were also pleased that I took a liking to their dog, Flinta, a small, short-haired, friendly mutt who was almost an equal member of the family.

One meal time Ewa's father, who worked as an engineer, was absent.

"Where's your father?" I asked.

"He's out hunting. He should be home soon."

It wasn't long before father appeared. Wearing a camouflage outfit and a bandoleer across his chest, he reminded me of a freedom fighter. In one hand he held his shotgun, in the other two limp rabbits. He looked tired, but greeted us cheerfully. "Good evening everyone! Here's supper for tomorrow."

When the holiday season arrived, I was delighted to accept the family's invitation to Christmas dinner. Guests also included Ewa's husband, Darek, and her sister and brother-in-law. The meal was a variety of typically Polish dishes—soup, fish, chicken, pork, potatoes, vegetables, rolls, and two kinds of cake for dessert. I especially remember a drink Ryszard made, vodka flavored with lemon and honey. It was delicious. I drank more than I should have.

My gift to the family was a boxed bottle of brandy, considered a luxury. Their gift to me was a wool scarf, to make sure, they said, that I stayed warm on the long walk back to my school.

Later, I presented the family with a small album of photographs I took that evening, with Flinta prominently included.

Two days after Christmas I took the train to Berlin for a five-day visit that included seeing in the New Year. I was amazed by the contrast to the city I had seen in the 1980s when East Berlin, isolated by the Wall, was a relative wasteland and could be reached only through Checkpoint Charlie. I can recall how subdued the people seemed and how dreary the city was with little traffic and store windows almost empty. Now it was full of life. I wandered all over the reunited city and felt almost at home being able to speak the language. Among Berlin's many outstanding museums, one of my favorites is the Egyptian Museum. There, in a darkened room under special lighting, I saw the fabulous painted limestone head of Nefertiti, the ancient Egyptian queen, whose compelling beauty almost defies description.

It began with a mild fever. Next there was rumbling in my chest. Then frequent coughing. It was late January, on a Wednesday in the waning days of the first semester. By the time I had finished teaching, I was feeling increasingly ill. I didn't sleep well that night, and when morning arrived I was pretty sure I was coming down with bronchitis. Not wanting to miss my classes, I forced myself to eat a meager breakfast and drag myself down the hall to my classroom. By noon I was feeling worse and still had two more classes. Sitting at my desk with flushed cheeks, chills, and aching limbs, I stared out at my students and told them they could do whatever they wanted.

Later that afternoon I called the nurse at the Peace Corps office in Warsaw. She thought I might have the flu, since several volunteers had called in with similar symptoms. It would pass in a few days, she told me. I wasn't convinced. Whatever I had, I went to the drugstore to get over-the-counter medication, hoping for some relief. With no classes on Friday, I looked forward to rest. I would have called my physician friend, but she was out of town.

By Saturday I was miserable. My chest was congested. My coughing had grown worse. I felt weak and I had no appetite. I forget why, but in the afternoon I left my apartment and went downstairs. By chance I found Mr. Zawada, the director, in his office.

"You don't look well," he said, frowning.

"I'm not," I replied feebly. "I think I have bronchitis."

"Then we must find you a doctor. I will make some calls."

Within the hour I was being examined by not just one, but two physicians, a short, middle-aged woman and her son, who looked to be in his thirties. The tidy, attractive office was in their home, very near to the school as it turned out. They took my temperature, felt my pulse, listened to my chest, and looked down my throat. Then a third physician appeared, the husband and father, who came downstairs apparently to see what was going on, since they didn't usually have Saturday afternoon office hours. Speaking first to his wife and son, he came over to me and felt my forehead. Slightly raising his bushy eyebrows and offering a friendly smile, he said in Polish, "Yes, you have quite a fever."

The three doctors agreed I had bronchitis and should be started on an antibiotic. They called in Mr. Zawada from the waiting room and handed him a prescription. He in turn gave the prescription and some money to the school custodian who had accompanied us, with instructions as to which drugstore he should go. By late afternoon I had taken my first dose of medication.

When I telephoned the nurse again in Warsaw, she said I would need twice the amount of antibiotics that was prescribed. She would send it along with other analgesics.

"The package will arrive early next week," she said. "Sorry to hear you're so ill. You should start to feel better within a few days."

When Monday morning arrived, the director called my apartment at eight o'clock to ask if I was well enough to teach my classes. I said I wasn't. He called the next day. Same answer. I wasn't able to return to class until Thursday. Except for calling Anita to cancel my lesson, I didn't talk to a soul for three days. It was the worst time of my second year.

In the teachers' room, I told Grażyna that I had been ill.

"Yes, we knew." That was all she or anyone said. There had been no phone calls, no inquiries.

Fortunately, I was well enough to attend the senior dance that weekend. I didn't want to miss it because I had been looking forward to seeing my students of last year dressed in their finery. Sylwia looked lovely in her long dress. I went over to say hello while her date went to get them food.

"Anita told me you've been sick. I was sorry to hear that. Did you get my e-mail?"

"Yes. Thank you. I'm much better now."

We chatted for a few minutes, and as I was about to return to my table she said, "By the way, I was thinking, why don't you stay another year?"

I laughed. "Really? Why do you say that?"

"Well, your Polish is improving, you seem to like teaching, and you've made some close friends."

"It's very nice of you to suggest it. I'll certainly give it some thought."

CHAPTER FOURTEEN
Świdnica, Poland: February to July 1999

On a bitterly cold morning in February 1999, the first major snowstorm of the winter blew in from Russia. Already Świdnica lay under a six-inch blanket of white that muffled the sounds of traffic. Even the gregarious crows that usually socialized in the wooded park across the street were silent. My students would have a hard time getting home in the afternoon. I reminded myself that there were certainly advantages to living in the school building. In contrast to the storm outside, the atmosphere inside my classroom was almost cozy.

The school building was an impressive edifice, built at the turn of the twentieth century by the Germans who lived in this part of Poland until the end of World War II. For such an old structure, it still gave a good impression, though many little things had been neglected, such as peeling paint in some hallways and plasterboard falling down in my classroom. I occasionally heard from other teachers that our school, like every other one in the country, struggled to make do with the limited funds parceled out by the Ministry of Education in Warsaw. During the communist era the school had served as the officers' club for a Russian military unit billeted in Świdnica until 1989. One story I heard was that there had been a swimming pool in the school basement, and before the Russians left they filled it in and then took whatever they could dismantle, such as doorknobs and chandeliers.

I had assumed that my students paid little attention to how the building looked or what it lacked. I was definitely wrong. From a casual conversation in one of my classes about the condition of the school building, a serious discussion developed. This was the first time I had heard any negative comments.

"Imagine that you had a million dollars," I said. "How would you spend it on the school?"

I asked them to write their suggestions on the board. They included a range of improvements, from fixing the wall of our classroom and cosmetic painting in the hallways, to installing a chemistry lab, buying more computers, upgrading the resources in the library, and improving the gymnasium with locker rooms and showers. In spite of these deficiencies, however, the students were proud of their school and its traditions. Our discussion took me back to my own high school years.

———◆◆◆◆———

I liked school and most of the time took it seriously. I was a good student, but not exceptional. It was a surprise when my father told me as a freshman in high school that he thought it would be a good idea for me to go to a private school. He had in mind Western Reserve Academy, fifty miles away, which would mean living away from home. I knew about the school because my brother John was there, as were two friends of my oldest brother. But I had no wish to go there myself. What seems strange to me in hindsight is that I don't remember being asked my opinion. I have wondered many times why I was so unassertive in expressing my feelings. My father was probably right that I was not working hard enough for the grades I was getting, though I could have remedied that. He was not in the least authoritarian, but it seemed that he had made up his mind. I dutifully complied.

I entered Western Reserve Academy* as a sophomore in the fall of 1945. I found that keeping up with the heavy academic load was a huge challenge. In the beginning I had to string a light bulb into my tiny closet after lights out to get my homework finished. I had to repeat first year Latin. It soon became obvious that I wasn't going to get the grades I was used to.

I also found it hard to adjust to the formality and rigidity of the school, which at that time enrolled only boys. Besides being required to wear a coat and tie, it felt as if almost every minute of the day was scheduled and my time closely monitored. The policy that allowed only

---

* Western Reserve Academy, located in Hudson, Ohio, occupies the original campus of Western Reserve College, founded in 1826. The town was settled in 1799 by David Hudson and other pioneers in what was called the Connecticut Western Reserve. After the college moved to Cleveland a half century later, its Preparatory Department remained and eventually became Western Reserve Academy.

so many weekends away was strictly enforced. On top of that, I was separated from my friends at home. It was not an easy transition.

The teachers, or masters as they were referred to, lived on campus and it seemed as though they watched our every move. Most were well liked, but a few were feared. We had nicknames among ourselves for some of them, passed down from upperclassmen. We called one of the Latin teachers, The Toad.

My favorite teacher, who taught English, had the nickname of Jiggs, I assume from the comic strip, "Maggie and Jiggs." A short, middle-aged single man with thinning gray hair, he was beyond casual in his dress. I can still see him in his rumpled wool jacket, half-pressed trousers, the ends of his shirt collar turned up, and the narrow end of his brown knit tie hanging several inches below the front. He was the resident master in the dormitory known as the Athenaeum, one of the original structures on campus. I roomed there during my sophomore and senior years and remember having occasional chats with Jiggs in his small, cluttered apartment that smelled of cigarette smoke and old books. He revered the written word and did his best to teach us how to write a good essay and understand literature. I recall one time in my first year when he called on me in class. We were discussing Tess of the D'Urbervilles, *by Thomas Hardy.*

"Larry, what insight did you gain from the chapter you read last night?"

I couldn't answer. I didn't know what insight meant.

"So, that's a new word for you, is it? Well, let's all take a few minutes to talk about this indispensable word."

Sports played an important part in the life of the school. I liked the fact that we were required to participate in a sport each season, either through the intramural program or on a varsity team. I was on the football team, but because I was small I didn't play enough to earn a letter, which was a big disappointment. I would have done much better going out for soccer where my size would not have mattered. I did get letters in wrestling and track. The mile relay team I was on my senior year missed breaking the school record by only half a second.

Coming from small-town Oberlin, it took time to adjust to a different social life. The majority of students came from more sophisticated communities around Cleveland and Akron, and many of the girls who came to our dances also attended private schools. I eventually got to know one of these girls and invited her to several social events. She turned out to be a terrific dancer. We had a great time jitterbugging to music like "One O'clock Jump" and "Stomping at the Savoy."

While I developed close relationships with several classmates, I felt cut off from my friends at home. Even though I saw them during vacations, I could tell that I wasn't as much a part of their social life as I used to be.

I completed three years at Reserve, graduating in 1948. While I didn't receive any academic honors, I was recognized in other ways. In my senior year I was a class officer and a member of the student council. I was also selected by the faculty to be a dormitory counselor to underclassmen, called a prefect (borrowing the British term). A prefect had a number of privileges that included the freedom to go off campus whenever you had free time.

One of the most important things I learned about myself during those years was that I had the capacity to stick with something in spite of it being difficult. All told it was a good experience. In the beginning I had some lonely times, but in my last two years I felt very much a part of the school. I never complained. In fact I kept most of my feelings to myself. My parents had little idea what it was like for me. In any case, I was well prepared for college.

Likewise, despite peeling paint and a lack of classroom equipment, the students at my school in Świdnica also experienced a rigorous academic program. Those who worked hard were well prepared to go on to the university.

◆•✕•◆

For one of my after-school projects, I organized a monthly discussion group for teachers of English from other schools in Świdnica. In response to the twenty letters I sent, eight teachers came to a meeting at my school. From this group, six teachers (including my friend Urszula) plus myself, met monthly on a late Friday afternoon at the Park Hotel for drinks and conversation. It was a lively group. Besides sharing ideas about teaching English and some of the problems they encountered with their students, they had personal stories to tell. I had a few entertaining stories of my own about adjusting to my new life in Świdnica.

I also met with students who wanted extra English conversation. One girl brought along her younger brother; he was not yet in high school but was becoming almost as fluent as his sister. Three girls came from another high school to learn, among other things, an American accent, preferring it to the British way of speaking. I was surprised when a boy from the previous year, who I remembered as an indifferent student, asked for help with two of his friends. He never revealed what prompted his turnaround in motivation.

One boy I remember well, a bright eighteen-year-old, did mediocre work in class but had a passion for the movies. His ambition was to be a documentary film director. He could talk for hours about the Polish film industry. When he was absent for two days, I asked the class if they knew why.

"He had a fall while hiking in the mountains over the weekend."

"He has a broken arm and is in the hospital."

He finally showed up two weeks later. If asked, he would show you the large stitch marks on his elbow as a result of extensive surgery. Though I doubted the veracity of his story, he also told us that patients in the hospital were not only allowed to smoke, but could secretly buy alcohol from one of the aides. (My physician friend, Wioletta, was shocked when I related this to her. "We would never allow that in our hospital," she said vehemently.) He was good-natured about his experience and voiced no complaints about his medical care. What he really wanted to talk about was making films.

———◆◆◆◆◆◆———

I enjoyed the freedom to choose a variety of activities in class. As was true the year before, many of my students liked music. It was mostly the girls, however, who liked to sing. I found that singing helped to improve pronunciation. Also, I often used songs to get students to write brief stories, both together in class and individually as homework. One of their favorites was "Oh!

Susanna." They liked the sound of names like Louisiana, Alabama, and banjo, and came up with some wild adventures for the young man on his way to see Susanna.

I introduced my students to classical music at Christmas time when I played a recording of the "Hallelujah Chorus" from Handel's *Messiah*. I handed out a copy of the words so they could follow along, and explained that the *Messiah* was the only major work of its kind that was originally written in English.

When I had a lesson on the geography of the United States, I referred to a large map in front of the classroom. I had the students' attention when I pointed out that Poland was about the size of New Mexico. There were expressions of disbelief when I said that if they were to drive across the country, it would take five or six days. They were surprised that I had twice hitchhiked across two-thirds of the country.

The war in the former Yugoslavia offered an opportunity for several lessons on European politics. When the NATO bombing in Kosovo took place, I had several classes hold debates on the issue. I divided them in half, one in favor of the bombing, the other against, and asked them to prepare a statement in twenty minutes. Then each side chose one student to read out loud their statement. They had some very heated discussions.

◆━◆✕◆━◆

With the coming of spring, the students in IIIB still offered me little respite from their annoying behavior. There were days when my patience wore thin. It was difficult to keep from raising my voice or yelling at some of them. One tactic I employed was simply to ignore their troublesome behavior, but it did little to alleviate my annoyance. What worked best was engaging a student individually and inquiring about non-school interests. When I had my party in the teachers' room at the beginning of the year, it was from this class that I asked four girls to help me. I'm sure they liked being singled out and performed their duties in a very grown-up fashion. Once, after I was asked what I had done for a living, several students requested to meet after class to learn more about psychotherapy. They were attentive and asked thoughtful questions. One girl had a friend who was depressed and found it difficult to find a therapist.

Deciding to tough it out on my own with IIIB, I didn't consult with Grażyna as I had done the year before. However, I still chatted with her during our breaks in the teachers' room, as I did with other colleagues. One day I asked her, "What do you think about IIIB? Do you have problems with them?"

"Yes, I do. They're terrible."

I laughed. "Really? I'm glad to hear I'm not the only teacher with problems." I paused a moment. "Does the director know how difficult they can be?"

"Oh yes, he does."

Then to my astonishment IIIB told me several days later that Grażyna had come to their classroom and yelled at them. "She told us you didn't like us."

"I didn't say I didn't like you. I said you could be difficult at times."

As the saying goes, it was déjà vu all over again—Grażyna had done almost the same thing the year before. My surprise was greater this time because I hadn't complained to her or anyone about IIIB. I couldn't tell if any of the students were offended by what happened. Most gave me the impression that they took it more as a joke. I said no more about it to Grażyna. It occurred to me that while she was trying to be supportive, without realizing it she may have also used me as an excuse to vent her own feelings of frustration.

In spite of the difficulties this class presented, they did some good work. I gave them many writing assignments, often as homework. Once, partly to learn more about their homeland, I had them write short essays about famous Polish people, with each student selecting a different person. Some of the papers I remember were about the scientist and Nobel Prize winner, Maria Skłodowska (Marie Curie, 1867-1934); the musician and composer, Fryderyk Szopen (Frederick Chopin, 1810-1849); the astronomer, Mikołaj Kopernik (Nicolaus Copernicus, 1473-1543);

Tadeusz Kościuszko (1746-1817), military hero in Poland and aid to General Washington in the American Revolutionary War; and Teodor Józef Konrad Korzeniowski (Joseph Conrad, 1857-1924), writer and novelist.

———◆•»◦«•◆———

The last Peace Corps meeting for all volunteers was a three-day gathering in March held at a conference center near Warsaw. This was the time when the staff explained about the forms to fill out and reports to write prior to our "close of service" (COS) in June.

We had finished unloading our luggage from the chartered bus that had brought us from Warsaw. As we were getting our room assignments, Paula waved to me from where she and Jenni were standing near the reception desk. I went over to them. "What's up?"

"Hey," Paula said, "we have room for one more person. Why don't you stay with us?"

"Really? Are you sure?"

"Why not?" she said.

Jenni added, "You couldn't ask for nicer roommates. Besides, Paula says you're a silent sleeper."

"I'd be delighted." I still hadn't gotten used to the ways of my young friends, but who was I to object?

The next morning I was up first. "I'll see you two at breakfast."

Paula soon came down dressed in jeans and a sweatshirt. After pouring a cup of coffee, she asked, "What are you doing for Easter? Got any plans?"

"No, not really. I thought you said you and Jenni were going somewhere."

"Well, that's changed. I'm thinking I'd like to go to Dresden. How about coming with me?"

"It's a deal."

Dresden, on the banks of the Elbe River in eastern Germany, was not far from the Polish border. It is a city known for art, music, and beautiful Baroque architecture, and in times past it was often called the "Florence of the North." That was before World War II. Since then, what one is most likely to associate with Dresden is the tragic bombing by allied airplanes toward the end of the war, which many authorities say was militarily unjustified. One of the best-known accounts of this event is told in the novel, *Slaughterhouse-Five*, by Kurt Vonnegut, who as a young P.O.W. survived the firestorm that swept the city and killed over 35,000 people.

Paula and I were having lunch at an outdoor café on one of the city's promenades that overlooked the river. Barges and tourist boats passed slowly up and down. It was a delightful spring day, sunny and warm. We had been discussing the memorial exhibit about the bombing, which we had seen in the morning.

"That was a sobering experience, I must say," Paula said. "Can we do something more uplifting this afternoon?"

"Well, we have our choice of two art museums. They're among the best in Europe I've been told."

"And how about this evening? I'd like to hear the Dresden Boys Choir. The guide book says it was founded over 700 years ago."

"Fine by me. Also, we have to decide how we will celebrate Easter tomorrow."

Paula and I found a Dresden that had been almost completely rebuilt, but it lacked the architectural beauty of the former city. Fortunately, some Baroque-style homes and buildings survived in a few of the city's outlying neighborhoods. Restoration of Dresden's landmarks was slow after the war, but one exception was the magnificent opera house, an absolute jewel among still-visible ruins. More money flowed into the city following Germany's reunification, and with added donations from around the world, Dresden's famous *Frauenkirche* (Church of Our Lady), with its massive dome, was in the midst of a ten-year-long reconstruction.

Peeking out from behind her sunglasses Paula said, "I haven't told you my news yet. I've been asked to be one of the Peace Corps staff this summer to help train the next group."

"That's terrific," I said. "Congratulations! When do you start?"

"Next month. It means leaving my school early. They were informed last week and weren't too happy. But I'm psyched!"

"From what you've told me, you've had a good experience at your school."

"Yeah. I'll really miss my kids. And my counterpart and her husband. They've been great to me."

"Aren't they the couple you went to Paris with, when you took your own food?"

"Oh, you remember that story? We had a great time."

"Well, this summer you'll have the new volunteers to take under your wing. They'll be fortunate to have you on the staff. Remember when we first arrived?"

Paula and I met again a few weeks later in the small city of Opole where there was a store noted for its Polish pottery. She wanted to buy a set of dishes to send home to her parents. After making her choice she said, "Aren't they beautiful, though?"

The floral pattern was a deep blue on a white background, with a touch of red and yellow here and there. "Yes. Excellent decision."

After we had lunch and did some sightseeing, we wandered down to the train station. Paula would be leaving first; my train was thirty minutes later. As we were waiting on the platform I said, "Do you realize that we probably won't see each other again?"

"Really? But you just mean here in Poland, right?"

"Yes, that's what I mean."

Hearing the train's whistle in the distance, Paula looked down the track, squinting into the late afternoon sun. Then turning to me she smiled and said, "I hope so. Because someday when I'm back home next fall I'll be looking to get a phone call."

<hr>

In May of 1999, a month before I left Świdnica, I received an e-mail from Marianne von Lieres Kreutzer, who in 1956 had accompanied John Westergaard and me from Munich to Istanbul. In 1992 I visited her and her husband in Regensburg, Germany, where he was a professor of German Literature at the university. I saw them again in 1997 after I arrived in Poland, spending New Year's Eve with them on my way back from Italy, where I had gone during my first Christmas vacation.

In her e-mail, Marianne wrote that she would be coming through Świdnica the following week on her way to Golkowice, eighty miles further. Her family had an estate there prior to World War II, when this part of Poland belonged to Germany. She would be traveling by car with her nephew and his wife. There would be time for a two-hour visit.

We agreed to meet outside the Peace Church. After she introduced her brother's son and his wife, a delightful young couple, we went inside where I gave them a brief tour and we listened to the recording in English I had made for visitors.

Over lunch at a restaurant on the *Rynek*, Marianne related how, at the end of the war, her family had to evacuate their home ahead of the rapidly advancing Russian army. They had no motorized transportation, only a horse-drawn cart to carry whatever household goods they could manage to bring. She was fourteen.

"On the way my father became ill and needed to be hospitalized," she said. "And where did we stop, but right here in Świdnica. It was called Schweidnitz then. My mother, brother and I went on ahead, and eventually my father joined us in Munich. It was a hard time."

"I remember your telling me some of this story when we were in Yugoslavia."

"I had forgotten all about that."

"Isn't it amazing, Marianne, that you and I first become acquainted in Munich in 1955, travel together to Turkey the next year, reunite in Regensburg thirty-six years later, and then meet again in Poland where we discover that my home here and where you grew up are so near one another?"

"It is amazing. I was so surprised when you wrote that you were living here." She told us that she always had fond memories of her childhood, which was why over the years she came back to visit and bring "what you Americans call care packages" to the poor people in the village. "There's no chance for any of us Germans to reclaim our property, but I'm glad to see that the young Polish couple living on our former estate are taking good care of it."

———◆•◆••◆———

With the semester coming to a close, my last few weeks in Świdnica flew by in a flurry of year-end classroom activities and last meetings with friends. Ashraf had offered to let me use his computer to send a few e-mails, since I had already shipped my laptop home. He had not done any conducting, but kept busy upgrading his website and looking for work. Afterward, I stayed for lunch with him and his girlfriend. We sat at the kitchen table. Their usually yapping dog rested quietly in one corner. We reminisced about the past two years.

"Here's wishing our American friend a safe journey home," Ashraf said, as the three of us clinked our glasses of beer.

"Thank you both again for your hospitality."

"It's been a pleasure," Ashraf replied.

◆ ▸▮◂ ◆

Urszula invited me to what she called a "farewell supper" with her family and several friends whom I had met before. In true Polish fashion there were more dishes of food than I could count, and what seemed like an endless supply of beer and vodka. On such occasions dining took place in the living room, with its familiar ornate lampshades and colorful drapes by the window. Well into the meal Urszula announced that she and her family had a gift for me. "We wanted you to have something from Poland that you can use everyday." What they gave me was a fine black leather wallet. "As you can see, it has a change purse sewed right in."

"Thank you so much. I'll definitely use it."

When it was time to leave, Urszula saw me to their apartment door. A few minutes remained while I waited for my taxi. "My family and I will miss you," she said. "I'm not much of a letter writer, but I hope we can keep in touch."

"I hope so, too. You've been a good friend." I paused a moment. "Who knows? Maybe someday I'll be knocking again at your door."

◆ ▸▮◂ ◆

My cell phone rang late one afternoon. It was Wioletta calling from the hospital. "When are you leaving Świdnica?"

"In ten days."

"Then we must meet soon. How about this weekend? I'll take you to dinner. I have a castle in mind."

The castle turned out to be more like a country estate. It had been recently restored to its former elegance, and a restaurant had been added. According to the back of the menu, the original structure dated from the late 1700s.

"Do you like my choice for our last meeting?" Wioletta asked.

"Excellent. But you always make good choices."

"They have a reputation for excellent fish. Shall I order for us both?

"Please do."

Like the surroundings, Wioletta also looked elegant, dressed in a beige blouse, black skirt, with a gold necklace and matching bracelet. I was reminded of our first meeting the year before at the Park Hotel, when I thought she looked like a film star. As we were finishing the last of our fruit dessert, Wioletta said, "So that you will think of me when you're home in America, I have something for you." It was a book of beautiful color photographs of Poland. Inside she had written, "Remember about the places where we visited together. From Wioletta."

———◆◆◆◆◆———

Sylwia and I agreed to meet one last time at the Piast Hotel. It was two days before her graduation. Unlike in America, the ceremony takes place in the morning and is an all-school event rather than a family-oriented evening occasion. I was eager to see my students from my first year receive their diplomas.

I had bought her a box of stationery illustrated with scenes of lily ponds from Monet's paintings. "This is just a little something to commemorate your graduation. And it's a reminder to keep in touch."

"Thank you. I've something for you, too." Inside tissue paper wrapping was a dark blue ceramic mug. "When you have your coffee in the morning back in America, you can think about me and Świdnica."

"Oh, I like it! It will be one of my favorite souvenirs. Before I forget it, I'll look for you after graduation so I can take pictures of you and your friends. We certainly want to document the occasion."

We spent the rest of our visit talking about her plans for the summer and my trip home.

"You're going to stop in Ireland?" she asked, her eyes lighting up. "How I envy you. I've always wanted to go there."

"I have, too."

"Promise you'll send me a postcard?"

"I promise." As we were finishing the last of our tea I said, "You know, Sylwia, we might not have become friends if it hadn't been for the rain shower that afternoon. Remember—the bookstore?"

"Yes. How could I forget? I think it was what you call a chance meeting."

◆◆◆◆◆◆

My final assignment of the year for all my students was to write a brief autobiography. I prepared a short outline, which I had each class copy into their notebooks. I made it clear that this was only a guide, and that they could decide what they wanted to write about. The outline included where they were born, where they grew up, who was in their family, memories of early family life, what elementary school was like, what they felt about their high school experience, and thoughts about their future. With a few exceptions, they worked diligently on this project and were far more revealing about themselves than I anticipated. Some accounts were poignant, some philosophical, a few were confessional; one girl even wrote about having been sexually abused. As a group they were optimistic about what they would be doing in five years. I thoroughly enjoyed reading these papers—over 200 of them— that more than compensated for the long hours it took to grade them. My only regret is that I didn't think to get permission to keep copies of a few of these life stories.

I wasn't able to return the autobiographies to two classes until the very last day. My congratulating them on their work was a pleasant way to end the year. Other students spent their last day differently. Two classes had parties, with soft drinks and pastries the students had baked at home. One class wanted to sing—their last chance for "Oh! Susanna."

The class I remember most vividly was IIIB. I asked for suggestions about how they wanted to spend their last hour. Agnieszka raised her hand.

"Yes, what is it?" I asked.

"The class has written a letter to you. They would like me to read it."

"Of course. Please do."

Agnieszka took a sheet of paper from her notebook and stood up at her desk. She was a good student and popular with her classmates. I could see why they chose her to represent them. Clearing her throat she began to read.

Dear Mr. Siddall,

Today is the last time when we are on your lesson and we think it is a good opportunity to thank you. We really appreciate your devotion. We know you had many difficult moments and problems with us, but we hope you will forget about them and you will remember only nice meetings. We would like you to know that lessons with you were really interesting for us. We would listen to you and, for many of us, it was enough to improve our English. You told us many exciting things and we know that they weren't only lessons of English, but also lessons about life. Besides, you always had time to talk to us after lessons and we thank you for your involvement.

Really, we hope that also for you lessons with us were a kind of experience. We are sorry for all our mistakes. So thank you and goodbye.

III "b"

I was really touched.

I had an appointment in Warsaw on June 24 to complete the paperwork to terminate my Peace Corps commitment. Until then there were only a few days in which to tie up loose ends after classes ended. I said my official goodbye to school colleagues the last week of classes, for which I had a very brief speech prepared. They knew of my interest in photography, since over the last six months I had taken individual portraits of them in the teachers' room. I was delighted when they presented me with a book of color photographs of the Polish countryside.

The next day there was a message on my cell phone to call Anita. I reached her at work. "I have a few hours free tomorrow afternoon," she said. "Let's meet for lunch. My treat. How about on the *Rynek*, at the restaurant near your bank."

I found Anita waiting for me inside the entrance. Seeing her dressed in a matching light blue suit jacket and skirt, with small star-shaped earrings that highlighted her short hair style, I was reminded that I rarely saw her in her professional attire. Usually, when I had a lesson at her apartment, she wore jeans and a sweater. "I like your outfit," I said. "As we might say in America, you look real sharp."

Anita smiled. "I don't know that expression, but it sounds like a compliment. Thank you."

As we followed the hostess to our table, Anita paused twice to say hello to acquaintances. After we were seated she said, "The two gentlemen work in the mayor's office, and the wife of the couple I spoke to is a manager with a new firm. I interviewed her recently for an article. It's a part of my job that I especially enjoy."

"As we might also say in America, you are a woman-about-town."

She laughed. "I don't know about that, but as a newspaper reporter and editor, I've gotten to know many interesting people in Świdnica."

"How are you today?" I asked.

"I'm fine, but as usual, very busy at work. There's never enough time. Too many deadlines."

We perused the menu. Anita chose veal cutlet with potato salad. I decided on an order of *pierogi*, small dumplings with cheese inside, and a cucumber salad.

"Shall we have a small glass of beer for the occasion?" Anita asked.

"Yes, let's do."

I found it hard to believe that within three days I would no longer be in Poland. I was looking forward to going home, but now I found myself feeling reluctant to leave Świdnica. I hadn't realized how attached I had become.

"Sylwia was at work today. She said to say hello."

"I'm so pleased that you and she have become friends," I said. "To me you two seem alike in many ways. Almost like sisters."

"I like her a lot. We get along very well. People at work like her, too. She sometimes visits Artur and me."

"When do you think you and Artur will get married?"

"We don't know. It's hard to save enough money for a Polish wedding. Traditionally it's a two-day affair, and of course very expensive. Neither of us has family who can help. But things are changing. A lot of people these days are having smaller weddings, something less elaborate. That's what we're thinking about."

"I hope I'll get an invitation."

"Absolutely. Wedding or not, to make sure you come back to Świdnica, Sylwia and I will find a reason."

After lunch we strolled around the *Rynek*, with Anita pointing out the many changes she had seen in the last few years, including the restoration of the Baroque-style façades of the town houses facing the square. "It's much more attractive now than it used to be, especially since cars are not allowed. You can see how people enjoy walking here."

Soon it came time for Anita to return to work. Leaving the city square behind, we walked together for several blocks. When we reached the corner of her street, we paused a moment, unaware of traffic and passersby. The day had turned out to be sunny and warm. Clouds drifted lazily overhead.

"Goodbye," I said.

We hugged. "Don't forget about us here," she said softly.

I crossed the street to the next corner and turned around. Anita was still standing where we parted. We waved. The next time I looked back she was gone.

POSTSCRIPT

After my official separation from the Peace Corps in Warsaw, I flew to Amsterdam where I spent two days wandering in art museums and drinking wine in sidewalk cafés that overlooked the city's canals. From there I went by train and ferry to London, pausing only long enough to buy a bus ticket to Cardiff, the capital of Wales. Besides the beautiful countryside, the Welsh are known for their male choruses. I had hoped to attend a concert, but missed one by a day. At the bed and breakfast where I stayed, I was interested to learn from the husband of the host couple that his father was the chief engineer in charge of rebuilding Poland's railway system after World War II. Then on to Ireland for a delightful stay. I finally arrived home on July 22, a day before my birthday.

A year after leaving Poland I invited Sylwia for a three-week visit. We had perfect late-August weather for drives around New England and visits to Boston and New York. She was a delightful guest. She now had a serious boyfriend, and that fall would begin her second year at the university in Wrocław.

In September of 2002, I returned to Świdnica to attend Sylwia's wedding. I also saw friends. In a visit to my school I found Grażyna and my former colleagues doing well. Urszula and her family were fine; she was teaching English in another school and invited me to meet with one of her classes. Ashraff was living in a different apartment with a different girlfriend. Anita and Artur, with whom I stayed, now had a ten-month-old daughter. Also, Anita and two colleagues had each recently received an award similar to our Pulitzer Prize for journalism and traveled to Warsaw for the ceremony. My one disappointment was not seeing Wioletta, who the year before had terminated her medical practice and left town with her partner and young son, her destination unknown.

I returned to Świdnica again in October, 2005 to see friends, attend a school reunion, and be an official witness at Anita and Artur's wedding. Sylwia and I were honored to be among the four signers of their marriage certificate.

SELECTED BIBLIOGRAPHY

Books

Bird, Isabella L. *Journeys in Persia and Kurdistan*. London: John Murray, 1891. Re-published by Virago Press, London, 1988.

Blair, Sheila S. and Jonathan M Blum. *The Art and Architecture of Islam*. New Haven and London: Yale University Press, 1994.

Blunt, Wilfrid. *Isfahan: Pearl of Persia*. New York: Stein & Day Publishers, 1966.

Curzon, George N. *Persia and the Persian Question*, Vol. I & II. London: Frank Cass & Co., 1892. Second Impression, Barnes & Noble, New York, 1966.

Davies, Norman. *Rising '44: The Battle for Warsaw*. New York: Viking Penguin, 2004.

Doughty, Charles M. *Arabia Deserta*. Cambridge, UK: Cambridge University Press, 1888. 2nd Edition, Phillips & Co. Books, 1989.

Ettinghausen, Richard, Oleg Graber, and Marilyn Jenkins-Madina. *Islamic Art and Architecture*. New Haven & London: Yale University Press, 2001.

Friedman, Thomas L. *From Beirut to Jerusalem*. New York: Farrar Straus Giroux, 1989.

Holoman, D. Kern. *Evenings with the Orchestra*. New York and London: W.W. Norton & Co., 1992.

Kimmerling, Baruch, and Joel S. Migdal. *Palestine: The Making of a People*. New York: The Free Press, 1993.

Morton, H.V. *Middle East*. New York: Dodd, Mead & Co., 1941.

Nyrop, Richard F., Ed. *Yugoslavia: A Country Study*. Washington, D.C.: U.S. Government Printing Office, 1982.

Payne, Robert. *Journey to Persia*. New York: E.P. Dutton & Co., 1952.

Stokstad, Marilyn. *Art History*, 2nd Edition. New York: Prentice Hall and Harry N. Abrams, 2002.

Townsend, Peter. *Earth, My Friend*. London: Hodder & Stoughton, 1959.

Tripp, Charles. *A History of Iraq*. Cambridge, UK: Cambridge University Press, 2000.

Zamoyski, Adam. *The Polish Way*. New York: Hippocrene Books, 1987.

Articles

Chelminski, Rudolph. "Warsaw: The City That Would Not Die," *Smithsonian*, (November, 1997)

Covington, Richard. "Mighty Macedonian: Alexander the Great," *Smithsonian*, (November, 2004)

Loos, Ted. "Polish Treasures Visit a Kindred Culture," *New York Times*, (October 27, 2002)

Lyall, Sarah. "Peter Townsend Dies at 80; Princess Margaret's Love," Obituary, *New York Times*, (June 21, 1995)

Meisler, Stanley. "Splendors of Topkapi," *Smithsonian*, (February, 2000)

Roach, John. "Delphic Oracle's Lips May Have Been Loosened by Gas Vapors," *National Geographic News*, (August 14, 2001)

Siddall, A. Clair. "Family Life in China, 1923-1932," Unpublished memoir, (1974)

Siddall, Lawrence B. "The Sad, Short Life of Elizabeth Siddal, Pre-Raphaelite Model and Artist," *The Review of the Pre-Raphaelite Society*, (Autumn 2002)

Walsh, Mary Williams. "John Westergaard, 72, Dies; Started a Mutual Fund," Obituary, *New York Times*, (February 10, 2003)

Zamoyski, Zygmunt. "Really So Ridiculous?" *The Warsaw Voice*, (August 3, 1997). The author advocates for stricter rules against cheating in Polish universities.

Encyclopedias

Encyclopedia Britannica

Microsoft Encarta Encyclopedia

Travel Guides

Lonely Planet Guides: *Greece, Turkey, Middle East, India and Pakistan,* Lonely Planet Publications, Victoria, Australia.

The Rough Guide: *Poland*, London, UK, 1996.

Insight Guide: *Poland*, APA Publications, Houghton Mifflin Co., Boston, 1996.

Internet Websites

"The Suez Crisis of 1956," www.historylearningsite.co.uk

"The Big 3 at Tehran-Europe 1943," www.history.acusd.edu

"The Suez War of 1956," www.jewishvirtuallibrary.org

"Britain, France, Israel, Egypt War, 1956," www.onwar.com

"Majdanek Museum Exhibits," www.scrapbookpages.com/Poland/Majdanek

"Black Madonna, Our Lady of Czestochowa," www.udayton.edu

"The Warsaw Uprising 1944," www.warsawuprising.com

"When the Sun Goes Down," www.2.warsawvoice.pl About cheating in Polish schools.

"Churches of Peace in Jawor and Swidnica," www.whc.unesco.org

"Point Four Program," www.wikipedia.org

"1948 Arab-Israeli War," www.wordiq.com